# Debugging Machine Learning Models with Python

Develop high-performance, low-bias, and explainable machine learning and deep learning models

**Ali Madani**

BIRMINGHAM—MUMBAI

# Debugging Machine Learning Models with Python

**Group Product Manager**: Niranjan Naikwadi

**Publishing Product Manager**: Anant Jain

**Book Project Manager**: Hemangi Lotlikar

**Senior Editor**: Rohit Singh

**Technical Editor**: Sweety Pagaria

**Copy Editor**: Safis Editing

**Proofreader**: Safis Editing

**Indexer**: Sejal Dsilva

**Production Designer**: Joshua Misquitta

**DevRel Marketing Executive**: Vinishka Kalra

First published: Sep 2023

Production reference: 1180823

Published by Packt Publishing Ltd.

Grosvenor House

11 St Paul's Square

Birmingham

B3 1RB, UK.

ISBN 978-1-80020-858-2

www.packtpub.com

*To my mother, Fatemeh Bekali, and my father, Razi, whose sacrifices and unwavering support have been my foundation. To my loving partner, Parand, whose constant understanding and love have been my inspiration and strength.*

*– Ali Madani*

# Foreword

Ali Madani is a global expert in ML-based drug discovery, where he has led the development of multiple robust ML products with real-world applications in the life sciences. Ali is a skilled communicator and he is passionate about practical applications of ML development. He rose to popularity over social media through his educational series on applied ML, distilling complex state-of-the-art AI research topics into brief descriptions and diagrams, which could be easily understood by ML learners and non-technical professionals interested in the scientific and business applications of new technologies. Through his role as Director of Machine Learning at Cyclica (acquired by Recursion Pharmaceuticals), Ali was involved in all phases of the ML product life cycle, from ideation to continuous development, field testing, and commercialization. He was a mentor to ML-oriented staff developing their technical skillsets as well as scientific-oriented staff and field experts seeking to reconcile their interpretation of ML model evaluations with real-world applications.

In this book, *Debugging Machine Learning Models with Python*, Ali shares his first-hand experience with readers, covering the practical elements of ML development that are critical for progressing ML technologies from first-pass data science experiments into refined, commercial ML solutions, aimed at real-world performance. This book covers a broad spectrum of topics – from modularizing components of ML life cycles to correctly assessing the performance of ML models and devising improvement strategies. This book extends beyond ML model training and testing, and provides you with technical details on how to detect biases in your models and plan to achieve fairness through different techniques such as methods aiming for local and global ML explainability. You will also practice with Deep Learning supervised, generative, and self-supervised modeling for different data modalities, such as images, texts, and graphs. In this book, you will practice with different Python libraries, such as `scikit-learn`, `PyTorch`, `Transformers`, `Ray`, `imblearn`, `Shap`, `AIF360`, and many more to gain hands-on experience in implementing these techniques and concepts.

With this book, you'll learn how to maximize the value of ML technologies, leading the way in developing *best-in-class* technologies in any domain. Here, Ali provides you with engineering aspects of ML technology development as well as covers topics, such as data and model versioning to achieve reproducibility, data, and concept drift detection to have reliable models in production, and test-driven development to reduce risks of having untrustworthy ML models. You will also learn about different techniques for increasing the security and privacy of your data and models.

**Stephen MacKinnon**

*Vice President, Digital Chemistry*

# Contributors

## About the author

**Ali Madani** worked as the director of machine learning at Cyclica Inc, leading AI technology development front of Cyclica for drug discovery before its acquisition by Recursion Pharmaceuticals, where Ali continues focusing on the applications of machine learning for drug discovery. Ali completed his Ph.D. at the University of Toronto, focusing on machine learning modeling in a cancer setting, and attained a Master of Mathematics degree from the University of Waterloo. As a believer in industry-oriented education and pro-democratization of knowledge, Ali has actively educated students and professionals through international workshops and courses on basic and advanced high-quality machine learning modeling. When not immersed in machine learning modeling and teaching, Ali enjoys exercising, cooking, and traveling with his partner.

*I would like to extend my heartfelt thanks to my partner, Parand, and my parents for their unwavering support and love. I'm also deeply grateful to my mentors throughout the years, whose wisdom and guidance have been invaluable. Thank you all for being an essential part of this journey.*

# About the reviewers

**Krishnan Raghavan** is an IT Professional with over 20 years of experience in the field of software development and delivery excellence across multiple domains and technologies, ranging from C++ to Java, Python, Data Warehousing, and Big Data tools and technologies. In his free time, Krishnan likes to spend time with his wife and daughter besides reading fiction, non-fiction as well as technical books. Krishnan tries to give back to the community by being a part of GDG – Pune Volunteer Group and helping the team in organizing events. Currently, he is unsuccessfully trying to learn to play the guitar.

You can connect with him at `mailtokrishnan@gmail.com` or via LinkedIn

*I would like to thank my wife, Anita, and daughter, Ananya, for giving me the time and space to review this book.*

**Amreth Chandrasehar** is a Director at Informatica responsible for ML Engineering, Observability, and SRE teams. Over the last few years, he has played a key role in Cloud migration, CNCF architecture, Generative AI, Observability, and machine learning adoption at various organizations. He is also a co-creator of the Conducktor Platform, serving T-Mobile's 140+ million customers, and a Tech/ Customer Advisory board member at various companies. He has also co-developed and open sourced Kardio.io. Amreth has been invited and spoken at several key conferences and has won several awards within the company. He was recently awarded a Gold Award at the 15th Annual 2023 Golden Bridge Business and Innovation Awards for his contributions to the field of Observability and Generative AI.

*I would like to thank my wife, Ashwinya Mani, and my son, Athvik A, for their patience and support during my review of this book.*

# Table of Contents

# 2

## Machine Learning Life Cycle                                                23

# 3

## Debugging toward Responsible AI                                           45

# Part 2: Improving Machine Learning Models

## 4

## 5

## 6

## 7

# Part 3: Low-Bug Machine Learning Development and Deployment

## 8

# 9

## Testing and Debugging for Production                              177

# 10

## Versioning and Reproducible Machine Learning Modeling              189

# 11

## Avoiding and Detecting Data and Concept Drifts                     197

# Part 4: Deep Learning Modeling

## 12

## 13

## 14

# Part 5: Advanced Topics in Model Debugging

## 15

## Correlation versus Causality                                    267

## 16

## Security and Privacy in Machine Learning                        279

## 17

## Human-in-the-Loop Machine Learning                              289

# Preface

Welcome to *Debugging Machine Learning Models with Python* – your comprehensive guide for mastering machine learning. This book is designed to help you advance from basic concepts in machine learning to the complexities of expert-level model development, ensuring that your journey is both educational and practical. In this book, we go beyond simple code snippets, delving into the holistic process of crafting reliable, industrial-grade models. From the nuances of modular data preparation to the seamless integration of models into broader technological ecosystems, every chapter is curated to bridge the gap between basic understanding and advanced expertise.

Our journey doesn't stop at mere model creation. We'll dive deep into evaluating model performance, pinpoint challenges, and provide you with effective solutions. Emphasizing the importance of bringing and maintaining reliable models in a production environment, this book will equip you with techniques to tackle data processing and modeling issues. You'll learn the importance of reproducibility and acquire skills to achieve it, ensuring that your models are both consistent and trustworthy. Furthermore, we will underscore the criticality of fairness, the elimination of bias, and the art of model explainability, ensuring that your machine learning solutions are ethical, transparent, and comprehensible. As we progress, we'll also explore the frontier of deep learning and generative modeling, enriched with hands-on exercises using renowned Python libraries such as PyTorch and scikit-learn.

In the ever-evolving landscape of machine learning, continuous learning and adaptation are essential. This book not only serves as a repository of knowledge but also as a motivator, inspiring you to experiment and innovate. As we delve into each topic, I invite you to approach it with curiosity and a willingness to explore, ensuring that the knowledge you gain is deep and actionable. Together, let's shape the future of machine learning, one model at a time.

## Who this book is for

This book is for data scientists, analysts, machine learning engineers, Python developers, and students looking to build reliable, high-performance, reproducible, trustworthy, and explainable machine learning models for production across diverse industrial applications. Fundamental Python skills are all you need to dive into the concepts and practical examples covered. Whether you're new to machine learning or an experienced practitioner, this book offers a breadth of knowledge and practical insights to elevate your modeling skills.

## What this book covers

*Chapter 1*, *Beyond Code Debugging*, covers a brief review of code debugging and why debugging machine learning models goes beyond that.

*Chapter 2, Machine Learning Life Cycle*, teaches you how to design a modular machine learning life cycle for your projects.

*Chapter 3, Debugging toward Responsible AI*, explains concerns, challenges, and some of the techniques in responsible machine learning modeling.

*Chapter 4, Detecting Performance and Efficiency Issues in Machine Learning Models*, teaches you how to correctly assess the performance of your machine learning models.

*Chapter 5, Improving the Performance of Machine Learning Models*, teaches you different techniques to improve the performance and generalizability of your machine learning models.

*Chapter 6, Interpretability and Explainability in Machine Learning Modeling*, covers some machine learning explainability techniques.

*Chapter 7, Decreasing Bias and Achieving Fairness*, explains some technical details and tools that you can use to assess fairness and reduce biases in your models.

*Chapter 8, Controlling Risks Using Test-Driven Development*, shows how to reduce the risk of unreliable modeling using test-driven development tools and techniques.

*Chapter 9, Testing and Debugging for Production*, explains testing and model monitoring techniques to have reliable models in production.

*Chapter 10, Versioning and Reproducible Machine Learning Modeling*, teaches you how to use data and model versioning to achieve reproducibility in your machine learning projects.

*Chapter 11, Avoiding and Detecting Data and Concept Drifts*, teaches you how to detect drifts in your machine learning models to have reliable models in production.

*Chapter 12, Going Beyond ML Debugging with Deep Learning*, covers an introduction to deep learning modeling.

*Chapter 13, Advanced Deep Learning Techniques*, covers convolutional neural networks, transformers, and graph neural networks for deep learning modeling of different data types.

*Chapter 14, Introduction to Recent Advancements in Machine Learning*, explains an introduction to recent advancements in generative modeling, reinforcement learning, and self-supervised learning.

*Chapter 15, Correlation versus Causality*, explains the benefits of, and some practical techniques for, causal modeling.

*Chapter 16, Security and Privacy in Machine Learning*, shows some of the challenges in preserving privacy and ensuring security in machine learning settings, and teaches you a few techniques to tackle those challenges.

*Chapter 17, Human-in-the-Loop Machine Learning*, explains the benefits and challenges of human-in-the-loop modeling.

# To get the most out of this book

In order to follow the instructions given in this book, you will need basic knowledge of the following:

- Access to Python via **Integrated Development Environments** (IDE), Jupyter notebook, or Colab notebook.

- Basics of Python programming.

- Basic understanding of machine learning modeling and terminologies, such as supervised learning, unsupervised learning, and model training and testing.

Having a virtual environment with all the required libraries would help you to run the code in each chapter, which is provided as Jupyter notebooks in the associated GitHub repository of the book.

The Python libraries required for the book are: sklearn >= 1.2.2, numpy >= 1.22.4, pandas >= 1.4.4, matplotlib >= 3.5.3, collections >= 3.8.16, xgboost >= 1.7.5, sklearn >= 1.2.2, ray >= 2.3.1, tune_sklearn >= 0.4.5, bayesian_optimization >= 1.4.2, imblearn, pytest >= 7.2.2, shap >= 0.41.0, aif360 >= 0.5.0, fairlearn >= 0.8.0, pytest >= 3.6.4, ipytest >= 0.13.0, mlflow >= 2.1.1, libi_detect >= 0.11.1, lightgbm >= 3.3.5, evidently >= 0.2.8, torch >= 2.0.0, torchvision >= 0.15.1, transformers >= 4.28.0, datasets >= 2.12.0, torch_geometric == 2.3.1, dowhy == 0.5.1, bnlearn == 0.7.16, tenseal >= 0.3.14, pycryptodome = 3.18.0, pycryptodomex = 3.18.0

Alternatively, you can use online services, such as Colab, and run the notebooks as Colab notebooks.

| Software/hardware covered in the book | Operating system requirements |
|---|---|
| Python >=3.6 | Windows, macOS, or Linux |
| DVC >= 1.10.0 | |

Importing the required libraries is omitted for every single code cell to eliminate the repetition and keep the book as short as possible. Having the GitHub repository of the book on the side will help you to be sure about the required libraries for each piece of code and learn how to install them. As this book is not a single command tutorial book, the majority of the examples include multi-line processes. As a result, you cannot copy-paste individual lines, in most chapters, without paying attention to the required libraries, their installation, and the code lines before that.

**If you are using the digital version of this book, we advise you to type the code yourself or access the code from the book's GitHub repository (a link is available in the next section). Doing so will help you avoid any potential errors related to the copying and pasting of code.**

# Download the example code files

You can download the example code files for this book from GitHub at `https://github.com/PacktPublishing/Debugging-Machine-Learning-Models-with-Python`. If there's an update to the code, it will be updated in the GitHub repository.

We also have other code bundles from our rich catalog of books and videos available at `https://github.com/PacktPublishing/`. Check them out!

## Conventions used

There are a number of text conventions used throughout this book.

`Code in text`: Indicates code words in text, database table names, folder names, filenames, file extensions, pathnames, dummy URLs, user input, and Twitter handles. Here is an example: "Mount the downloaded `WebStorm-10*.dmg` disk image file as another disk in your system."

A block of code is set as follows:

```
import pandas as pd
orig_df = pd.DataFrame({
    'age': [45, 43, 54, 56, 54, 52, 41],
    'gender': ['M', 'F', 'F', 'M', 'M', 'F', 'M'],
    'group': ['H1', 'H1', 'H2', 'H3', 'H2', 'H1', 'H3'],
    'target': [0, 0, 1, 0, 1, 1, 0]})
```

When we wish to draw your attention to a particular part of a code block, the relevant lines or items are set in bold:

```
in_encrypt = open("molecule_enc.bin", "rb")
nonce, tag, ciphertext = [in_encrypt.read(x) for x in (16, 16, -1) ]
in_encrypt.close()
```

Any command-line input or output is written as follows:

```
python -m pytest
```

**Bold**: Indicates a new term, an important word, or words that you see onscreen. For instance, words in menus or dialog boxes appear in **bold**. Here is an example: "You might be able to find other images of cracked products or you could generate new images using a process called **data augmentation**."

> **Tips or important notes**
> Appear like this.

## Get in touch

Feedback from our readers is always welcome.

**General feedback**: If you have questions about any aspect of this book, email us at `customercare@packtpub.com` and mention the book title in the subject of your message.

**Errata**: Although we have taken every care to ensure the accuracy of our content, mistakes do happen. If you have found a mistake in this book, we would be grateful if you would report this to us. Please visit www.packtpub.com/support/errata and fill in the form.

**Piracy**: If you come across any illegal copies of our works in any form on the internet, we would be grateful if you would provide us with the location address or website name. Please contact us at copyright@packt.com with a link to the material.

**If you are interested in becoming an author**: If there is a topic that you have expertise in and you are interested in either writing or contributing to a book, please visit authors.packtpub.com.

## Share your thoughts

Once you've read *Debugging Machine Learning Models with Python*, we'd love to hear your thoughts! Scan the QR code below to go straight to the Amazon review page for this book and share your feedback.

https://packt.link/r/1-800-20858-8

Your review is important to us and the tech community and will help us make sure we're delivering excellent quality content.

# Download a free PDF copy of this book

Thanks for purchasing this book!

Do you like to read on the go but are unable to carry your print books everywhere?

Is your eBook purchase not compatible with the device of your choice?

Don't worry, now with every Packt book you get a DRM-free PDF version of that book at no cost.

Read anywhere, any place, on any device. Search, copy, and paste code from your favorite technical books directly into your application.

The perks don't stop there, you can get exclusive access to discounts, newsletters, and great free content in your inbox daily

Follow these simple steps to get the benefits:

1.  Scan the QR code or visit the link below

https://packt.link/free-ebook/978-1-80020-858-2

2.  Submit your proof of purchase
3.  That's it! We'll send your free PDF and other benefits to your email directly

# Part 1:
# Debugging for
# Machine Learning Modeling

In this part of the book, we will delve into the different aspects of machine learning development that extend beyond traditional paradigms. The first chapter illuminates the nuances between conventional code debugging and the specialized realm of machine learning debugging, emphasizing that the challenges in ML transcend mere code errors. The next chapter provides a comprehensive overview of the machine learning life cycle, highlighting the role of modularization in streamlining and enhancing model development. Finally, we will underscore the importance of model debugging in the pursuit of Responsible AI, emphasizing its role in ensuring ethical, transparent, and effective machine learning solutions.

This part has the following chapters:

- *Chapter 1, Beyond Code Debugging*
- *Chapter 2, Machine Learning Life Cycle*
- *Chapter 3, Debugging toward Responsible AI*

# 1
# Beyond Code Debugging

**Artificial intelligence** (**AI**), like human intelligence, is a capability and tool that can be used for decision-making and task accomplishment. As humans, we use our intelligence in making our daily decisions and thinking about the challenges and problems we deal with. We use our brains and central nervous systems to receive information from our surroundings and process them for decision-making and reactions.

Machine learning models are the AI techniques that are used nowadays to tackle problems across healthcare and finance. Machine learning models have been used in robotic systems in manufacturing facilities to package products or identify products that might have been damaged. They have been used in our smartphones to identify our faces for security purposes, by e-commerce companies to suggest the most suited products or movies to us, and even for improving healthcare and drug development to bring new more effective drugs onto the market for severe diseases.

In this chapter, we will provide a quick review of different types of machine learning modeling. You will learn about different techniques and challenges in debugging your machine learning code. We will also discuss why debugging machine learning modeling goes far beyond just code debugging.

We will cover the following topics in this chapter:

- Machine learning at a glance
- Types of machine learning modeling
- Debugging in software development
- Flaws in data used for modeling
- Model and prediction-centric debugging

This chapter is an introduction to this book to prepare you for more advanced concepts that will be presented later. This will help you improve your models and move toward becoming an expert in the machine learning era.

## Technical requirements

You can find the code files for this chapter on GitHub at `https://github.com/PacktPublishing/Debugging-Machine-Learning-Models-with-Python/tree/main/Chapter01`.

## Machine learning at a glance

You need three fundamental elements to build a machine learning model: an algorithm, data, and computing power (*Figure 1.1*). A machine learning algorithm needs to be fed with the right data and trained using the necessary computing power. It can then be used to predict what it has been trained on for unseen data:

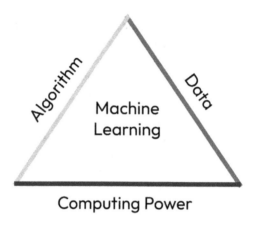

Figure 1.1 – The three elements in the machine learning triangle

Machine learning applications can be generally categorized as **automation** and **discovery**. In the automation category, the goal of the machine learning model and the software and hardware systems built around it is to do the tasks that are possible and usually easy but tedious, repetitive, boring, or dangerous for human beings. Some examples of this include recognizing damaged products in manufacturing lines or recognizing employees' faces at entrances in high-security facilities. Sometimes, it is not possible to use human beings for some of these tasks, although the task would be easy. For example, for face recognition on your phone, if your phone was stolen, you would not be there to recognize that the person who is trying to log into your phone is not you and your phone should be able to do it by itself. But we cannot come up with a generalizable mathematical formulation for these tasks to tell the machine what to do in each situation. So, the machine learning model learns how to come up with its prediction, for example, in terms of recognizing faces, according to the identified patterns in the data.

On the other hand, in the discovery category of machine learning modeling, we want the models to provide information and insight about unknowns that are either not easy or fully discovered, or even impossible, for human experts or non-experts to extract. For example, discovering new drugs for cancer patients is not a task where you can learn all aspects of it by going through a couple of courses and books. In such cases, machine learning can help us come up with new insights to help discover new drugs.

For both discovery and automation, different types of machine learning modeling can help us achieve our goals. We will explore this in the next section.

## Types of machine learning modeling

Machine learning contains multiple modeling types that may rely on output data, a variable type of model output, and learning from prerecorded data or experience. Although the examples in this book focus on supervised learning, we will review other types of modeling, including unsupervised learning, self-supervised learning, semi-supervised learning, **reinforcement learning** (**RL**), and generative machine learning to cover the six major categories of machine learning modeling (*Figure 1.2*). We will also talk about techniques in machine learning modeling and provide code examples that are not parallel to these categories, such as active learning, transfer learning, ensemble learning, and deep learning:

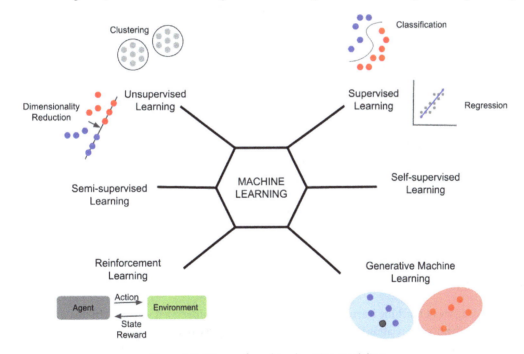

Figure 1.2 – Types of machine learning modeling

Self-supervised and semi-supervised learning are sometimes considered sub-categories of supervised learning. However, we will separate them here so that we can establish the differences between the usual supervised learning models you are familiar with and these two types of modeling.

## Supervised learning

Supervised learning is about identifying the relationship between inputs/features and the output for each data point. But what do input and output mean?

Imagine that we want to build a machine learning model to predict whether a person is likely to get breast cancer or not. The output of the model could be 1 for *getting breast cancer* and 0 for *not getting breast cancer* and the inputs could be the characteristics of the people, such as their age, weight, and whether they smoke or not. There could even be inputs that are measured using advanced technologies, such as the genetic information of each person. In this case, we want to use our machine learning model to predict which patient will get cancer in the future.

You can also design a machine learning model to estimate the price of houses in a city. Here, your model could use characteristics of houses, such as the number of bedrooms and size of the house, the neighborhood, and access to schools, to estimate house prices.

In both of these examples, we have models trying to identify patterns within input features, such as a high number of bedrooms but only one bathroom, and associate those with the output. Depending on the output variable type, your model can be categorized as a classification model, in which the output is categorical, such as *getting* or *not getting cancer*, or a regression model, in which the output is continuous, such as house prices.

## Unsupervised learning

The majority of our life, at least in childhood, has been spent using our five senses (eyesight, hearing, taste, touch, and smell) to collect information about our surroundings, food, and so on, without us trying to find supervised learning style relationships such as whether a banana is ripe or not based on its color and shape. Similarly, in unsupervised learning, we are not seeking to identify the relationship between the features (input) and the output. Instead, the goal is to identify relationships between data points, as in clustering, extract new features (that is, embeddings or representations), and, if needed, reduce the dimensionality (that is, the number of features) of our data without using any output for the data points.

## Self-supervised learning

The third category of machine learning modeling is called self-supervised learning. In this category, the goal is to identify the relationship between inputs and outputs, but the difference with supervised learning is the source of outputs. For example, if the goal of the supervised machine learning model is to translate from English to French, the inputs come from English words and sentences and the outputs come from French words and sentences. However, we can have a self-supervised learning model within English sentences to try to predict the next word or a missing word in a sentence. For example, let's say we aim to recognize that "talking" is a good candidate to fill the gap in "Jack is ____ with Julie." Self-supervised learning models have been used in recent years across different fields to identify new features. This is commonly called representation learning. We will talk about some examples of self-supervised learning in *Chapter 14, Introduction to Recent Advancements in Machine Learning*.

## Semi-supervised learning

Semi-supervised learning can help us benefit from supervised learning without throwing out the data points that don't have output values. Sometimes, we have data points for which we don't have the output values and only their feature values are available. In such cases, semi-supervised learning helps us use data points with or without output. One simple process to do so is to group data points that are similar to each other and use known outputs of the data points in each group to assign output for other data points of the same group that don't have output value.

## Reinforcement learning

In RL, a model is rewarded according to its experience in an environment (real or virtual). In other words, RL is about identifying relationships with piecewise example addition. In RL, data is not considered part of the model and is independent of the model itself. We will go through some details of RL in *Chapter 14, Introduction to Recent Advancements in Machine Learning*.

## Generative machine learning

Generative machine learning modeling helps us develop models that can generate images, text, or any data point that is close to the probability distribution of data provided in the training process. ChatGPT is one of the most famous tools that's built on top of a generative model to generate realistic and meaningful text in response to user questions and answers (https://openai.com/blog/chatgpt). We will go through more details about generative modeling and the available tools built on top of it in *Chapter 14, Introduction to Recent Advancements in Machine Learning*.

In this section, we provided a brief review of the basic components for building machine learning models and different types of modeling. But if you want to develop machine learning models for automation or discovery, for healthcare or any other application, with a low or high number of data points, on your laptop or the cloud, using a **central processing unit** (**CPU**) or **graphics processing unit** (**GPU**), you need to develop high-quality code that works as expected. Although this book is not a software debugging book, an overview of software debugging challenges and techniques could help you in developing your machine learning models.

## Debugging in software development

If you want to use Python and its libraries to build machine learning and deep learning models, you need to make sure your code works as expected. Let's consider the following examples of the same function for returning the multiplication of two variables:

- Correct code:

```
def multiply(x, y):
    z = x * y
    return z
```

- Code with a typo:

```
def multiply(x, y):
    z = x * y
    returnr z
```

- Code with an indentation issue:

```
def multiply(x, y):
z = x * y
    return z
```

- Incorrect use of ** for multiplication:

```
def multiply(x, y):
    z = x ** y
    return z
```

As you can see, there could be typos in the code and issues with indentation that prevent the code from running. You might also face issues because of an incorrect operator being used, such as ** for multiplication instead of *. In this case, your code will run but the expected result will be different than what the function is supposed to do, which is multiplying the input variables.

### Error messages in Python

Sometimes, there are issues with our code that don't let it continue running. These issues could result in different error messages in Python. Here are some examples of error messages you might face when you're running your Python code:

- `SyntaxError`: This is a type of error you'll get when the syntax you used in your code is not the correct Python syntax. It could be caused by a typo, such as having `returnr` instead of `return`, as shown previously, or using a command that doesn't exist, such as using `giveme` instead of `return`.

- TypeError: This error will be raised when your code tries to perform an operation on an object or variable that cannot be done in Python. For example, if your code tries to multiply two numbers while the variables are in string format instead of float or integer format.

- AttributeError: This type of error is raised when an attribute is used for an object that it is not defined for. For example, isnull is not defined for a list. So, my_list.isnull() results in AttributeError.

- NameError: This error is raised when you try to call a function, class, or other names and modules that are not defined in your code. For example, if you haven't defined a neural_network class in your code but call it in your code as neural_network(), you will get a NameError message.

- IndentationError: Python is a programming language that relies on correct indentation – that is, the necessary spaces at the beginning of each line of code – to understand relationships between the lines. It also helps with code readability. IndentationError is the result of the wrong type of indentation being used in your code. But not all wrong indentation, based on the objective you have in mind, results in IndentationError. For example, the following code examples work without any error, but only the first one meets the objective of counting the number of odd numbers in a list. The bottom function returns the length of the input list instead. As a result, if you run the top part of the code, you will get 3 as the output, which is the total number of odd numbers in the input list, while the bottom part of the code returns 5, which is the length of the list. These types of errors, which don't stop the code from running but generate an incorrect output, are called *logical errors*.

Here is some example code in which using the wrong indention results in wrong results without any error message:

```python
def odd_counter(num_list: list):
    """
    :param num_list: list of integers to be checked for identifying
    odd numbers
    :return: return an integer as the number of odd numbers in the
    input list
    """
    odd_count = 0
    for num in num_list:
        if (num % 2) == 0:
            print("{} is even".format(num))
        else:
            print("{} is even".format(num))
            odd_count += 1
    return odd_count

num_list = [1, 2, 5, 8, 9]
```

```
print(f'Total number of odd numbers in the list:
    {odd_counter(num_list)}')
```

The following code runs but generates unintended results:

```
def odd_counter(num_list: list):
    """
    :param num_list: list of integers to be checked for identifying
    odd numbers
    :return: return an integer as the number of odd numbers in the
    input list
    """
    odd_count = 0
    for num in num_list:
        if (num % 2) == 0:
            print("{} is even".format(num))
        else:
            print("{} is even".format(num))
        odd_count += 1
    return odd_count

num_list = [1, 2, 5, 8, 9]
print(f'Total number of odd numbers in the list:
    {odd_counter(num_list)}')
```

There are other errors whose meanings are clear based on their name, such as `ZeroDivisionError` when your code tries to return division by zero, `IndexError` if your code tries to get a value based on an index that is greater than the length of a list, or `ImportError` when you're trying to import a function or class that cannot be found.

In the previous code examples, we used `docstring` to specify the type of input parameter (that is, a list) and the intended output. Having this information helps you and new users of your code to better understand the code and resolve any issue with it quickly.

These are simple examples of issues that can happen in your software and pipelines. In machine learning modeling, you need to conduct debugging to deal with hundreds or thousands of lines of code and tens or hundreds of functions and classes. However, debugging could be much more challenging compared to these examples. It could be even more difficult if you need to start working on a piece of code that you have not written yourself when, for example, you're joining a new team in the industry or academia. You need to use techniques and tools that help you debug your code with minimum effort and time. Although this book is not designed for code debugging, reviewing some debugging techniques could help you in developing high-quality code that runs as planned.

## Debugging techniques

There are techniques to help you in the process of debugging a piece of code or software. You might have used one or more of these techniques, even without remembering or knowing their names. We will review four of them here.

### *Traceback*

When you get an error message in Python, it usually provides you with the necessary information to find the issue. This information creates a report-like message about the lines of your code that the error occurred in, as well as the types of error and function or class calls that resulted in such errors. This report-like message is called a **traceback** in Python.

Consider the following code, in which the reverse_multiply function is supposed to return a list of element-wise multiplication of an input list and its reverse. Here, reverse_multiply uses the multiply command to multiply the two lists. Since multiply is designed for multiplying two float numbers, not two lists, the code returns the traceback message with the necessary information for finding the issue, starting from the bottom operation. It specifies that TypeError occurred on line 8 within multiply, which is the bottom operation, and then lets us know that this issue results in an error occurring on line 21, in reverse_multiply, and eventually line 27 in the whole code module. Both the PyCharm IDE and Jupyter return this information. The following code examples show you how to use traceback to find necessary information so that you can debug a small and simple piece of Python code in both PyCharm and Jupyter Notebook:

```python
def multiply(x: float, y: float):
    """

    :param x: input variable of type float
    :param y: input variable of type float
    return: returning multiplications of the input variables
    """

    z = x * y
    return z
def reverse_multiply(num_list: list):
    """

    :param num_list: list of integers to be checked for identifying
    odd numbers
    :return: return a list containing element-wise multiplication of
    the input list and its reverse
    """
    rev_list = num_list.copy()
    rev_list.reverse()
    mult_list = multiply(num_list, rev_list)

    return mult_list
```

```
num_list = [1, 2, 5, 8, 9]
print(reverse_multiply(num_list))
```

The following lines show you the **traceback** error message when you run the previous code in Jupyter Notebook:

```
TypeError                         Traceback (most recent call last)
<ipython-input-1-4ceb9b77c7b5> in <module>()
      25
      26 num_list = [1, 2, 5, 8, 9]
---> 27 print(reverse_multiply(num_list))
<ipython-input-1-4ceb9b77c7b5> in reverse_multiply(num_list)
      19    rev_list.reverse()
      20
---> 21    mult_list = multiply(num_list, rev_list)
      22
      23    return mult_list
<ipython-input-1-4ceb9b77c7b5> in multiply(x, y)
       6    return: returning multiplications of the input variables
       7    """
----> 8    z = x * y
       9    return z
      10
TypeError: can't multiply sequence by non-int of type 'list'
```

**Traceback error message in Pycharm**
```
Traceback (most recent call last):
  File "<input>", line 27, in <module>
  File "<input>", line 21, in reverse_multiply
  File "<input>", line 8, in multiply
TypeError: can't multiply sequence by non-int of type 'list'
```

Python traceback messages seem to be very useful for debugging our code. However, they are not enough for debugging large code bases that contain many functions and classes. You need to use complementary techniques to help you in the debugging process.

## Induction and deduction

When you have found an error in your code, you can either start by collecting as much information as you can and try to find potential issues using the information, or you can jump into checking your suspicions. These two approaches differentiate induction from the deduction process in terms of code debugging:

- **Induction**: In the induction process, you start collecting information and data about the problem in your code that helps you come up with a list of potential issues resulting from the error. Then, you can narrow the list down and, if necessary, collect more information and data from the process until you fix the error.

- **Deduction**: In the deduction process, you come up with a short list of your points of suspicion regarding the issues in your code and try to find if any one of them is the actual source of the issue. You continue this process and gather more information and come up with new potential sources of the problem. You continue this process until you fix the problem.

In both approaches, you go through an iterative process of coming up with potential sources of issues and building hypotheses and then collect the necessary information until you fix the error in your code. If a piece of code or software is new to you, this process could take time. In such cases, try to get help from your teammates with more experience with the code to collect more data and come up with more relevant hypotheses.

## Bug clustering

As stated in the Pareto principle, named after Vilfredo Pareto, a famous Italian sociologist and economist, 80% of the results originate from 20% of the causes. The exact number is not the point here. This principle helps us better understand that the majority of the problems and errors in our code are caused by a minority of its modules. By grouping bugs, we can hit multiple birds with one stone as resolving an issue in a group of bugs could potentially resolve most others within the same group.

## Problem simplification

The idea here is to simplify the code so that you can identify the cause of the error and fix it. You could replace big data objects with smaller and even synthetic ones or limit function calling in a big module. This process could help you quickly eliminate the options for identifying the causes of the issues in your code, or even in the data format you have used as inputs of functions or classes in your code. Especially in a machine learning setting, where you might deal with complex data processes, big data files, or streams of data, this simplification process for debugging could be very useful.

## Debuggers

Each IDE you might use, such as PyCharm, or if you use Jupyter Notebook to experiment with your ideas using Python, has built-in features for debugging. There are also free or paid tools you can benefit from to facilitate your debugging processes. For example, in PyCharm and most other IDEs, you can use breakpoints as pausing places when running a big piece of code so that you can follow the operations in your code (*Figure 1.3*) and eventually find the cause of the issue:

```python
def multiply(x: float, y: float):
    """

    :param x: input variable of type float
    :param y: input variable of type float

    return: returning multiplications of the input variables
    """

    z = x * y
    return z

def reverse_multiply(num_list: list):
    """

    :param num_list: list of integers to be checked for identifying odd numbers

    :return: return a list containing element-wise multiplication of the input list and its reverse
    """

    rev_list = num_list.copy()
    rev_list.reverse()

    mult_list = multiply(num_list, rev_list)

    return mult_list

num_list = [1, 2, 5, 8, 9]
print(reverse_multiply(num_list))
```

Figure 1.3 – Using breakpoints in PyCharm for code debugging

The breakpoint capabilities in different IDEs are not the same. For example, you can use PyCharm's conditional breakpoints to speed up your debugging process, which helps you not execute a line of code in a loop or repeat function calls manually. Read more about the debugging features of the IDE you use and consider them as another tool in your toolbox for better and easier Python programming and machine learning modeling.

The debugging techniques and tools we've briefly explained here, or those you already know about, could help you develop a piece of code that runs and provides the intended results. You could also follow some best practices for high-quality Python programming and building your machine learning models.

# Best practices for high-quality Python programming

Prevention is better than a cure. There are practices you can follow to prevent or decrease the chance of bugs occurring in your code. In this section, we will talk about three of those practices: **incremental programming**, **logging**, and **defensive programming**. Let's look at each in detail.

## *Incremental programming*

Machine learning modeling in practice, in academia or industry, is beyond writing a few lines of code to train a simple model such as a logistic regression model using datasets that already exist in `scikit-learn`. It requires many modules for processing data, training and testing model and postprocessing inferences, or predictions to assess the reliability of the models. Writing code for every small component, then testing it and writing test code using PyTest, for example, could help you avoid issues with each function or class you wrote. It also helps you make sure that the outputs of one module that feed another module as its input are compatible. This process is what is called **incremental programming**. When you write a piece of software or pipeline, try to write and test it piece by piece.

## *Logging*

Every car has a series of dashboard lights that get turned on when there is a problem with the car. These problems could stop the car from running or cause serious damage if they're not acted upon, such as low gas or engine oil change lights. Now, imagine there was no light or warning, and all of a sudden, the car you are driving stops or makes a terrible sound, and you don't know what to do. When you develop functions and classes in Python, you can benefit from **logging** to log information, errors, and other kinds of messages that help you in identifying potential sources of issues when you get an error message. The following example showcases how to use **error** and **info** as two attributes of logging. You can benefit from different attributes of logging in terms of the functions and classes you write to improve data and information gathering while running your code. You can also export the log information in a file using `basicConfig()`, which does the basic configuration for the logging system:

```
import logging
def multiply(x: float, y: float):
    """
    :param x: input variable of type float
    :param y: input variable of type float
    return: returning multiplications of
    the input variables
    """
    if not isinstance(x, (int, float)) or not isinstance(y,
    (int, float)):
        logging.error('Input variables are not of type float or
integer!')
```

```
        z = x * y
        return z
def reverse_multiply(num_list: list):
        """
        :param num_list: list of integers to be checked
        for identifying odd numbers
        :return: return a list containing element-wise multiplication
        of the input list and its reverse
        """
        logging.info("Length of {num_list} is {
        list_len}".format(num_list=num_list,
            list_len = len(num_list)))
        rev_list = num_list.copy()
        rev_list.reverse()
        mult_list = [multiply(num_list[iter], rev_list[iter])
        for iter in range(0, len(num_list))]
        return mult_list
num_list = [1, 'no', 5, 8, 9]
print(reverse_multiply(num_list))
```

When you run the previous code, you will get the following messages and output:

```
ERROR:root:Input variables are not of type float or integer!
ERROR:root:Input variables are not of type float or integer!
[9, 'nononononononono', 25, 'nononononononono', 9]
```

The logged error messages are the results of attempting to multiply 'no', which is a string with another number.

### Defensive programming

Defensive programming is about preparing yourself for mistakes that can be made by you, your teammates, and your collaborators. There are tools, techniques, and Python classes to defend the code against such mistakes, such as **assertions**. For example, using the following line in your code stops it, if the conditions are met, and returns an error message stating AssertionError: Variable should be of type float:

```
assert isinstance(num, float), 'Variable should be of type float'
```

## Version control

The tools and practices we covered here are just examples of how you can improve the quality of your programming and decrease the amount of time needed to eliminate issues and errors in your code. Another important tool in improving your machine learning modeling is **versioning**. We will talk about data and model versioning in *Chapter 10, Versioning and Reproducible Machine Learning Modeling*, but let's briefly talk about code versioning here.

Version control systems allow you to manage changes in your code and files that exist in a code base and help you in tracking those changes, gain access to the history of changes, and collaborate in developing different components of a machine learning pipeline. You can use version control systems such as **Git** and its associated hosting services such as **GitHub**, **GitLab**, and **BitBucket** for your projects. These tools let you and your teammates and collaborators work on different branches of code without disrupting each other's work. It also lets you easily go back to the history of changes and find out when a change happened in the code.

If you have not used version control systems, don't consider them as a new complicated tool or programming language you need to start learning. There are a couple of core concepts and terms you need to learn first, such as `commit`, `push`, `pull`, and `merge`, when using Git. Using these functionalities could be even as simple as a few clicks in an IDE such as PyCharm if you don't want to or know how to use the **command-line interface** (**CLI**).

We reviewed some commonly used techniques and tools to help you in debugging your code and high-quality Python programming. However, there are more advanced tools built on top of models such as GPT, such as ChatGPT (`https://openai.com/blog/chatgpt`) and GitHub Copilot (`https://github.com/features/copilot`), that you can use to develop your code faster and increase the quality of your code and even your code debugging efforts. We will talk about some of these tools in *Chapter 14, Introduction to Recent Advancements in Machine Learning*.

Although using the preceding debugging techniques or best practices to avoid issues in your Python code helps you have a low-bug code base, it doesn't prevent all the problems with machine learning models. This book is about going beyond Python programming for machine learning to help you identify problems with your machine learning models and develop high-quality models.

## Debugging beyond Python

Eliminating code issues doesn't resolve all the issues that may exist in a machine learning model or a pipeline for data preparation and modeling. There could be issues that don't result in any error message, such as problems that originate from data used for modeling, and differences between test data and production data (that is, data that the model needs to be used for eventually).

> **Production versus development environments**
>
> The **development environment** is where we develop our models, such as our computers or cloud environments we use for development. It is where we develop our code, debug it, process data, train models, and validate them. But what we do in this stage doesn't affect users directly.
>
> The **production environment** is where the model is ready to be used by end users or could affect them. For example, a model could get into production in the Amazon platform for recommending products, be delivered to other teams in a banking system for fraud detection, or even be used in hospitals to help clinicians in diagnosing patients' conditions better.

# Flaws in data used for modeling

Data is one of the core components of machine learning modeling (*Figure 1.1*). Applications of machine learning across different industries such as healthcare, finance, automotive, retail, and marketing are made possible by getting access to the necessary data for training and testing machine learning models. As the data gets fed into machine learning models for training (that is, identifying optimal model parameters) and testing, flaws in data could result in problems in models, such as low performance in training (for example, high bias), low generalizability (for example high variance), or socioeconomic biases. Here, we will discuss examples of flaws and properties of data that need to be considered when designing a machine learning model.

## Data format and structure

There could be issues with how data is stored, read, and moved through different functions and classes in your code or pipeline. You might need to work with structured or tabular data or unstructured data such as videos and text documents. This data could be stored in relational databases such as **MySQL** or **NoSQL** (that is, non-relational) databases, data warehouses, and data lakes, or even stored locally in different file formats, such as **CSV**. Either way, the expected and existing file data structure and formats need to match. For example, if your code is expecting a tab-separated file format but instead the input file of the corresponding function is comma-separated, then all the columns could be lumped together. Luckily, most of the time, these kinds of issues result in errors in the code.

There could also be mismatches in the provided and expected data that wouldn't cause any errors if the code is not defended against them and not enough information is logged. For example, imagine a scikit-learn `fit` function that expects training data with 100 features and at the same time, you have 100 data points. In this case, your code will not return any errors if features are in rows or columns of an input DataFrame. Then, your code needs to check if each row of an input DataFrame contains values of one feature across all data points or the feature values of one data point. The following figure shows how switching features with data points, such as transposing a DataFrame that switches rows with columns, could provide wrong input files but result in no error. In this figure, we have considered four columns and rows for simplicity. Here, F and D are used as abbreviations for feature and data point, respectively:

|     | F₁ | F₂ | F₃ | F₄ |
|-----|-----|-----|-----|-----|
| D₁ | 0.3 | 0.4 | 0.2 | 0.1 |
| D₂ | 0.2 | 0.6 | 0.4 | 0.2 |
| D₃ | 0.4 | 0.8 | 0.6 | 0.1 |
| D₄ | 0.2 | 0.3 | 0.5 | 0.7 |

|     | D₁ | D₂ | D₃ | D₄ |
|-----|-----|-----|-----|-----|
| F₁ | 0.3 | 0.2 | 0.4 | 0.2 |
| F₂ | 0.4 | 0.6 | 0.8 | 0.3 |
| F₃ | 0.2 | 0.4 | 0.6 | 0.5 |
| F₄ | 0.1 | 0.2 | 0.1 | 0.7 |

Figure 1.4 – Simplified example showcasing how the transpose of a DataFrame can be used by mistake in a scikit-learn fit function that expects four features

Data flaws are not restricted to structure and format issues. Some data characteristics need to be considered when you're trying to build and improve a machine learning model.

## Data quantity and quality

Despite machine learning being a more than half-century-old concept, the rise of excitement around machine learning started in 2012. Although there were algorithmic advancements for image classification between 2010 and 2015, it was the availability of 1.2 million high-resolution images in the ImageNet LSVRC-2010 contest and the necessary computing power that played a crucial role in the development of the first high-performance image classification models, such as AlexNet (Krizhevsky et al., 2012) and VGG (Simonyan and Zisserman, 2014).

In addition to data quantity, the quality of the data also plays a very important role. In some applications, such as clinical cancer settings, a high quantity of high-quality data is not accessible. Benefitting from both quantity and quality could also become a tradeoff as we could have access to more data but with lower quality. We can choose to stick to high-quality data or low-quality ones or try to benefit from both high-quality and low-quality data if possible. Selecting the right approach is domain-specific and depends on the data and algorithm used for modeling.

## Data biases

Machine learning models can have different kinds of biases, depending on the data we feed them. **Correctional Offender Management Profiling for Alternative Sanctions (COMPAS)** is a famous example of machine learning models with reported biases. COMPAS is designed to estimate the likelihood of a defendant to re-offend based on their response to more than 100 survey questions. A summary of the responses to the questions results in a risk score, which includes questions such as whether one of the prisoner's parents was ever in prison. Although the tool has been successful in many examples, when it has been wrong in terms of prediction, the results for white and black offenders were not the same. The developer company of COMPAS presented data that supports its algorithm's findings. You can find articles and blog posts to read more about its current status and whether it is still used or still has biases or not.

These were some examples of issues in data and their consequences in the resulting machine learning models. But there are other problems in models that do not originate from data.

# Model and prediction-centric debugging

The predictions of a model in the training, testing, and production stages could help us detect issues with the models and find opportunities to improve them. Here, we will briefly review some aspects of model- and prediction-centric model debugging. You can read more details about these problems and other considerations in achieving a reliable model, how to identify the source of the issues, and how to resolve them in future chapters of this book.

## Underfitting and overfitting

When we train a model, such as a supervised learning model, the goal is to have high performance not just in training but also in testing. When a model has low performance even in a training set, we need to deal with the issue of **underfitting**. We can develop more complicated models, such as a random forest or deep learning model, instead of linear and logistic regression models. More complex models might result in lower underfitting, but they might cause **overfitting** and result in lower generalizability of the prediction to test or production data (*Figure 1.5*):

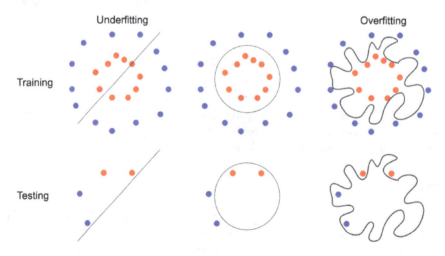

Figure 1.5 – Schematic illustration of underfitting and overfitting

Algorithm and hyperparameter selection determine the level of complexity and the chance of underfitting or overfitting when training and testing a machine learning model. For example, by choosing a model that can learn nonlinear patterns instead of linear models, your model could have a higher chance of low underfitting as it could identify more complex patterns in training data. But at the same time, you could increase the chance of overfitting as some of the complex patterns in the training data might not be generalizable to the test data (*Figure 1.5*). There are approaches to assess underfitting and overfitting that will help you develop a high-performance and generalizable model. We will discuss these in future chapters.

> **Model hyperparameters**
>
> Some parameters can affect the performance of a machine learning model that usually do not get optimized automatically in the training process. These are called hyperparameters. We will go through examples of such hyperparameters, such as the number of trees in a random forest model or the size of hidden layers in neural network models, in future chapters.

## Inference in model testing and production

The eventual goal of machine learning modeling is to have a highly effective model in production. When we test the model, we are assessing its generalizability, but we cannot be sure about its performance on the data it has not seen. The data that's used for training machine learning models could become out of date. For example, the changes in the trends of the clothing market could make predictions of a model for clothing recommendation unreliable.

There are different concepts in this topic, such as data variance, data drift, and model drift, all of which we will cover in the next few chapters.

## Data or hyperparameters for changing landscapes

When we train a machine learning model with specific training data and a set of hyperparameters, the values of model parameters get changed so that they're as close to an optimum point as possible for a defined objective or loss function. The two other tools to achieve a better model are providing better data for training and selecting better hyperparameters. Each algorithm has a capacity for performance improvement. By playing with model hyperparameters alone, you cannot develop the best possible model. In the same way, by increasing the quality and quantity of your data and keeping your model hyperparameters the same, you could also not achieve the best performance possible. So, data and hyperparameters come hand in hand. Before you read the next chapters, remember that by spending more time and money on hyperparameter optimization alone, you cannot necessarily get a better model. We will look at this in more detail later in this book.

# Summary

In this chapter, we reviewed important concepts and approaches for debugging in software development and their differences with machine learning model debugging. You learned that debugging in machine learning modeling is beyond software debugging and how data and algorithms, in addition to code, could cause flawed or low-performance models and unreliable predictions. You can benefit from these understandings and the tools and techniques you will learn about throughout this book to develop reliable machine learning models.

In the next chapter, you will learn about the different components of the machine learning life cycle. You will also learn how modularizing machine learning modeling with these components helps us in identifying opportunities for improving our models before and after training and testing.

## Questions

1. Could your code have unintended indentation but not return any error message?

2. What is the difference between `AttributeError` and `NameError` in Python?

3. How does data dimensionality affect model performance?

4. What information do *traceback* messages in Python provide you about the errors in your code?

5. Could you explain two best practices for high-quality Python programming?

6. Could you explain why you might have features or data points with different levels of confidence?

7. Could you provide suggestions on how to reduce underfitting or overfitting when building a model for a given dataset?

8. Could we have a model with significantly lower performance in production than testing?

9. Is it a good idea to focus on hyperparameter optimization when we can also improve the quality or quantity of the training data?

## References

- Widyasari, Ratnadira, et al. *BugsInPy: A database of existing bugs in Python programs to enable controlled testing and debugging studies.* Proceedings of the 28th ACM joint meeting on European software engineering conference and symposium on the foundations of software engineering. 2020.

- *The Art of Software Testing, Second Edition*, by Glenford J. Myers, Corey Sandler, Tom Badgett, Todd M. Thomas.

- Krizhevsky, Alex, Ilya Sutskever, and Geoffrey E. Hinton. *Imagenet classification with deep convolutional neural networks.* Advances in neural information processing systems 25 (2012).

- Simonyan, Karen, and Andrew Zisserman. "Very deep convolutional networks for large-scale image recognition." arXiv preprint arXiv:1409.1556 (2014). https://arxiv.org/abs/1409.1556.

# 2
# Machine Learning Life Cycle

Machine learning modeling in practice, either at the industrial level or in academic research, is beyond writing a couple of lines of Python code to train and evaluate a model on a public dataset. Learning to write a piece of Python program to train a machine learning model using Python and `scikit-learn` or a deep learning model using `PyTorch` is a starting point for becoming a machine learning developer and specialist. In this chapter, you will learn about the components of the machine learning life cycle and how, while considering this life cycle when planning for machine learning modeling, it helps you in designing a valuable and scalable model.

Here are the topics, including the main components of the machine learning life cycle, that will be covered in this chapter:

- Before we start modeling
- Data collection
- Data selection
- Data exploration
- Data wrangling
- Modeling data preparation
- Model training and evaluation
- Testing the code and the model
- Model deployment and monitoring

By the end of this chapter, you will have learned how to design a machine learning life cycle for your projects and why modularizing your projects into the components of a life cycle helps you in your collaborative model developments. You will have also learned about some of the techniques and their Python implementations for different components of a machine learning life cycle, such as data wrangling and model training and evaluation.

# Technical requirements

The following requirements should be considered for this chapter as they will help you better understand the concepts, use them in your projects, and practice with the provided code:

- Python library requirements:

  - `sklearn` >= 1.2.2

  - `numpy` >= 1.22.4

  - `pandas` >= 1.4.4

  - `matplotlib` >= 3.5.3

You can find the code files for this chapter on GitHub at `https://github.com/PacktPublishing/Debugging-Machine-Learning-Models-with-Python/tree/main/Chapter02`.

# Before we start modeling

Before collecting data as the starting point of a machine learning life cycle, you need to know your objectives. You need to know what problems you want to solve and then define smaller subproblems that would be machine learning solvable. For example, in the case of a problem such as, *"How could we reduce the number of fragile products returned to a manufacturing facility?,"* the subproblems could be as follows:

- *How could we detect the cracks before packaging?*

- *How could we design better packaging to protect the products and reduce transportation-caused cracks?*

- *Could we use better materials to reduce the risk of cracking?*

- *Could we apply small design changes to our product that do not change its functionality but reduce the risk of cracking?*

Once you have identified your subproblems, you can find out how you can use machine learning for each and go through a machine learning life cycle for the defined subproblems. Each of the subproblems may need specific data processing and machine learning modeling, and some of them could be easier to solve compared to the rest.

*Figure 2.1* shows the major steps in machine learning life cycles. Some of these names are not universally defined. For example, data exploration sometimes gets included in data wrangling. But all these steps are required, even if they are named differently in different resources:

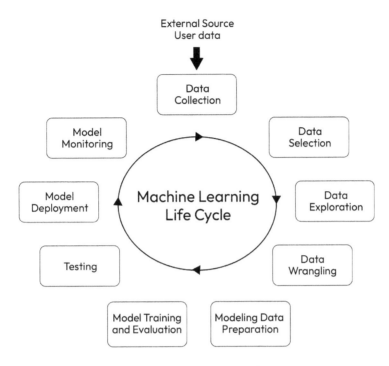

Figure 2.1 – Machine learning life cycle

When you rely on a dataset that's already available in Python, through `scikit-learn` or `PyTorch`, for example, or a dataset that is ready for modeling in public repositories, you don't need to worry about the early steps, such as data collection, selection, and wrangling. These steps have already been taken care of for you. Or if you are just doing modeling for practice and don't want to provide your model in a production system, you don't need to worry about model deployment and monitoring. But understanding the meaning, importance, and benefits of all these steps helps you develop or design a functional technology with continuous improvement to be provided for users. It also helps you better understand your role as a machine learning developer or find your first job or a better job in this field.

## Data collection

The first step in the machine learning life cycle is data collection. It could be about collecting data from different public or commercial databases, storing user data back into your database or any data storage system you have, or even using commercial entities that take care of data collection and annotation for you. If you are relying on free resources, the main consideration for you could be the space the data will get in your local or cloud-based storage system and the time you need to spend to collect the data and analyze it in future steps. But for paid data, either provided in commercial resources or generated by data collection, generation, and annotation companies, you need to assess the value of the data for modeling before you decide to pay for it.

# Data selection

Depending on the objectives of the corresponding projects, we need to select the required data for model training and testing. For example, you might have access to information about cancer patients in one or multiple hospitals, such as their age, gender, whether they smoke or not, their genetic information if available, their MRI or CT scans if available, history of their medication, their response to cancer drugs, whether they had surgery or not, their prescriptions, either handwritten or in PDF format, and much more. When you want to build a machine learning model to predict the response of patients to therapy using their CT scans, you need to select different data for each patient compared to when you want to build a model using their information, such as age, gender, and smoking status. You also need to select patients from whom you have the input and output data available if you are building a supervised learning model.

> **Note**
> It is possible to combine data points with and without outputs in a semi-supervised learning model.

Selecting relevant data for your models is not an easy task as the information that separates data as *relevant* and *irrelevant* from your model objective is not necessarily available in this binary way. Imagine you need to extract data from a chemical, biological, or physical database, which could be a collection of data from different smaller datasets, supplementary materials of papers, or even data coming from within scientific articles. Or perhaps you want to extract information from the medical records of patients or even from written answers to an economical or sociological survey. In all such examples, separation of data for your model, or querying relevant data from relevant databases, is not as simple as searching for one keyword. Each keyword could have synonyms, either in plain English or in technical terms, could be written in different ways, or even sometimes the relevant information could exist in different columns of a data file or a relational database. Proper data selection and query systems provide you with a huge opportunity to improve your models.

You can benefit from a literature review and asking experts, if needed, to extend the keywords you are using. You can benefit from known data selection methods for specific tasks you have or even license tools or pay for services to help you in extracting more relevant data for your objectives. There are also advanced natural language processing techniques to help you in your query system from text. We will discuss these in *Chapter 13, Advanced Deep Learning Techniques*, and *Chapter 14, Introduction to Recent Advancements in Machine Learning*.

# Data exploration

In this stage, your data is selected and you can explore the quantity, quality, sparsity, and format of the data. You can find the number of data points in each class if you have categorical output in supervised learning, distribution of features, confidence in output variables, if available, and other characteristics of the data you get out of the *data selection* stage. This process helps you identify issues with your data that need to be fixed in *data wrangling*, which is the next step in the life cycle, or opportunities for improving your data by revising your *data selection* process.

# Data wrangling

Your data needs to go through structuring and enriching processes and be transformed and cleaned up, if necessary. All these aspects are part of data wrangling.

## Structuring

The raw data might come in different formats and sizes. You might have access to handwritten notes, Excel sheets, or even images of tables that contain information that needs to be extracted and put in the right format for further analysis and used for modeling. This process is not about transforming all data into a table-like format. In the process of data structuring, you need to be careful regarding information loss. For example, you could have features that are in a specific order, such as based on time, date, or the sequence of information coming through a device.

## Enriching

After structuring and formatting your data, you need to assess whether you have the right data to build a machine learning model of that cycle. You might identify opportunities to add or generate new data before continuing the wrangling process. For example, you might find out that in the data for identifying cracks in images of products in a manufacturing pipeline, you only have 50 out of 10,000 images that are labeled as images of cracked products. You might be able to find other images of cracked products or you could generate new images using a process called **data augmentation**.

> **Data augmentation**
>
> Data augmentation is a series of techniques for generating new data points, computationally, using the original dataset we have at hand. For example, if you rotate your portrait, or change the quality of an image by adding Gaussian noise to it, the new image will still show your face. But it could help your model to be more generalizable. We will talk about different data augmentation techniques in *Chapter 5, Improving the Performance of Machine Learning Models*.

# Data transformation

The features and the output of datasets could be different types of variables, including the following:

- **Quantitative or numerical:**

  - **Discrete:** For example, the number of houses in a neighborhood

  - **Continuous:** For example, the age or weight of patients

- **Qualitative or categorical:**

  - **Nominal (no order):** For example, different colors of cars

  - **Ordinal (qualitative variable with order):** For example, grades of students, such as A, B, C, or D

When we train a machine learning model, the model needs to use numerical values to calculate the loss function in each iteration of the optimization process. Hence, we need to transform categorical variables into numerical alternatives. There are multiple feature encoding techniques, three of which are one-hot encoding, target encoding (Micci-Barreca, 2001), and label encoding. A one-hot, label, and target encoding calculation for an example matrix of four columns, including age, gender, group, and target, and seven rows, as seven example data points, is shown in *Figure 2.2*:

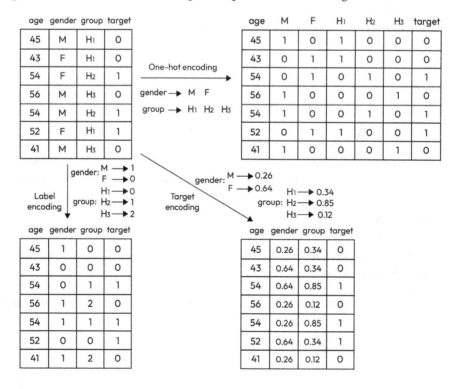

Figure 2.2 – Manual calculations for one-hot, target, and label encoding using
a simple example dataset with four features and seven data points

This is an imaginary dataset for predicting the response of patients to a drug, with the target column as the output. Variable categories are abbreviated as F: Female, M: Male, H1: Hospital 1, H2: Hospital 2, and H3: Hospital 3. In reality, many more variables need to be considered and more data points are necessary to have a reliable model for drug response prediction and assess whether there are biases in the response of patients to drugs between male and female groups or in different hospitals.

Each of these techniques has its benefits and caveats. For example, one-hot encoding increases the number of features (that is, the dimensionality of the dataset) and increases the chance of overfitting. Label encoding assigns integer values to each category, which do not necessarily have a meaning. For example, considering male as 1 and female as 0 is arbitrary and doesn't have any real meaning. Target encoding is an alternative approach that considers the probabilities of each category concerning the target. You can read the mathematical details of this process in Micci-Barreca, 2001. Python's implementation of these approaches is provided in the following code snippets.

Let's define a synthetic DataFrame to use for feature encoding:

```
import pandas as pd
orig_df = pd.DataFrame({
    'age': [45, 43, 54, 56, 54, 52, 41],
    'gender': ['M', 'F', 'F', 'M', 'M', 'F', 'M'],
    'group': ['H1', 'H1', 'H2', 'H3', 'H2', 'H1', 'H3'],
    'target': [0, 0, 1, 0, 1, 1, 0]})
```

First, we will use label encoding to encode the categorical features in the defined DataFrame:

```
# encoding using label encoding
from sklearn.preprocessing import LabelEncoder
# initializing LabelEncoder
le = LabelEncoder()
# encoding gender and group columns
label_encoded_df = orig_df.copy()
label_encoded_df['gender'] = le.fit_transform(
    label_encoded_df.gender)
label_encoded_df['group'] = le.fit_transform(
    label_encoded_df.group)
```

Then, we will try to perform one-hot encoding for categorical feature transformation:

```
# encoding using one hot encoding
from sklearn.preprocessing import OneHotEncoder
# initializing OneHotEncoder
ohe = OneHotEncoder(categories = 'auto')
# encoding gender column
gender_ohe = ohe.fit_transform(
    orig_df['gender'].values.reshape(-1,1)).toarray()
```

```
gender_ohe_df = pd.DataFrame(gender_ohe)
# encoding group column
group_ohe = ohe.fit_transform(
    orig_df['group'].values.reshape(-1,1)).toarray()
group_ohe_df = pd.DataFrame(group_ohe)
# generating the new dataframe with one hot encoded features
onehot_encoded_df = pd.concat(
    [orig_df, gender_ohe_df, group_ohe_df], axis =1)
onehot_encoded_df = onehot_encoded_df.drop(
    ['gender', 'group'], axis=1)
onehot_encoded_df.columns = [
    'age','target','M', 'F','H1','H2', 'H3']
```

Now, we will implement target encoding in Python, after installing the `category_encoders` library, as the third encoding approach, as follows:

```
# encoding using target encoding
from category_encoders import TargetEncoder
# initializing LabelEncoder
te = TargetEncoder()
# encoding gender and group columns
target_encoded_df = orig_df.copy()
target_encoded_df['gender'] = te.fit_transform(
    orig_df['gender'], orig_df['target'])
target_encoded_df['group'] = te.fit_transform(
    orig_df['group'], orig_df['target'])
```

Ordinal variables can also be transformed using the `OrdinalEncoder` class as part of `sklearn.preprocessing`. The difference between ordinal and nominal transformation is the meaning behind the order of categories in ordinal variables. For example, if we are encoding grades of students, A, B, C, and D could be transformed into 1, 2, 3, and 4, or 4, 3, 2, and 1, but transforming them into 1, 3, 4, and 2 will not be acceptable as it is changing the meaning behind the order of the grades.

Output variables can also be categorical. You can use label encoding to transform a nominal output into a numerical variable for classification models.

## Cleaning

After structuring the data, it needs to be cleaned. Cleaning data helps increase the quality of your data and makes it closer to being ready for modeling. An example of a cleaning process is filling in missing values in your data. For example, if you want to use patients' living habits to predict their risk of getting diabetes using their responses to a survey, you might find out some of the participants didn't respond to the questions about their smoking habits.

## Feature imputation for filling in missing values

The features of a dataset we have at hand could contain missing values. The majority of machine learning models and their corresponding Python implementations cannot handle missing values. In these cases, we need to either remove data points with missing feature values or somehow fill in those missing values. There are feature imputation techniques we can use to calculate the values of features that are missing in our dataset. Examples of such methods are shown in *Figure 2.3*:

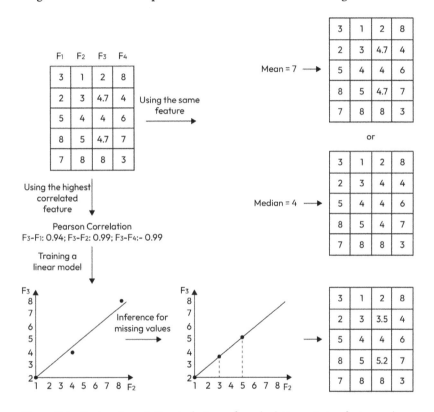

Figure 2.3 – Feature imputation techniques for calculating missing feature values

As you can see, either we can use other values of the same features and replace the missing values with the mean or median of the available values, or we can use other features with low or no missing values that have a high correlation with the feature with missing values. In the second case, we can use the feature with the highest correlation, with the target feature with missing values, to build a linear model. The linear model considers the correlated feature as input and the feature with missing values as output and then uses the predictions of the linear model to calculate the missing values.

When we use a statistical summary of the values of the same feature, such as the mean or median, we are reducing the variance of the feature values as those summary values will be used for all the missing values of the same feature (*Figure 2.3*). On the other hand, when we use a linear model between the feature with missing values and a highly correlated feature with low or no missing values, we are assuming a linear relationship between them. Alternatively, we can build more complex models between features for missing value calculation. All these approaches have their benefits and limitations, and you need to choose the one that works best for your dataset, depending on the distribution of feature values, the fraction of data points with missing features values, the correlation range between features, the existence of features with low or no missing value, and other relevant factors.

We used a very simple case of four features and five data points in *Figure 2.3* to showcase the discussed feature imputation techniques. But in reality, we need to build models with more than four features. We can use Python libraries such as `scikit-learn` for feature imputation by using the mean of the same feature values, as follows. First, we will import the required libraries:

```
import numpy as np
from sklearn.impute import SimpleImputer
```

Then, we must define the two-dimensional input list, where each internal list shows the feature values of a data point:

```
X = [[5, 1, 2, 8],
     [2, 3, np.nan, 4],
     [5, 4, 4, 6],
     [8, 5, np.nan, 7],
     [7, 8, 8, 3]]
```

Now, we are ready to fit a `SimpleImputer` function by specifying what needs to be considered as a missing value and what strategy to be used for imputation:

```
# strategy options: mean, median, most_frequent, constant
imp = SimpleImputer(missing_values=np.nan, strategy='mean')
imp.fit(X)
# calculate missing values of the input
X_no_missing = imp.transform(X)
```

We can also use `scikit-learn` to make a linear regression model that calculates missing feature values:

```
import numpy as np
from sklearn.linear_model import LinearRegression as LR

# defining input variables for feature 2 and 3
f2 = np.array([1, 4, 8]).reshape((-1, 1))
f3 = np.array([2, 4, 8])

# initializing a linear regression model with sklearn LinearRegression
model = LR()
```

```
# fitting the linear regression model using f2 and f3 as input and
output variables, respectively
model.fit(f2, f3)

# predicting missing values of feature 3
model.predict(np.array([3, 5]).reshape((-1, 1)))
```

## Outlier removal

Numerical variables in our datasets could have values that are far away from the rest of the data. They could be real values that are dissimilar to the rest of the data points or caused by errors in data generation, such as in experimental measurement processes. You can visually see and detect them using a boxplot (*Figure 2.4*). The circles of the plot are the outliers that get automatically detected by the plotting functions in Python, such as `matplotlib.pyplot.boxplot` (*Figure 2.4*). Although visualization is a good way of exploring our data and understanding the distribution of numerical variables, we need to have a quantitative way of detecting outliers without the need to plot the values of all the variables in our datasets.

The simplest way of detecting outliers is by using quantiles of the distribution of variable values. Data points that are beyond the upper and lower bounds are considered outliers (*Figure 2.4*). Lower and upper bounds can be calculated as $Q_1 - a.IQR$ and $Q_3 - a.IQR$, where  can be a real value between 1.5 and 3. The common value of $a$, which is also used by default in drawing boxplots, is 1.5, but having higher values makes the process of outlier identification less stringent and lets fewer data points be detected as outliers. For example, by changing the stringency of outlier detection from the default (that is, $a = 1.5$) to $a = 3$, none of the data points in *Figure 2.4* would be detected as outliers. This approach for outlier identification is non-parametric, meaning it doesn't have any assumptions regarding the distribution of data points. Hence, it can be applied to non-normal distributions, such as the data shown in *Figure 2.4*:

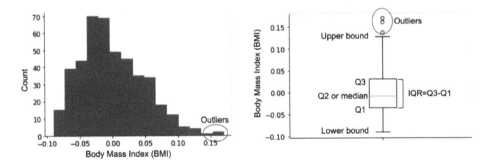

Figure 2.4 – Outliers in histograms and boxplots

In the preceding figure, the plots were generated using the values of features in the diabetes dataset of the `scikit-learn` package, which was loaded via `sklearn.datasets.load_diabetes()`.

## Data scaling

The values of features, either originally numerical or after transformation, could have different ranges. Many machine learning models perform better, or at least their optimization processes converge faster, if their feature values get scaled and normalized properly. For example, if you have a feature ranging from 0.001 to 0.05 and another one from 1,000 to 5,000, bringing both of them to a reasonable range such as [0, 1] or [-1, 1] could help improve the speed of convergence or the performance of your model. You need to make sure the scaling and normalizations you implement don't cause ties in your feature values, meaning data points don't lose their difference based on features that went under transformation.

The objective of scaling is to change the range of values of a variable. In normalization, the shape of the distribution of values could also change. You can use examples of these methods and the corresponding classes available in `scikit-learn` in your projects to improve the scale and distribution of your features (*Table 2.1*). The resulting scaled variables after using each of these classes have specific characteristics. For example, the values of a variable after using the `StandardScalar` class of `scikit-learn` will be centered around zero with a standard deviation of one.

Some of these techniques, such as robust scaling, which can be done using the `RobustScaler` class of `scikit-learn`, are less likely to be affected by outliers (*Table 2.1*). In robust scaling, outliers, based on the definition we provided, don't affect how the median and *IQR* are calculated and, therefore, do not affect the scaling process. Outliers themselves then be scaled using the calculated median and *IQR*. Outliers can be either kept or removed before or after scaling, depending on the machine learning method used and the task at hand. But the important point is to detect them and be aware of them when you're trying to prepare data for modeling and, if required, scale or remove them:

| Python Class | Mathematical Definition | Value Limits |
|---|---|---|
| `sklearn.preprocessing.`<br>`StandardScaler()` | $Z = (X - u) / s$<br><br>u: Mean<br><br>s: Standard deviation | No limit<br><br>>99% of data between -3 and 3 |
| `sklearn.preprocessing.`<br>`MinMaxScaler()` | X_scaled = $(X - X_{min})/(X_{max} - X_{min})$ | [0,1] |
| `sklearn.preprocessing.`<br>`MaxAbsScaler()` | X_scaled = $X/\|X\|_{max}$ | [-1,1] |
| `sklearn.preprocessing.`<br>`RobustScaler()` | $Z_{robust} = (X - Q_2) / IQR$<br><br>$Q_2$: Median<br><br>IQR: Interquartile range | No limit<br><br>Majority of data between -3 and 3 |

Table 2.1 – Example of Python classes for scaling and normalizing feature values

Other forms of exploratory data analysis are conducted after data wrangling before machine learning modeling is started. Domain expertise could also help in identifying patterns whose interpretations need to be better understood regarding the subject domain for which the problem has been defined. To increase the likelihood of success for machine learning modeling, you may need feature engineering to build new features or learn new features through representation learning. These new features could be as simple as body mass index, defined as the ratio of someone's weight in kilograms to the square of their height in meters. Or they could be new features and representations that are learned through complicated processes or extra machine learning modeling. We will talk about this later in *Chapter 14, Introduction to Recent Advancements in Machine Learning*.

# Modeling data preparation

In this stage of a machine learning life cycle, we need to finalize the features and data points we want to use for modeling, as well as our model evaluation and testing strategies.

## Feature selection and extraction

The original features that were normalized and scaled in previous steps can be now processed further to increase the likelihood of having a high-performance model. In general, features can either be sub-selected, meaning some of the features get thrown out, using a *feature selection* method, or be used to generate new features, which is traditionally called *feature extraction*.

### Feature selection

The goal of feature selection is to reduce the number of features, or the dimensionality of your data, and keep features that are information-rich. For example, if we have 20,000 features and 500 data points, there is a high chance that most of the original 20,000 features are not informative when used to build a supervised learning model. The following list explains some simple techniques for feature selection:

- Keeping features with a high variance or MAD across the data points
- Keeping features with the highest number of unique values across the data points
- Keeping representative features from groups of highly correlated features

These processes can be conducted using all the data points or just training data to avoid potential information leakage between the training and test data.

### Feature extraction

Combining original features linearly or nonlinearly could result in more informative features for building a predictive model. This process is called feature extraction and could be conducted based on domain knowledge or through different statistical or machine learning models. For example, you can use principal component analysis or isometric mapping to reduce the dimensionality of your data in a linear or non-linear way, respectively. Then, you can use these new features in your training and testing process. The Python implementation of these two approaches is provided in the following code snippets.

First, let's import the required libraries and load the `scikit-learn` digit dataset:

```python
import numpy as np
import matplotlib.pyplot as plt
from sklearn.decomposition import PCA
from sklearn.manifold import Isomap
from sklearn.datasets import load_digits

# loading digit dataset from sklearn
X, _ = load_digits(return_X_y=True)
print('Number of features: {}'.format(X.shape[1]))
```

Now, let's use `isomap` and `pca`, both of which are available in `scikit-learn`:

```python
# fitting isomap and build new dataframe of feature with 5 components
embedding = Isomap(n_components=5)
X_transformed_isomap = embedding.fit_transform(X)
print('Number of features: {}'.format(
    X_transformed_isomap.shape[1]))
# fitting pca and build new dataframe of feature with 5 components
pca = PCA(n_components=5)
X_transformed_pca = pca.fit_transform(X)
print('Number of features: {}'.format(
    X_transformed_pca.shape[1]))
# plotting ratio of variance explained by the first n, being between 1
and 5, components
plt.bar(x = np.arange(0, len(
    pca.explained_variance_ratio_)),
    height = np.cumsum(pca.explained_variance_ratio_))
plt.ylabel('Explained variance ratio')
plt.xlabel('Number of components')
plt.show()
```

The number of components you can select from each such method can be determined through different techniques. For example, the explained variance ratio is a commonly used approach to select the number of principal components. These are identified through principal component analysis and collectively explain more than a specific percentage, such as 70% of the total variance in a dataset.

There are also more advanced techniques that are part of self-supervised pre-training and representation learning for identifying new features. In these techniques, large amounts of data are used to calculate new features, representations, or embeddings. For example, the English version of Wikipedia can be used to come up with better representations of English words rather than performing one-hot encoding for each word. We will talk about self-supervised learning models in *Chapter 14, Introduction to Recent Advancements in Machine Learning*.

## Designing an evaluation and testing strategy

We need to specify our testing strategy before we train our model to identify its parameters or optimal hyperparameters. Model testing could be done by another team on separate datasets if you are working in a big organization. Alternatively, you can dedicate one or multiple datasets, separate from your training set, or separate part of your data so that you can test it separately from the training set. You also need to list the ways you want to assess the performance of your model in the testing stage. For example, you may need to specify the performance plots or measures you want to use, such as the **receiver operating curve** (**ROC**) and **precision-recall** (**PR**) curve, or other criteria, to select a new classification model.

Once your testing strategy has been defined, you can use the rest of the data to specify training and validation sets. Validation and training sets don't need to be one series of fixed data points. We can use *k*-fold **cross-validation** (**CV**) to split a dataset into *k* chunks and use one chunk at a time as a validation set and the rest as the training set. Then, the average of the performance across all *k* chunks can be used as a validation set to calculate the validation's performance. Training performance is important for finding optimal values for model parameters based on the objective of the model. You can also use validation performance to identify optimal hyperparameter values. If you specify one validation set or use *k*-fold CV, you can use the validation performance of different hyperparameter combinations to identify the best one. Then, the best hyperparameter set can be used to train the model on all data, excluding test data, so that you can come up with the final model to be tested in the testing stage.

There are some common practices for each application regarding the number of folds (that is, *k*) or fraction of data points to be separated as validation and test sets. For small datasets, 60%, 30%, and 10% are commonly used to specify the training, validation, and testing fraction of data points, respectively. But both the number of data points and their diversity are important factors in deciding on the number of data points within validation and test sets or specifying *k* in CV. You can also use available Python classes that perform training and validation using *k*-fold CV with your choice of *k*, as follows:

```
from sklearn.model_selection import cross_val_score,KFold
from sklearn.neighbors import KNeighborsClassifier
from sklearn.datasets import load_breast_cancer
# loading breast cancer dataset
X, y = load_breast_cancer(return_X_y=True)

# defining the k-fold CV
k_CV = KFold(n_splits=5)

# initializing a k nearest neighbor model
```

```
knn = KNeighborsClassifier()

# outputting validation performances using average precision across
different folds of the designed CV
scores = cross_val_score(
    estimator = knn, X = X, y = y, cv = k_CV,
    scoring = 'average_precision')
print("Average cross validation score: {}".format(
    round(scores.mean(),4)))
```

This returns the following output:

```
Average Cross Validation score: 0.9496
```

> **Note**
>
> Preferably, the data you prepared in each of these stages shouldn't just get dumped in the
> cloud or a hard drive, or get added to a database after each of the previous steps in a life cycle.
> It is beneficial to have a report attached to the data to track historical efforts in each step and
> provide that information for other individuals or teams within your team or organization.
> Proper reporting, such as on data wrangling, could provide feedback-seeking opportunities
> to help you improve data provided for machine learning modeling.

## Model training and evaluation

The process of training and validating or testing a model consists of the following three major steps
if you use `scikit-learn` or `PyTorch` and TensorFlow for neural network modeling:

1. **Initializing the model**: Initializing a model is about specifying the method, its hyperparameters,
   and the random state to be used for modeling.

2. **Training the model**: In model training, the initialized model in *Step 1* gets used on the training
   data to train a machine learning model.

3. **Inference, assignment, and performance assessment**: In this step, the trained model can be
   used for inference (for example, predicting outputs) in supervised learning or, for example,
   assigning new data points to identified clusters in unsupervised learning. In supervised learning,
   you can use these predictions for model performance assessment.

These steps are similar for both supervised learning and unsupervised learning models. In *Steps 1* and
*2*, both types of models can be trained. Python's implementation of these three steps using `scikit-learn` is provided in the following code snippets for the random forest classifier and *k*-means clustering.

First, let's import the required libraries and load the `scikit-learn` breast cancer dataset:

```
from sklearn.datasets import load_breast_cancer
from sklearn.model_selection import train_test_split
from sklearn import metrics

# loading breast cancer dataset
X, y = load_breast_cancer(return_X_y=True)
X_train, X_test, y_train, y_test = train_test_split(X, y,
    test_size=0.30, random_state=5)
```

Now, we can use a random forest to train and test a supervised learning model:

```
from sklearn.ensemble import RandomForestClassifier
# initializing a random forest model
rf_model = RandomForestClassifier(n_estimators=10,
    max_features=10, max_depth=4)
# training the random forest model using training set
rf_model.fit(X_train, y_train)
# predicting values of test set using the trained random forest model
y_pred_rf = rf_model.predict(X_test)
# assessing performance of the model on test setprint("Balanced
accuracy of the predictions:",
    metrics.balanced_accuracy_score(y_test, y_pred_rf))
```

This code prints out the following performance on the test set:

```
Balanced accuracy of the predictions: 0.9572
```

We can also build a *k*-means clustering model, as follows:

```
from sklearn import cluster
# initializing a random forest model
kmeans_model = cluster.KMeans(n_clusters=2, n_init = 10)
# training the kmeans clustering model using training set
kmeans_model.fit(X_train)
# assigning new observations, that are test set datapoints here, to
the identified clusters
y_pred_kmeans = kmeans_model.predict(X_test)
```

If you don't have enough experience in machine learning modeling, the methodologies and corresponding Python classes provided in *Table 2.2* could be a good starting point:

| Type | Method | Python Class |
|---|---|---|
| Classification | Logistic regression | `sklearn.linear_model.LogisticRegression()` |
| | K-nearest neighbors | `sklearn.neighbors.KNeighborsClassifier()` |
| | Support vector machine classifier | `sklearn.svm.SVC()` |
| | Random forest classifier | `sklearn.ensemble.RandomForestClassifier()` |
| | XGBoost classifier | `xgboost.XGBClassifier()` |
| | LightGBM classifier | `Lightgbm.LGBMClassifier()` |
| Regression | Linear regression | `sklearn.linear_model.LinearRegression()` |
| | Support vector machine regressor | `sklearn.svm.SVR()` |
| | Random forest regressor | `sklearn.ensemble.RandomForestRegressor()` |
| | XGBoost regressor | `xgboost.XGBRegressor()` |
| | LightGBM regressor | `Lightgbm.LGBMRegressor()` |
| Clustering | K-means clustering | `sklearn.cluster.KMeans()` |
| | Agglomerative clustering | `sklearn.cluster.AgglomerativeClustering()` |
| | DBSCAN clustering | `sklearn.cluster.DBSCAN()` |
| | UMAP | `umap.UMAP()` |

Table 2.2 – Starting methods and their Python classes for your supervised learning or clustering problems with tabular data

**Note**

UMAP is a dimensionality reduction approach that provides lower dimensional visualization, such as a 2D plot of a series of data points. The resulting groups of data points in the lower dimensional space can also be used as reliable clusters.

# Testing the code and the model

Although the performance of a machine learning model that is selected and brought to this stage of the life cycle can be further tested using one or multiple datasets, there are a series of tests that need to be done in this stage to make sure of this:

- Ensuring the process of deployment and bringing the model into production goes smoothly

- Ensuring the model will work as expected from a performance and computational cost perspective

- Ensuring that using the model in production will not have legal and financial implications

Here are some such tests that can be used in this stage:

- **Unit tests**: These are fast tests that make sure our code runs correctly. These tests are not specific to machine learning modeling and not even to this stage. Throughout the life cycle, you need to design unit tests to make sure your data processing and modeling code runs as expected.

- **A/B testing**: This type of testing helps you, your team, and your organization in deciding whether to select a model or reject it. The idea of this test is to assess two possible scenarios, such as two models, or two different designs of the frontend, and check which one is more favorable. But you need to quantitatively assess the result by deciding *what needs to be measured* and your *selection criteria*.

- **Regression tests**: This type of test assesses whether your code and model perform as expected after a change in dependencies and environment variables. For example, if your version of Python, `scikit-learn`, `PyTorch`, or TensorFlow changes, this test makes sure your code runs and checks the effects of those changes on model performance and predictions.

- **Security tests**: Security testing is an important part of programming and modeling at an industrial level. You need to make sure your code and dependencies are not vulnerable. However, you need to design a test for advanced adversarial attacks. We will discuss this in *Chapter 3, Debugging toward Responsible AI*.

- **Responsible AI test**: We need to design tests to assess the important factors of responsible AI, such as transparency, privacy, and fairness. We will go through some important aspects of responsible AI in the next chapter.

Although these kinds of tests need to be designed for this stage, similar ones could be integrated as part of previous steps of the life cycle. For example, you can have security testing in all steps of the life cycle, especially if you are using different tools or code bases. There could be other tests such as checking the memory size and prediction runtime of a model or whether the format and structure of data in production and what is expected in the deployed model are the same.

## Model deployment and monitoring

If you are new to deployment, you might think of it as how to develop a frontend, mobile application, or API for end users of your models. But that is not what we want to talk about in this book. There are two important aspects of deployment that we want to cover here and in future chapters: the actions needed to provide a model in production and integrating a model into a process that is supposed to benefit the users.

When you deploy your model, your code should run properly in the designated environment and have access to the required hardware, such as the GPU, and users' data needs to be accessible in the right format for your model to work. Some of the tests that we talked about in the *testing* stage of the life cycle make sure that your model runs as expected in the production environment.

When we talk about providing a model in a production environment, it either gets used behind the scenes for the benefit of the user, such as when Netflix and Amazon Prime suggest movies to you using their machine learning models, or gets used directly by the user as a standalone process or as part of a bigger system, such as when machine learning models get used in hospitals to help clinicians in disease diagnosis. The considerations for these two different use cases are not the same. If you want to deploy a model in hospitals to be used directly by clinicians, you need to consider all the difficulties and planning needed to set up the proper production environment and all the software dependencies. You also need to make sure their local system has the necessary hardware requirements. Alternatively, you can provide your model through web applications. In this case, you need to ensure the security and privacy of the data that gets uploaded into your database.

Model mentoring is a critical part of the machine learning life cycle when it comes to collecting the necessary information and feedback. This feedback can then be used to improve or correct the data that's used for modeling or improve the model's training and testing. Monitoring machine learning models helps us ensure that the models in production provide predictions according to expectations. Three of the issues that could cause unreliable predictions by a machine learning model are data variance, data drift, and concept drift. Data drift and concept drift are considered two different types of model drift. Model drift is about different kinds of changes in the data, either features or output variables, that make predictions of a model irrelevant or ineffective on the new user data.

We will talk more about model deployment and monitoring and the engineering aspects of the machine learning life cycles in future chapters of this book, such as *Chapter 10, Versioning and Reproducible Machine Learning Modeling*.

## Summary

In this chapter, we talked about different components of a machine learning life cycle, from data collection and selection to model training and evaluation and, finally, model deployment and monitoring. We also showed how modularizing the data processing, modeling, and deployment aspects of the machine learning life cycle helps in identifying opportunities for improving machine learning models.

In the next chapter, you will learn about concepts beyond improving the performance of machine learning models, such as impartial modeling and fairness, accountability, and transparency toward achieving responsible AI systems.

## Questions

1. Can you provide two examples of data cleaning processes?

2. Can you explain the difference between the one-hot and label encoding methods?

3. How can you use quantiles of a distribution to detect its outliers?

4. What comes to your mind regarding the differences between the considerations of deploying a model locally for doctors versus deploying models behind chatbots in a banking system?

## References

- Micci-Barreca, Daniele. *A preprocessing scheme for high-cardinality categorical attributes in classification and prediction problems*. ACM SIGKDD Explorations Newsletter 3.1 (2001): 27-32.

- Basu, Anirban, *Software Quality Assurance, Testing and Metrics*, PRENTICE HALL, January 1, 2015.

# 3
# Debugging toward Responsible AI

Developing successful machine learning models is not solely about achieving high performance. We all get excited when we improve the performance of our models. We feel responsible for developing a high-performance model. But we are also responsible for building fair and secure models. These goals, which are beyond performance improvement, are among the objectives of *responsible machine learning*, or more broadly, *responsible artificial intelligence*. As part of responsible machine learning modeling, we should consider transparency and accountability when training and making predictions for our models and consider governance systems for our data and modeling processes.

In this chapter, we will cover the following topics:

- Impartial modeling fairness in machine learning
- Security and privacy in machine learning
- Transparency in machine learning modeling
- Accountable and open to inspection modeling
- Data and model governance

By the end of this chapter, you will understand the need and different concerns and challenges in responsible machine learning modeling. You will have also learned about different techniques that can help us in responsible modeling and ensuring privacy and security while developing machine learning models.

## Technical requirements

You need to understand the components of machine learning life cycles before reading this chapter as this will help you better understand the concepts and be able to use them in your projects.

# Impartial modeling fairness in machine learning

Machine learning models make mistakes. But when a mistake happens, they could have biases, such as in the COMPAS example provided in *Chapter 1, Beyond Code Debugging*. We need to investigate our models for the existence of such biases and revise them to eliminate these biases. Let's go through more examples to clarify the importance of investigating our data and models for the existence of such biases.

Recruiting is a challenging process for every company as they must identify the most suitable candidates to interview from hundreds of applicants who have submitted resumes and cover letters. In 2014, Amazon started to develop a hiring tool using machine learning to screen job applicants and select the best ones to pursue based on the information provided in their resumes. This was a text processing model that used the text in resumes to identify the key information and select the top candidates. But eventually, Amazon decided to abandon the system as the model was biased in selecting men over women in the hiring process. The main reason behind this bias was the data, which contained mainly resumes of men, that was fed into the machine learning model. The model learned how to identify language and key information in men's resumes, but it was not effective when it came to women's resumes. Hence, the model couldn't rank candidates for a job application while remaining unbiased in terms of gender.

Some machine learning models are designed to predict the likelihood of hospitalization. These models can help reduce individual and population healthcare costs. However, such beneficial models can have their own biases. For example, hospitalization requires access to and the use of health care services, which is influenced by differences in socioeconomic conditions. This means that the datasets that are available for building models to predict the likelihood of hospitalization would have more positive data on people of high socioeconomic conditions compared to poor families. This inequality could cause biases in decision-making by machine learning models for hospitalization, which results in limiting the access of low socioeconomic people to hospitalization even further.

Another example of biases in machine learning applications in the healthcare setting has been in genetic studies. These studies have been criticized for biases due to them not properly accounting for diversity in populations, which could result in misdiagnosis in the studied diseases.

Two main sources of bias include data, which either originated from the data source or was introduced in data processing before model training, and algorithmic bias. Let's review both.

## Data bias

You might have heard of the "garbage in, garbage out" concept in computer science. This concept is about the fact that if nonsense data gets into a computer tool, such as a machine learning model, the output will be nonsense. The data that gets fed to help train machine learning algorithms could have all sorts of issues that eventually result in biases, as mentioned previously. For example, the data could under-represent a group, similar to women in the hiring data fed into the Amazon model. Recall that having this biased data shouldn't stop us from building models, but we have to design our life cycle components, such as data selection and wrangling or model training, while considering these biases and testing our models for bias detection before bringing a model into production. The following are some of the sources of data biases.

### Data collection bias

Data that is collected could contain biases, such as gender bias, as in the Amazon applicant sorting example, race bias, as in COMPAS, socioeconomic biases, as in hospitalization examples, or other kinds of biases. As another example, imagine that a machine learning model for autonomous driving is trained only on images of streets, cars, people, and traffic signs taken in the daytime. The model will be biased and not reliable in the nighttime. This kind of bias can be removed after providing feedback from data exploration or data wrangling steps to data collection and selection in the machine learning life cycle. But if it is not revised before a model gets trained, tested, and deployed, then the feedback needs to be immediately provided from model monitoring, when biases in predictions get detected, and used in the life cycle to provide less biased data for modeling.

### Sampling bias

Another source of data bias could be in the process of sampling data points or sampling the population in the *data collection* stage of the life cycle. For example, when sampling students to fill in a survey, our sampling process could be biased toward girls or boys, rich or poor student families, or high versus low-grade students. These kinds of biases cannot be easily fixed by adding samples of other groups. Sampling processes for filling surveys or designing clinical trials for new drug testing on patients are among examples of data collection processes where adding data to them is not necessarily allowed. Some of these data collection processes need a prior definition of the population that cannot be changed in the middle of the process. In such cases, different kinds of possible biases need to be determined and considered when designing the data sampling process.

### Exclusion bias

In the process of data cleaning and wrangling, before you start training and testing a machine learning model, features could be removed because of statistical reasoning, such as low information content or variance across data points or not having a desired characteristic. These feature removals can sometimes cause biases in our modeling. Although not excluded, some of the features could also cause biases in the eventual machine learning model predictions.

### Measurement or labeling bias

Measurement and annotation biases could be caused by issues or differences in terms of technologies, experts, or non-expert data annotators, who generated or annotated the data that's used for model training, testing, and prediction in production. For example, if one camera type is used to collect the data to train a machine learning model for image classification, predictions in production might have lower reliability if images in production will be captured by another camera that generates images with a different quality.

## Algorithmic bias

There could be systematic errors associated with the algorithm and training process of a machine learning model. For example, instead of the data being biased to a specific race or skin color in face recognition tools, the algorithm might result in biased predictions regarding a group with a specific skin color or race. Keeping the machine learning life cycle in mind, in the modular way it was presented in *Chapter 2*, *Machine Learning Life Cycle*, will help you identify the issues in a stage such as model monitoring. Then, the feedback can be provided for the relevant step, such as data collection or data wrangling, to eliminate the identified biases. There are methodologies to detect biases and resolve them that we will go through in future chapters. For example, we can use machine learning explainability techniques to identify the contributions of features, or their combinations, that could cause biases in predictions.

In addition to eliminating biases in our models, we also need to take into account security and privacy concerns while going through a machine learning life cycle, which is our next topic.

# Security and privacy in machine learning

Security is a concern for all businesses with physical or virtual products and services. 60 years ago, each bank had to ensure the security of physical assets, such as cash and important documents, in its branches. But after moving to the digital world, they had to build new security systems to make sure that the data of their clients and their money and assets, which can now be transferred and changed digitally, were secure. Machine learning products and technologies are no exception and need to have proper security systems. Security concerns in machine learning settings could be related to the security of the data, the models themselves, or model predictions. In this section, we will introduce three important subjects regarding security and privacy in machine learning modeling: **data privacy**, **data poisoning**, and **adversarial attacks**.

## Data privacy

The privacy of the user data in production or the data you have stored and used for model training and testing is an important aspect of security system design for machine learning technologies. The data needs to be secure for many reasons:

- If the data includes confidential information of users, people, or organizations the data has been received from

- If the data is licensed from a commercial data provider under legal contracts and should not become accessible through your services or technologies with others

- If the data is generated for you and considered one of the assets of your team and organization

In all these cases, you need to make sure the data is secure. You can use security systems for your databases and datasets. You can also design encryption processes on top of this if part of the data needs to be transferred digitally between two servers, for example.

### Data privacy attacks

Some attacks are designed to access private and confidential data in your datasets and databases, such as patient information in hospitals, customer data in banking systems, or the personal information of employees of governmental organizations. Three of these attacks are *data reconstruction attacks*, *identity recognition attacks*, and *individual tracing attacks*, all of which can be done through **internet protocol** (**IP**) tracking, for example.

## Data poisoning

Change in the meaning and quality of data is another concern in data security. Data could be poisoned and the resulting changes in prediction could have drastic consequences financially, legally, and ethically for individuals, teams, and organizations. Imagine you designed a machine learning model with your friends for stock market prediction and your model uses news feeds and stock prices in previous days as input features. This data gets extracted from different resources such as Yahoo Finance and different sources of news. If your database gets poisoned, by changing the values of some of the features or changes in the collected data, such as the price history of a piece of stock, you might go through serious financial losses as your model might suggest that you buy stocks that will lose their value by more than 50% in a week rather than going up. This is an example that has financial consequences. However, data poisoning could have life-threatening consequences if, for example, it happens in healthcare or military systems.

## Adversarial attacks

Sometimes, you can fool machine learning models by making very simple changes, such as adding small amounts of noise or perturbation to feature values. This is the concept behind generating adversarial examples and adversarial attacks.

For example, in a medical AI system, an image of a benign (that is, not harmful) mole could be diagnosed as malignant (that is, harmful and dangerous in general terms) by adding adversarial noise in the image that would not be recognizable by the human eye or simply rotating the image. Synonymous text substitution such as changing *"The patient has a history of back pain and chronic alcohol abuse and more recently has been seen in several..."* to *"The patient has a history of lumbago and chronic alcohol dependence and more recently has been seen in several..."* could change the diagnosis from benign to malignant (Finlayson et al., 2019). In other applications of image classification, such as in self-driving cars, simple black and white stickers could sometimes fool models into classifying images of stop signs or frames of videos of stop signs (Eykholt et al., 2018).

Adversarial examples could mislead your system in inference or training and validating whether they get injected into your modeling data and poison it. There are three important aspects of knowing your adversary that can help you in protecting your systems – that is, the attacker's goal, knowledge, and capability (*Table 3.1*):

| Type of Knowledge about the Adversary | Aspects of Different Types of Knowledge | Definition |
| --- | --- | --- |
| The attacker's goal | Security violation | The attacker tries to do the following:<br><br>• Evade detection<br><br>• Compromise system functionalities<br><br>• Get access to private information |
| | Attack specificity | Targeting specific or random data points to generate wrong results |
| The attacker's knowledge | Perfect-knowledge white-box attacks | The attacker knows everything about the system |
| | Zero-knowledge black-box attacks | The attacker doesn't have any knowledge of the system itself but collects information through predictions of the model in production |
| | Limited-knowledge gray-box attacks | The attacker has limited knowledge |
| The attacker's capability | Attack influence | Causative: Attackers can poison train data and manipulate test data<br><br>Exploratory: The attacker can manipulate test data only |
| | Data manipulation constraints | Constraints on data manipulation to eliminate data manipulation or make it challenging |

Table 3.1 – Types of knowledge about adversaries (Biggio et al., 2018)

## Output integrity attacks

This type of attack usually doesn't affect data processing, model training and testing, or even prediction in production. It comes between the output of your model and what will be shown to the user. Based on this definition, this attack is not specific to machine learning settings. But in our machine learning systems, understanding this type of attack solely based on the outputs shown to the users might be challenging. For example, if the prediction probabilities or labels of your model in classification settings get changed once in a while, the results that are shown to the users will be wrong, but the user might accept them if they believe in our systems. It is our responsibility to make sure such kinds of attacks don't challenge the integrity of the results of our model in production.

## System manipulation

Your machine learning system could be manipulated by intentionally designed synthetic data, which either does not exist or might not have existed in the model training and test sets. This manipulation in the prediction level could not only have consequences such as time wasted for investigating wrong predictions of the model, but it could also poison your models and change the performance of your model in testing and production if the data enters your training, evaluation, or test data.

## Secure and private machine learning techniques

Some techniques help us in developing secure and privacy-preserving processes and tools for data storage, transfer, and use in machine learning modeling:

- **Anonymization**: This technique focuses on removing information that helps in identifying individual data points, such as individual patients, within a healthcare dataset. This information could be very specific, such as health card numbers, which could have different names in different countries, or more general information, such as gender and age.

- **Pseudonymization**: Instead of removing information, as in anonymization, the personally identifiable data could be replaced with synthetic substitutes as part of pseudonymization.

- **Data and algorithm encryption**: The encryption process transforms the information – be it data or an algorithm – into a new (encrypted) form. The encrypted data can be decrypted (so that it becomes human-readable or machine understandable) if the individual has access to the encryption key (that is, a password-style key necessary for the decryption process). In this way, getting access to the data and algorithm without the encryption key will be almost impossible or very difficult. We will review encryption techniques such as **Advanced Encryption Standard (AES)** in *Chapter 16, Security and Privacy in Machine Learning*.

- **Homomorphic encryption**: This is an encryption technique that eliminates the need for data decryption at the time of prediction by a machine learning model. The model uses the encrypted data for predictions, so the data can be kept encrypted through the whole data transfer and usage process in a machine learning pipeline.

- **Federated machine learning**: Federated machine learning relies on the idea of decentralizing learning, data analysis, and inference, thus allowing the user data to be kept within individual devices or local databases.

- **Differential privacy**: Differential privacy tries to ensure that the removal or addition of individual data points does not affect the outcome of modeling. It attempts to learn from patterns within groups of data points. For example, by adding random noise from a normal distribution, it tries to make features of individual data points obscure. The effect of noise in learning could be eliminated based on the law of large numbers (`https://www.britannica.com/science/law-of-large-numbers`) if a large number of data points is accessible.

These techniques are not applicable and useful in all settings. For example, federated machine learning will not be helpful when you have an internal database and need to just be sure about its security. Differential privacy for small data sources could also be unreliable.

> **Encryption and decryption processes**
>
> Encryption is the process to transform readable data into a human-unreadable form. On the other hand, decryption is the process of transforming encrypted data back into its original readable format. You can find more information on this topic at `https://docs.oracle.com/` and `https://learn.microsoft.com/en-ca/`.

In this section, we talked about privacy and security in machine learning modeling. Even if we build a secure system with minimum privacy concerns, we need to consider other factors to build trust in our models. Transparency is one of those factors. We will introduce this next.

## Transparency in machine learning modeling

Transparency helps users of your model trust it by helping them understand how it works and how it was built. It also helps you, your team, your collaborators, and your organization to collect feedback on different components of your machine learning life cycle. It is worth understanding the transparency requirements in different stages of a life cycle and the challenges in achieving them:

- **Data collection**: Transparency in data collection needs to answer two major questions:

  - What data are you collecting?

  - What do you want to use that data for?

  For example, when users click on the agreement button for data usage when registering for a mobile phone app, they are giving consent for the information they provide in the app to be used. But the agreement needs to be clear on the part of the user data that is going to be used and for what purposes.

- **Data selection and exploration**: In these stages of the life cycle, your process of data selection and how you achieved your exploratory results need to be clear. This helps you collect feedback from other collaborators and colleagues on your project.

- **Data wrangling and modeling data preparation**: Before this step, data is almost like the so-called raw data, without any changes in feature definition or data being split into train and test sets. If you design these components of the life cycle as a black box and it's not transparent, you might lose both trust and the opportunity for feedback from other experts with future access to your data and results. For example, imagine you are supposed to not use the genetic information of patients in hospitals, and you provide features called Feature1, Feature2, and so on after these steps in the life cycle. Without explaining how those features were generated and using what original features, people cannot be sure if you used patients' genetic information or not. You also need to be transparent about how you designed your testing strategy and separated your training data from validation and testing.

- **Model training and evaluation**: Transparency in model training helps in understanding the decision-making and pattern recognition aspects of models when learning from data. Transparency in both training and evaluation builds trust for direct users, developers, and auditors to better assess these processes. It is true that, for example, >99% of Amazon Prime users never want to understand the machine learning modeling behind the scenes. However, our models are sometimes used directly by users, such as doctors in hospitals for diagnosis or employees of manufacturing facilities. *Explainability*, which we will discuss in *Chapter 6*, *Interpretability and Explainability in Machine Learning Modeling*, is an important concept in machine learning modeling that has a close relationship with transparency and helps users better understand how the model works.

- **Testing**: Transparency in decision-making in the testing stage of the life cycle that helps in better understanding the process of selecting or rejecting a model, or planning for improving and debugging the related code, data processing, or model training and evaluation.

- **Model deployment and monitoring**: In addition to getting feedback from other developers and experts in your organization and team, or public experts, you need to make the effect of the model in production and what data is collected for monitoring clear for users and auditors within or outside of your organization.

Despite the need for transparency, an increase in transparency might make your system vulnerable from the perspectives of security and privacy. So, you cannot aim for maximum transparency without keeping privacy and security in mind.

Fairness and bias removal, privacy, and transparency are all factors in responsible machine learning modeling. But we need to remember that the accountability for achieving fair and secure models and systems is on us.

## Accountable and open to inspection modeling

The models we develop as employees of different businesses or incorporations, research institutes or universities, or as freelancers could eventually get into production in different applications, such as healthcare, finance, manufacturing, marketing, retail, transportation, media, and entertainment. Our models could use patient data to predict whether they will get cancer or diabetes or whether they will respond to therapy. Alternatively, they could use the financial history and other information on the clients of a bank to assess their eligibility for loans. Another example is that our model can use the history of people's purchases to recommend new products to them.

As we discussed in this chapter, we have to take care of the privacy of data and models, provide a fair and impartial model, and make our models as transparent as possible. But we have to remember that we are accountable for managing all these concerns in developing reliable and responsible machine learning models. I asked ChatGPT, the famous machine learning chatbot developed by OpenAI, *"Are you accountable for your responses?"* It responded as follows:

*"As a machine learning model, I do not have the ability to be held accountable for my responses in the same way that a human would. I am designed to generate responses based on the input I receive, but I do not have personal beliefs, intentions, and motivations. I am not capable of making decisions or choices on my own. My responses are a reflection of the training data and algorithms that were used to create me, and my creators are responsible for ensuring that I am functioning as intended."*

> **Note**
>
> There are quotes in the next few paragraphs of this chapter from legal sources that haven't been changed to make sure the legal content is not rephrased inappropriately. However, this is not a legal book and no content of this book should be considered as legal advice.

But accountability is not optional. There have been legislations and regulations in the last few years to keep the developers and owners of machine learning models and products accountable regarding the concerns we talked about in this chapter. For example, the **European Union's (EU's) General Data Protection Regulation (GDPR)** lists the rights of the individuals whose personal data is being processed to give them control over their data. It does this through the following aspects:

- The need for an individual's clear consent to process their data
- Easier access for the data subject to their data
- The rights to rectification, to erasure, and to be forgotten
- The right to object, including to the use of personal data, for profiling
- The right to data portability from one service provider to another

The EU also established a judicial remedy and compensation system (source: https://www.consilium.europa.eu/en/policies/data-protection/).

The EU later developed the **Artificial Intelligence (AI) Act** as the first law on AI by a major regulator (source: https://artificialintelligenceact.eu/).

But these regulations are not limited to the EU. For example, the *White House Office of Science and Technology Policy* released the following blueprint for an AI Bill of Rights to protect the American public in the age of AI (source: `https://www.whitehouse.gov/ostp/ai-bill-of-rights/`).

Canada also later proposed the C-27 AI law, which "creates its baseline obligations through a set of primary offenses, protecting citizens from errant AI and a universal record-keeping obligation on the use of data" (source: `https://www.lexology.com/library/detail.aspx?g=4b960447-6a94-47d1-94e0-db35c72b4624`).

The last topic we want to discuss in this chapter is governance in machine learning modeling. In the next section, you will learn how governance can help you and your organizations in developing your machine learning models.

# Data and model governance

Governance in machine learning modeling is about the use of tools and procedures to help you, your team, and your organization in developing reliable and responsible machine learning models. You shouldn't consider it as any sort of restriction on how to conduct your projects but as an opportunity to reduce the risk of undetected mistakes. The governance in machine learning is supposed to be designed to help you and your organization achieve your objectives in helping humanity and business and avoid processes and models that could have ethical, legal, or financial consequences. Here are some examples of ways to establish governance systems in a team and organization:

- **Define guidelines and protocols**: As we want to detect issues in our models and improve our models in terms of both performance and responsibility, we need to design guidelines and protocols for simplification and consistency. We need to define criteria and methods for what are considered issues with models, such as from a security perspective, and what is considered an opportunity for model improvement that's worth spending time and effort on. We need to remember that machine learning modeling, considering the topics we talked about in this chapter and the different steps of the life cycle, is not an easy task and you shouldn't expect that every developer you work with will know all of them like a specialist.

- **Training and mentorship**: You need to look for mentorship and training programs and read books and articles, and then provide these opportunities for your team if you are a manager. But you also need to bring what you or your team learn into practice. Each concept in machine learning modeling has its challenges. For example, if you decide to use defense mechanisms against adversarial attacks, it is not as simple as loading a Python library and hoping nothing happens for eternity. So, practice what you learn and provide opportunities for your team to bring what they learn into practice.

- **Define responsibilities and accountabilities**: It is not a one-person job to take care of all aspects of the machine learning life cycle to build a technology and take care of all the responsibility topics we talked about in this chapter. That being said, the responsibilities and accountabilities of individuals within teams and organizations need to be clearly defined to reduce the redundancy of effort while making sure nothing gets missed.

- **Use feedback collection systems**: We need to design simple-to-use and preferably automated systems to collect feedback and act upon it throughout the machine learning life cycle. This feedback will help developers that are responsible for each step of a life cycle and eventually result in a better model being brought up in production.

- **Use a quality control process**: We need quantitative and predefined methods and protocols to assess the quality of machine learning models after training or in production or to assess processed data coming out of each stage of a machine learning life cycle. Having the quality control processes defined and documented help us in attaining a scalable system for a faster and more consistent quality assessment. However, these processes can be revised and adapted according to new criteria and the risks associated with data and the corresponding machine learning models.

Now that we understand the importance of responsible machine learning modeling and reviewed important factors and techniques to achieve it, we are ready to move on to the next part of this book and get into more technical details concerning developing reliable, high-performance, and fair machine learning models and technologies.

## Summary

In this chapter, we talked about the different elements of responsible AI, such as data privacy, security in machine learning systems, the different types of attacks and designing defense systems against them, transparency and accountability in the machine learning era, and how to use data and model governance to develop reliable and responsible models in practice.

This chapter and the two previous chapters, which make up *Part 1* of this book, introduced important concepts in machine learning modeling and model debugging. *Part 2* includes topics on *how* to improve machine learning models.

In the next chapter, you will learn about methods for detecting issues in machine learning models and opportunities for improving the performance and generalizability of such models. We will cover statistical, mathematical, and visualization techniques for model debugging with real-life examples to help you quickly start implementing these methods so that you can investigate and improve your models.

## Questions

1. Can you explain two types of data biases?
2. What is the difference between white-box and black-box adversarial attacks?
3. Can you explain how data and algorithm encryption can help in securing the privacy and security of your systems?
4. Can you explain the difference between differential privacy and federated machine learning?

5. How does transparency help you in increasing the number of users of your machine learning models?

# References

- Zou, James, and Londa Schiebinger. *AI can be sexist and racist – it's time to make it fair.* (2018): 324-326.

- Nushi, Besmira, Ece Kamar, and Eric Horvitz. *Towards accountable ai: Hybrid human-machine analyses for characterizing system failure.* Proceedings of the AAAI Conference on Human Computation and Crowdsourcing. Vol. 6. 2018.

- Busuioc, Madalina. *Accountable artificial intelligence: Holding algorithms to account.* Public Administration Review 81.5 (2021): 825-836.

- Unceta, Irene, Jordi Nin, and Oriol Pujol. *Risk mitigation in algorithmic accountability: The role of machine learning copies.* Plos one 15.11 (2020): e0241286.

- Leonelli, Sabina. *Data governance is key to interpretation: Reconceptualizing data in data science.* Harvard Data Science Review 1.1 (2019): 10-1162.

- Sridhar, Vinay, et al. *Model governance: Reducing the anarchy of production {ML}.* 2018 USENIX Annual Technical Conference (USENIX ATC 18). 2018.

- Stilgoe, Jack. *Machine learning, social learning, and the governance of self-driving cars.* Social studies of science 48.1 (2018): 25-56.

- Reddy, Sandeep, et al. *A governance model for the application of AI in health care.* Journal of the American Medical Informatics Association 27.3 (2020): 491-497.

- Gervasi, Stephanie S., et al. *The Potential For Bias In Machine Learning And Opportunities For Health Insurers To Address It: Article examines the potential for bias in machine learning and opportunities for health insurers to address it.* Health Affairs 41.2 (2022): 212-218.

- Gianfrancesco, M. A., Tamang, S., Yazdany, J., & Schmajuk, G. (2018). *Potential Biases in Machine Learning Algorithms Using Electronic Health Record Data.* JAMA internal medicine, 178(11), 1544.

- Finlayson, Samuel G., et al. *Adversarial attacks on medical machine learning.* Science 363.6433 (2019): 1287-1289.

- Eykholt, Kevin, et al. *Robust physical-world attacks on deep learning visual classification.* Proceedings of the IEEE conference on computer vision and pattern recognition. 2018.

- Biggio, Battista, and Fabio Roli. *Wild patterns: Ten years after the rise of adversarial machine learning.* Pattern Recognition 84 (2018): 317-331.

- Kaissis, Georgios A., et al. *Secure, privacy-preserving and federated machine learning in medical imaging.* Nature Machine Intelligence 2.6 (2020): 305-311.

- Acar, Abbas, et al. *A survey on homomorphic encryption schemes: Theory and implementation.* ACM Computing Surveys (Csur) 51.4 (2018): 1-35.

- Dwork, Cynthia. *Differential privacy: A survey of results.* International conference on theory and applications of models of computation. Springer, Berlin, Heidelberg, 2008.

- Abadi, Martin, et al. *Deep learning with differential privacy.* Proceedings of the 2016 ACM SIGSAC conference on computer and communications security. 2016.

- Yang, Qiang, et al. *Federated machine learning: Concept and applications.* ACM Transactions on Intelligent Systems and Technology (TIST) 10.2 (2019): 1-19.

# Part 2: Improving Machine Learning Models

This part will help us transition into the critical aspects of refining and understanding machine learning models. We will start with a deep dive into detecting performance and efficiency bottlenecks in models, followed by actionable strategies to enhance their performance. The narrative then shifts to the subject of interpretability and explainability, elucidating the importance of not just building models that work, but ones we can understand and trust. We will conclude this part by presenting the methods to reduce bias, emphasizing the imperative of fairness in machine learning.

This part has the following chapters:

- *Chapter 4, Detecting Performance and Efficiency Issues in Machine Learning Models*
- *Chapter 5, Improving the Performance of Machine Learning Models*
- *Chapter 6, Interpretability and Explainability in Machine Learning Modeling*
- *Chapter 7, Decreasing Bias and Achieving Fairness*

# 4

# Detecting Performance and Efficiency Issues in Machine Learning Models

One of the main objectives we must keep in mind is how to build a high-performance machine learning model with minimal errors on new data we want to use the model for. In this chapter, you will learn how to properly assess the performance of your models and identify opportunities for decreasing their errors.

This chapter includes many figures and code examples to help you better understand these concepts and start benefiting from them in your projects.

We will cover the following topics:

- Performance and error assessment measures
- Visualization
- Bias and variance diagnosis
- Model validation strategy
- Error analysis
- Beyond performance

By the end of this chapter, you will have learned about how to assess the performance of machine learning models and the benefits, limitations, and wrong usage of visualization in different machine learning problems. You will have also learned about bias and variance diagnosis and error analysis to help you identify opportunities so that you can improve your models.

# Technical requirements

The following requirements should be considered for this chapter as they will help you better understand the concepts, use them in your projects, and practice with the provided code:

- Python library requirements:

  - `sklearn` >= 1.2.2

  - `numpy` >= 1.22.4

  - `pandas` >= 1.4.4

  - `matplotlib` >= 3.5.3

  - `collections` >= 3.8.16

  - `xgboost` >= 1.7.5

- You should have basic knowledge of model validation and testing, as well as classification, regression, and clustering in machine learning

You can find the code files for this chapter on GitHub at `https://github.com/PacktPublishing/Debugging-Machine-Learning-Models-with-Python/tree/main/Chapter04`.

# Performance and error assessment measures

The metrics we use to assess the performance and calculate errors in our models, and how we interpret their values, determine the models we select, the decisions we make to improve a component of our machine learning life cycle, and determine if we have a reliable model to bring into production. Although many performance metrics can be used in one line of Python code to calculate errors and performance, we shouldn't blindly use them or try to improve our performance reports by implementing many of them together without knowing their limitations and how to correctly interpret them. In this section, we will talk about metrics for assessing the performance of classification, regression, and clustering models.

## Classification

Each classification model, either binary or multi-class, returns the probability of predictions, a number between 0 and 1, which then gets transformed into class labels. There are two major categories of performance metrics: **label-based performance metrics**, which rely on predicted labels, and **probability-based performance metrics**, which use the probability of predictions for performance or error calculation.

## Label-based performance metrics

The predicted probabilities of classification models get transformed into class labels by the Python classes we use for modeling. We can then use a confusion matrix, as shown in *Figure 4.1*, to identify four groups of data points, including **true positives (TPs)**, **false positives (FPs)**, **false negatives (FNs)**, and **true negatives (TNs)** for binary classification problems:

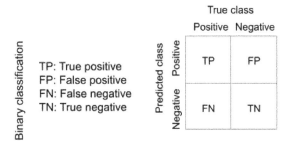

Figure 4.1 – Confusion matrix for binary classification

We can use `sklearn.metrics.confusion_matrix()` to extract these four groups of data points and then calculate performance metrics such as specificity according to the following mathematical definition:

$$Specificity = \frac{TN}{TN + FP}$$

Here is the Python implementation of extracting specificity, precision, and recall from a confusion matrix:

```
from sklearn.metrics import confusion_matrix as cm

def performance_from_cm(y_true, y_pred):
    # Calculating values of confusion matrix
    cm_values = cm(y_true, y_pred)
    # Extracting tn, fp, fn, and tp from calculated confusion matrix
    tn, fp, fn, tp = cm_values.ravel()
    # Calculating specificity
    specificity = tn/(tn+fp)
    # Calculating precision
    precision = tp/(tp+fp)
    # Calculating recall
    recall = tp/(tp+fn)

    return specificity, precision, recall
```

We can calculate other performance metrics, such as precision and recall, using TP, TN, FP, and FN, which have been extracted from the confusion matrix, or directly use functions available in Python (*Table 4.1*). In addition to the Python functions to calculate some of the common performance metrics for classification models, you can also find the mathematical definitions of the metrics and their interpretations in *Table 4.1*. This extra information will help you understand how to interpret each of these metrics and when to use them:

| Metric | Python Function | Formula | Description |
|---|---|---|---|
| Accuracy | `metrics.accuracy_score()` | $\frac{TP + TN}{n}$ <br> $n$: Number of data points | Number of correct predictions over the total number of data points <br><br> Range: [0, 1] <br><br> Higher values mean higher performance |
| Precision or positive predictive value (PPV) | `metrics.precision_score()` | $\frac{TP}{TP + FP}$ | Fraction of predicted positives that are positive <br><br> Range:[0, 1] <br><br> Higher values mean higher performance |
| Recall, sensitivity, or true positive rate (TPR) | `metrics.recall_score()` | $\frac{TP}{TP + FN}$ | Fraction of positives that are predicted as positive <br><br> Range:[0, 1] <br><br> Higher values mean higher performance |

| | | | |
|---|---|---|---|
| F1 score and its derivatives | `metrics.` `f1_` `score()` | $\dfrac{Precision * Recall}{\frac{Precision + Recall}{2}}$ | The harmonic mean of precision and recall<br><br>Range:[0, 1]<br><br>Higher values mean higher performance |
| Balanced accuracy | `metrics.` `balanced_` `accuracy_` `score()` | $\dfrac{Recall + Specificity}{2}$ | Average of the fraction of positives and negatives that are truly predicted<br><br>Range:[0, 1]<br><br>Higher values mean higher performance |
| Matthews correlation coefficient (MCC) | `sklearn.` `metrics.` `matthews_` `corrcoef()` | $\dfrac{TP*TN - FP*FN}{\sqrt{(TP + FP)(FP + TN)(TN + FN)(FN + TP)}}$ | The numerator aims to maximize diagonal and minimize off-diagonal elements of a confusion matrix<br><br>Range: [ − 1, 1]<br><br>Higher values mean higher performance |

Table 4.1 – Common metrics for assessing the performance of classification models

One aspect of selecting performance metrics for model selection and reporting is their relevance to the target problem. For example, if you are building a model for cancer detection, you could aim to maximize recall by maximizing the identification of all positive class members (that is, cancer patients) while controlling them for precision. This strategy helps you make sure patients with cancer will not remain undiagnosed with a deadly disease, although it would be ideal to have a model with high precision and recall at the same time.

Selecting performance metrics depends on whether we care about the true prediction of all classes with the same level of importance or whether there are one or more classes that would be more important. There are algorithmic ways to enforce the model to care more about one or multiple classes. Also, in reporting performance and model selection, we need to consider this imbalance between the classes and not solely rely on performance metrics that summarize the prediction performance of all classes with equal weights.

We also have to note that we define positive and negative classes in the case of binary classification. The data we generate or collect usually does not have such labeling. For example, your dataset could have "fraud" versus "not fraud," "cancer" versus "healthy," or digit names in strings such as "one," "two," and "three." So, we need to select the performance metrics according to our definition of classes if there are one or more we care more or less about.

The other aspect of selecting performance metrics is their reliability, and if they have biases that depend on the data, we use them for training, validation, or testing. For example, accuracy, one of the widely used performance metrics for classification models, should not be used on an imbalanced dataset. Accuracy is defined as the total number of correct predictions over the total number of data points (*Table 4.1*). Hence, if a model predicts all data points as the majority class, it returns a high value, even if it might not be a good model. *Figure 4.2* shows the values of different performance metrics, including accuracy, for a model that predicts all data points as negatives. The accuracy of this bad model is 0.8 if 80% of the data points in the dataset are negative (*Figure 4.2*). However, alternative performance metrics such as balanced accuracy or **Matthews correlation coefficient** (**MCC**) remain unchanged for such a bad model across datasets with different positive data point fractions. Data balance is only one of the parameters, although an important one, in selecting performance metrics for classification models.

Some of the performance metrics have derivatives that better behave in situations such as imbalanced data classification. For example, F1 is a widely used metric that is not the best choice when dealing with imbalanced data classification (*Figure 4.2*):

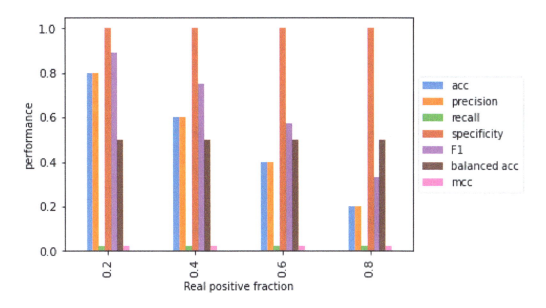

Figure 4.2 – Values of common classification metrics across different real positive
fractions for a model that returns all predictions as negatives

However, it has a general form of $F_\beta$ where a parameter, $\beta$, is used as a weight for increasing the effect of precision according to its mathematical definition. You can use the `sklearn.metrics.fbeta_score()` function to calculate this metric using true and predicted labels of a list of data points:

$$F_\beta = \frac{(1 + \beta^2)precision + recall}{\beta^2 \times precision + recall}$$

## Probability-based performance metrics

The probability outputs of classification models can be directly used to assess the performance of models, without the need for transformation to predict labels. An example of such a performance measure is **logistic loss**, known as **log-loss** or **cross-entropy loss**, which calculates the total loss over a dataset using probabilities of prediction for each data point and its true label, as follows. Log-loss is also a loss function that's used to train classification models:

$$L_{log}(y, p) = -(ylog(p) + (1 - y)log(1 - p))$$

There are other types of probability-based performance assessment methods such as the **receiver operating characteristic** (**ROC**) curve and the **precision recall** (**PR**) curve that consider different cutoffs for transforming probabilities into labels to predict the true positive rate, false positive rate, precision, and recall. Then, these values, across different cutoffs, get used to generate ROC and PR curves (*Figure 4.3*):

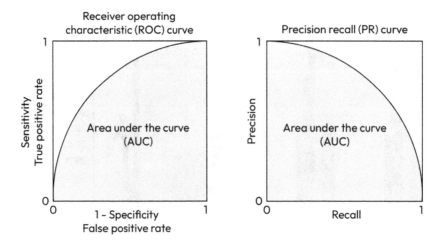

Figure 4.3 – Schematic illustration of ROC and PR curves

It is common to use the area under these curves, referred to as ROC-AUC and PR-AUC, to assess the performance of classification models. ROC-AUC and PR-AUC range from 0 to 1, with 1 being the performance of a perfect model.

In *Figure 4.2*, you saw how some performance metrics return high-performance values for a bad model that predicts everything as negative due to data imbalance. We can see the extension of this analysis in *Figure 4.4* for different fractions of positive data points among true labels and predicted labels. There is no training here and the data points are randomly generated to result in the specified fraction of positive data points in each panel of *Figure 4.4*. The randomly generated probabilities are then transformed into labels so that they can be compared with true labels using different performance metrics.

*Figures 4.4* and *4.5* show different biases in the performance metrics of classification models. For example, the median precision of random predictions is equal to the fraction of true positive data points, while the median recall of random predictions is equal to the fraction of positive predicted labels. You can also check the behavior of other performance metrics in *Figures 4.4* and *4.5* for different fractions of true or predicted positives:

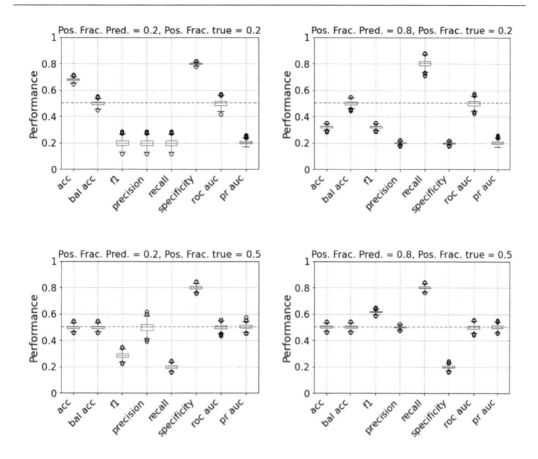

Figure 4.4 – Distribution of performance of 1,000 random binary predictions on 1,000 data points (part 1)

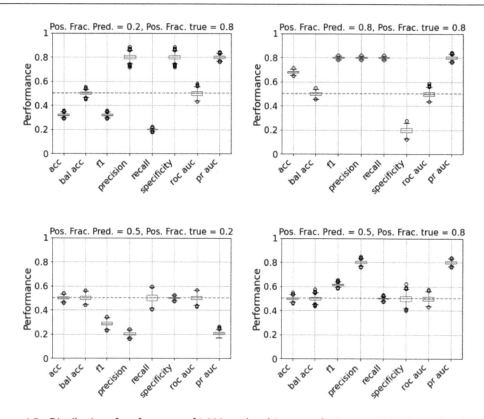

Figure 4.5 – Distribution of performance of 1,000 random binary predictions on 1,000 data points (part 2)

A combination of ROC-AUC and PR-AUC, or the use of MCC or balanced accuracy, are common approaches to have a low bias in performance assessment for classification models. But if you know your objectives, such as if you care more about precision than recall, then you can choose the performance metrics that would add the necessary information for decision-making. But avoid reporting 10 performance metrics for your models just for the sake of counting how many of them are better in one model versus another.

## Regression

You can assess the performance of your regression models using metrics that evaluate either the difference between the continuous predictions of your models and true values, such as **Root Mean Squared Error** (**RMSE**), or the agreement between the predictions and true values, such as the coefficient of determination $R^2$ (*Table 4.2*). Each of the metrics for regression model performance assessment has its assumptions, interpretation, and limitations. For example, $R^2$ doesn't take into account data dimensionality (that is, the number of features, inputs, or independent variables). So, if you have a regression model with multiple features, you should use adjusted $R^2$ instead of $R^2$. By adding new features, $R^2$ could increase but might not necessarily correspond to a better model. However, adjusted

$R^2$ increases when the new inputs improve model performance more than expectation by chance. This is an important consideration, especially if you want to compare models with different numbers of inputs for the sample problem:

| Metric | Python Function | Formula | Description |
|---|---|---|---|
| **Root Mean Squared Error (RMSE)**<br><br>**Mean Squared Error (MSE)** | ```sklearn. metrics. mean_squared_ error()``` | $MSE = \frac{1}{n}\sum_{i=1}^{n}(y_i - \hat{y}_i)^2$<br><br>$RMSE = \sqrt{MSE}$<br><br>$n$: Number of data points<br><br>$y_i$: The true value of the data point, $i$<br><br>$\hat{y}_i$: The predicted value of the data point, $i$ | Range: $[0, \infty)$<br><br>Lower values mean higher performance |
| **Mean Absolute Error (MAE)** | ```sklearn. metrics.mean_ absolute_ error()``` | $MAE = \frac{1}{n}\sum_{i=1}^{n}\lvert y_i - \hat{y}_i \rvert$ | Range: $[0, \infty)$<br><br>Lower values mean higher performance |
| Coefficient of determination ($R^2$) | ```sklearn. metrics.r2_ score()``` | $R^2 = 1 - \dfrac{\sum_{i=1}^{n}(y_i - \hat{y}_i)^2}{\sum_{i=1}^{n}(y_i - \underline{y})^2}$ ;<br><br>$\underline{y} = \frac{1}{n}\sum_{i=1}^{n}y_i$<br><br>$y$: Mean of the true values<br><br>$n$: Number of data points<br><br>$y_i$: The true value of the data point, $i$<br><br>$\hat{y}_i$: The predicted value of the data point, $i$ | Range: $[0, 1]$<br><br>Higher values mean higher performance<br><br>The proportion of the dependent variable that can be explained by the independent variables |
| Adjusted $R^2$ | Use ```sklearn. metrics. r2_score()``` to calculate $R^2$, then calculate the adjusted version using its formula. | $Adj\ R^2 = 1 - \dfrac{(1 - R^2)(n - 1)}{n - m - 1}$<br><br>$n$: Number of data points<br><br>$m$: Number of features | Adjusts to the number of features<br><br>Could be greater than 1 or less than 0 if $m$ is close to $n$<br><br>Higher values mean higher performance |

Table 4.2 – Common metrics for assessing the performance of regression models

Correlation coefficients are also used to report on the performance of regression models. Correlation coefficients use the predicted and true continuous values, or a transformation of those, and report values commonly between -1 and 1, with 1 corresponding to an ideal prediction with 100% agreement and -1 with full disagreement (*Table 4.3*). Correlation coefficients also have their own assumptions and cannot be selected randomly for reporting on the performance of regression models. For example, Pearson correlation is a parametric test that assumes a linear relationship between predicted and true continuous values, which does not always hold. Alternatively, the Spearman and Kendall rank correlations are non-parametric without such assumptions behind the relationship of variables or the distribution of each variable in comparison. Both the Spearman and Kendall rank correlations rely on the rank of predicted and true outputs instead of their actual values:

| Correlation Coefficient | Python Function | Formula | Description |
|---|---|---|---|
| Pearson correlation coefficient or Pearson's r | `scipy.stats.pearsonr()` | $r = \dfrac{\sum_{i=1}^{n}(\hat{y}_i - \hat{\bar{y}})(y_i - \bar{y})}{\sqrt{\sum_{i=1}^{n}(\hat{y}_i - \hat{\bar{y}})^2 (y_i - \bar{y})^2}}$ <br><br> $n$: Number of data points <br><br> $y_i$: The true value of the data point, $i$ <br><br> $\bar{y}$: Mean of the true values <br><br> $\hat{y}_i$: The predicted value of the data point, $i$ <br><br> $\hat{\bar{y}}$: Mean of the predicted values | Parametric <br><br> Looks for a linear relationship between predictions and true values <br><br> Range: <br><br> $[-1, 1]$ |
| Spearman's rank correlation coefficient or Spearman correlation coefficient | `scipy.stats.spearmanr()` | $\rho = 1 - \dfrac{6\sum_{i=1}^{n}d_i^2}{n(n^2 - 1)}$ <br><br> $n$: Number of data points <br><br> $d_i$: The difference between the rank of the data point, $i$, among true values and predicted values | Non-parametric <br><br> Looks for a monotonic relationship between predictions and true values <br><br> Range: <br><br> $[-1, 1]$ |

| Kendall rank correlation coefficient or Kendall's $\tau$ coefficient | `scipy.stats.`<br>`kendalltau()` | $\tau = \dfrac{C - D}{\sqrt{(C + D + T)(C + D + c)}}$<br><br>$C$: Number of concordant pairs (for example, $y_i > y_j$ and $\hat{y}_i > \hat{y}_j$; or $y_i < y_j$ and $\hat{y}_i < \hat{y}_j$)<br><br>$D$: Number of discordant pairs (for example, $y_i > y_j$ and $\hat{y}_i < \hat{y}_j$; or $y_i < y_j$ and $\hat{y}_i > \hat{y}_j$)<br><br>$T$: Number of ties only in predicted values<br><br>$U$: Number of ties only in true values | Non-parametric<br><br>Looks for a monotonic relationship between predictions and true values<br><br>Range:<br><br>$[-1, 1]$ |

Table 4.3 – Common correlation coefficients used for assessing the performance of regression models

## Clustering

Clustering is an unsupervised learning approach to identify groupings of data points using their feature values. However, to assess the performance of a clustering model, we need to have a dataset or example data points with available true labels. We don't use these labels when training the clustering model, as in supervised learning; instead, we use them to assess how well similar data points are grouped and separated from dissimilar data points. You can find some of the common metrics for assessing the performance of clustering models in *Table 4.4*. These metrics do not inform you about the quality of the clustering. For example, homogeneity tells you if the data points that are clustered together are similar to each other while completeness informs you if similar data points in your dataset are clustered together. There are also metrics such as V-measure and adjusted mutual information that try to assess both qualities at the same time:

| Metric | Python Function | Formula | Description |
|---|---|---|---|
| Homogeneity | `sklearn.metrics.homogeneity_score()` | Formula (1) provided in Rosenberg et al., EMNLP-CoNLL 2007 | Measures how many data points within the same clusters are similar to each other<br><br>Range: [0, 1]<br><br>Higher values mean higher performance |
| Completeness | `sklearn.metrics.completeness_score()` | Formula (2) provided in Rosenberg et al., EMNLP-CoNLL 2007 | Measures how similar the data points that are clustered together are<br><br>Range: [0, 1]<br><br>Higher values mean higher performance |
| V-measure or normalized mutual information score | `sklearn.metrics.v_measure_score()` | $v = \dfrac{(1 + \beta) \times h \times c}{(\beta \times h + c)}$<br><br>$h$: Homogeneity<br><br>$c$: Completeness<br><br>$\beta$: Ratio of weight attributed to homogeneity versus completeness | Measures both homogeneity and completeness at the same time<br><br>Range: [0, 1]<br><br>Higher values mean higher performance |
| Mutual information | `sklearn.metrics.mutual_info_score()` | $MI\left(U, V\right) = \sum\limits_{i=1}^{\lvert U \rvert} \sum\limits_{j=1}^{\lvert V \rvert} \dfrac{\lvert U_i \cap V_j \rvert}{N} log \dfrac{\lvert U_i \cap V_j \rvert}{\lvert U_i \rvert \lvert V_j \rvert}$ | Range:<br><br>[0, 1]<br><br>Higher values mean higher performance |
| Adjusted mutual information | `sklearn.metrics.adjusted_mutual_info_score()` | $AMI\left(U, V\right)$<br><br>$= \dfrac{[MI(U, V) - E(MI(U, V))]}{[avg(H(U), H(V)) - E(MI(U, V))]}$ | Range:<br><br>[0, 1]<br><br>Higher values mean higher performance |

Table 4.4 – Common metrics for assessing the performance of clustering models

In this section, we discussed the different performance measures for assessing the performance of machine learning models. But there are other important aspects of performance assessment to consider, such as data visualization, which we will discuss next.

# Visualization for performance assessment

Visualization is an important tool that helps us not only understand the characteristics of our data for modeling but also better assess the performance of our models. Visualization could provide complementary information to the aforementioned model performance metrics.

## Summary metrics are not enough

There are summary statistics such as ROC-AUC and PR-AUC that provide a one-number summary of their corresponding curves for assessing the performance of classification models. Although these summaries are more reliable than many other metrics such as accuracy, they do not completely capture the characteristics of their corresponding curves. For example, two different models with different ROC curves can have the same or very close ROC-AUCs (*Figure 4.6*):

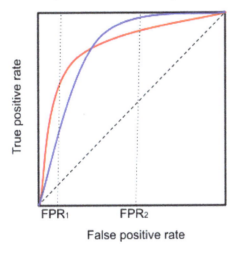

Figure 4.6 – Comparison of two arbitrary models with the same ROC-AUCs and different ROC curves

Comparing ROC-AUCs alone could result in deciding the equivalence of these models. However, they have different ROC curves and in most applications, a red curve is preferred over a blue one as it results in a higher true positive rate for low false positive rates such as $FPR_1$.

## Visualizations could be misleading

Using the proper visualization technique for your results is the key to analyzing the results of your models and reporting their performances. Plotting your data without having the model objective in mind could be misleading. For example, you might see time series plots such as the one shown in *Figure 4.7* that overlay predictions and real values over time in many blog posts. For such time series models, we want predictions and real values to be as close to each other as possible for each time point. Although the lines might seem to agree with each other in *Figure 4.7*, there is a two-time unit delay in predictions shown in orange compared to the true values shown in blue. This lag in predictions could have serious consequences in many applications such as stock price prediction:

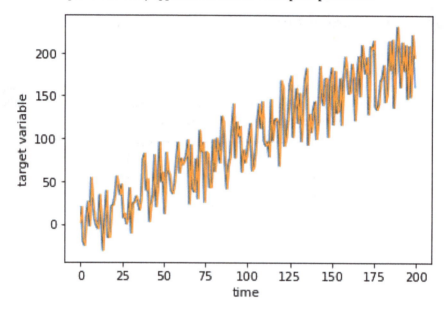

Figure 4.7 – Laying two time series diagrams on top of each other is misleading – the orange and blue curves represent predictions and true values for arbitrary time series data

## Don't interpret your plots as you wish

Each visualization has its assumptions and right way of interpretation. For example, if you want to compare the numerical values of data points in a 2D plot, you need to pay attention to the units of the $x$ and $y$ axes. Or when we use **t-distributed Stochastic Neighbor Embedding** (**t-SNE**), a dimensionality reduction method designed to help in visualizing high dimensional data in low dimensional space, we have to remind ourselves that large distances between data points and densities of each group are not representative of the distances and densities in the original high-dimensional space (*Figure 4.8*):

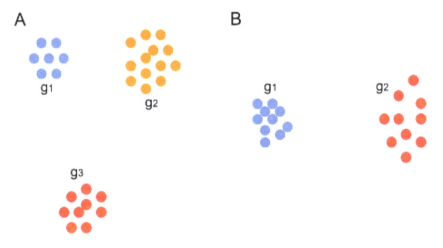

Figure 4.8 – Schematic t-SNE plots showing (A) three groups of data points with different distances and (B) two groups with different densities in two dimensions

You can use different performance measures to assess if your models are trained well and generalizable to new data points, which is the next topic in this chapter.

## Bias and variance diagnosis

We aim to have a model with high performance, or low error, in the training set (that is, a low bias model) while keeping the performance high, or error low, for new data points (that is, a low variance model). As we don't have access to unseen new data points, we must use validation and test sets to assess the variance or generalizability of our models. Model complexity is one of the important factors in determining the bias and variance of machine learning models. By increasing complexity, we let a model learn more complex patterns in training data that could reduce training errors or model bias (*Figure 4.9*):

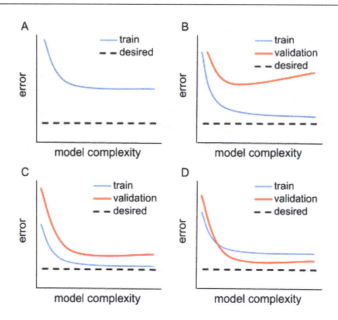

Figure 4.9 – Error versus model complexity for (A) high bias, (B) high variance,
and (C, D) two different cases of low bias and low variance models

This decrease in error helps build a better model, even for new data points. However, this trend changes after a point, and higher complexities could cause overfitting or higher variance and lower performance in validation and test sets compared to the training set (*Figure 4.9*). Assessing bias and variance concerning parameters such as model complexity or dataset size could help us identify opportunities for model performance improvements in training, validation, and test sets.

Four of the possible dependencies of model error in training and validation sets to model complexity are shown in *Figure 4.9*. Although the validation error is usually higher than the training error, you might experience a lower error in validation sets because of the data points you have in your training and validation sets. For example, a multiclass classifier could have a lower error in the validation set because of being better at predicting classes that form the majority of the data points in the validation set. In such cases, you need to investigate the distribution of data points in the training and validation sets before reporting performance assessments on training and validation datasets and deciding which model to select for production.

Let's practice a bias and variance analysis. You can find the results of training random forest models with different maximum depths on the breast cancer dataset from `scikit-learn` (*Figure 4.10*). The breast cancer data from `scikit-learn` is used for training and validating model performance, with 30% of the data randomly separated as the validation set and the rest kept as the training set. By increasing the maximum depth of the random forest models, log-loss error in the training set decreases while balanced accuracy as a measure of model performance increases. Validation errors also decrease up to a maximum depth of three and start increasing after that as a sign of overfitting. Although error decreases after the maximum depth of three, balanced accuracy can still be increased by increasing the maximum depth to four and five. The reason is the difference in the definition of log-loss based on the probability of predictions and the balanced accuracy on predicted labels:

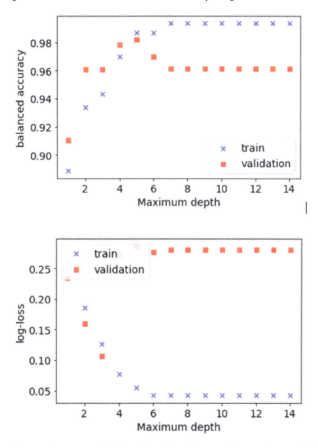

Figure 4.10 – Balanced accuracy (top) and log-loss (bottom) in training and validation sets separated from the breast cancer dataset of scikit-learn for a random forest model

Here is the code for the results shown in *Figure 4.10*. First, we must import the necessary Python libraries and load the breast cancer dataset:

```
from sklearn.datasets import load_breast_cancer
from sklearn.model_selection import train_test_split
from sklearn.metrics import balanced_accuracy_score as bacc
from sklearn.ensemble import RandomForestClassifier as RF
from sklearn.metrics import log_loss
from sklearn.metrics import roc_auc_score
import matplotlib.pyplot as plt
```

```
X, y = load_breast_cancer(return_X_y=True)
```

Then, we must split the data into train and test sets and train multiple random forest models with different maximum depths allowed for their decision trees:

```
X_train, X_test, y_train, y_test = train_test_split(X, y,
    test_size = 0.3, random_state=10)

maximum_depth = 15
depth_range = range(1, maximum_depth)

bacc_train = []
bacc_test = []
log_loss_train = []
log_loss_test = []
for depth_iter in depth_range:
# initializing an fitting a decision tree model
model_fit = RF(n_estimators = 5, max_depth = depth_iter,
    random_state=10).fit(X_train, y_train)
# generating label outputs of train and test set using the trained
model
train_y_labels = model_fit.predict(X_train)
test_y_labels = model_fit.predict(X_test)
# generating probability outputs of train and test set using the
trained model
train_y_probs = model_fit.predict_proba(X_train)
test_y_probs = model_fit.predict_proba(X_test)
# calculating balanced accuracy
bacc_train.append(bacc(y_train, train_y_labels))
bacc_test.append(bacc(y_test, test_y_labels))
# calculating log-loss
log_loss_train.append(log_loss(y_train, train_y_probs))
log_loss_test.append(log_loss(y_test, test_y_probs))
```

Now that you've learned about the concepts of bias and variance, we will introduce different techniques that you can use to validate your models.

# Model validation strategy

To validate our models, we can use separate datasets or split the dataset we have into training and validation sets using different techniques, as explained in *Table 4.5* and illustrated in *Figure 4.11*. In cross-validation strategies, we split the data into different subsets, then the performance score or error for each subset, since the validation set is calculated using the predictions of the model trained on the rest of the data. Then, we can use the mean of the performance across the subsets as the cross-validation performance:

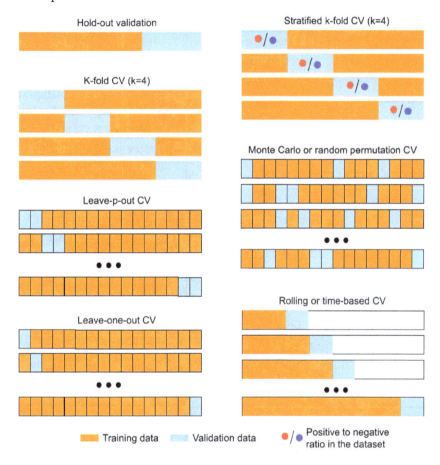

Figure 4.11 – Techniques for separating the validation and training sets within one dataset

Each of these validation techniques has its advantages and limitations. Using cross-validation techniques instead of hold-out validation has the benefit of covering all or the majority of the data in at least one validation subset. Stratified k-fold **cross-validation (CV)** is also a better choice compared to k-fold CV or leave-one-out CV as it keeps the same balance across the validation subsets as in the whole dataset.

The classification or regression hold-out or CV methods don't work for time series data. As the order of data points is important in time series data, shuffling the data or randomly selecting data points is not suitable in the process of training and validation subset selection. Randomly selecting data points for validation and training sets results in models trained on some future data points to predict the outcome in the past, which is not the intention of time series models. Rolling or time series CV is an appropriate validation technique for time series models as it rolls the validation set over time instead of randomly selecting the data point (*Table 4.5*):

| Validation Method | Python Function | Description |
| --- | --- | --- |
| Hold-out validation | `sklearn.model_ selection.train_ test_split()` | This splits all the data into one training and one validation set. 20-40% of the data commonly gets selected as a validation set but this percentage could be lower for large datasets. |
| k-fold cross-validation | `sklearn.model_ selection.KFold()` | This method splits the data into k different subsets and uses each as a validation set and the remaining data points as a training set. |
| Stratified k-fold cross-validation | `sklearn.model_ selection. StratifiedKFold()` | This is similar to k-fold CV but preserves the percentage of samples for each class, as in the whole dataset, in each of the k subsets. |
| Leave-p-out cross-validation (LOCV) | `sklearn.model_ selection. LeavePOut()` | This is similar to k-fold CV, with each subset having p data points instead of splitting the dataset into k subsets. |
| Leave-one-out cross-validation (LOOCV) | `sklearn.model_ selection. LeaveOneOut()` | This works exactly as k-fold CV, with k being equal to the total number of data points. Each validation subset has one data point that uses LOOCV. |
| Monte Carlo or random permutation cross-validation | `sklearn.model_ selection. ShuffleSplit()` | This splits the data randomly into a training and a validation set, similar to hold-out validation, and repeats this process many times. More iterations result in a better assessment of performance, although it increases the computational cost of validation. |

| Rolling or time-based cross-validation | `sklearn.model_selection.TimeSeriesSplit()` | A small subset of data gets selected as the training set and a smaller subset gets selected as the validation set. The validation set gets shifted in time and the data points that were previously considered for validation get added to the training set. |
|---|---|---|

Table 4.5 – Common validation techniques that use one dataset

Here is the Python implementation of hold-out, k-fold CV, and stratified k-fold CV to help you start using these methods in your projects.

First, we must import the necessary libraries, load the breast cancer dataset, and initialize a random forest model:

```
from sklearn.datasets import load_breast_cancer
from sklearn.ensemble import RandomForestClassifier as RF
from sklearn.metrics import roc_auc_score
from sklearn.model_selection import cross_val_score
# importing different cross-validation functions
from sklearn.model_selection import train_test_split
from sklearn.model_selection import KFold
from sklearn.model_selection import StratifiedKFold

modle_random_state = 42
X, y = load_breast_cancer(return_X_y=True)
rf_init = RF(random_state=modle_random_state)
```

Then, we must train and validate different random forest models using each validation technique:

```
# validating using hold-out validation
X_train, X_test, y_train, y_test = train_test_split(X, y,
    test_size = 0.3, random_state=10)
rf_fit = rf_init.fit(X_train, y_train)
# validating using k-fold (k=5) cross-validation
kfold_cv = KFold(n_splits = 5, shuffle=True,
    random_state=10)
scores_kfold_cv = cross_val_score(rf_init, X, y,
    cv = kfold_cv, scoring = "roc_auc")
# validating using stratified k-fold (k=5) cross-validation
stratified_kfold_cv = StratifiedKFold(n_splits = 5,
    shuffle=True, random_state=10)
```

```
scores_strat_kfold_cv = cross_val_score(rf_init, X, y, cv =
stratified_kfold_cv, scoring = "roc_auc")
```

Error analysis is another technique you can benefit from when seeking to develop reliable machine learning models, which we will introduce next.

## Error analysis

You can use error analysis to find common characteristics between data points with incorrectly predicted outputs. For example, the majority of images that are misclassified in image classification models might have darker backgrounds, or a disease diagnostic model might have lower performance for men compared to women. Although manually investigating the data points with incorrect predictions could be insightful, this process could cost you a lot of time. Instead, you can try to reduce the cost programmatically.

Here, we want to practice with a simple case of error analysis in which the number of misclassified data points from each class is counted for a random forest model that's been trained and validated using a 5-fold CV. For error analysis, only predictions for validation subsets are used.

First, we must import the necessary Python libraries and load the wine dataset:

```
from sklearn.datasets import load_wine
from sklearn.ensemble import RandomForestClassifier as RF
from sklearn.model_selection import KFold
from collections import Counter
# loading wine dataset and generating k-fold CV subsets
X, y = load_wine(return_X_y=True)
```

Then, we must initialize a random forest model and 5-fold CV object:

```
kfold_cv = KFold(n_splits = 5, shuffle=True,
    random_state=10)
# initializing the random forest model
rf_init = RF(n_estimators=3, max_depth=5, random_state=42)
```

Then, for each fold, we must train a random forest model using all the data, excluding that fold, and validate the model on the chunk of data considered in that fold:

```
misclass_ind_list = []
for fold_n, (train_idx, validation_idx) in enumerate(
    kfold_cv.split(X, y)):

        #get train and validation subsets for current fold
        X_train, y_train = X[train_idx], y[train_idx]
        X_validation, y_validation = X[validation_idx],
```

```
        y[validation_idx]

rf_fit = rf_init.fit(X_train, y_train)

# write results
match_list = rf_fit.predict(
    X_validation) != y_validation
wrong_pred_subset = [i for i, x in enumerate(
    match_list) if x]
misclass_ind_list.extend([validation_idx[
    iter] for iter in wrong_pred_subset])
```

This analysis shows that class 1 has nine misclassified data points, while classes 2 and 0 have only three and two misclassified examples, respectively. This simple example helps you start practicing with error analysis. But error analysis is not only about identifying misclassification count per class. You can also identify patterns in feature values for misclassified examples by comparing feature values between misclassified data points and the whole dataset.

There are other important factors, such as computational cost and time, that also need to be considered when developing machine learning models. Here, we will briefly talk about this important topic, but the details are beyond the scope of this book.

## Beyond performance

Paying any price for improving the performance of machine learning models is not the objective of modeling as part of bigger pipelines at the industrial level. Increasing the performance of models by a tenth of a percent could help you win machine learning competitions or publish papers by beating state-of-the-art models. But not all improvements result in models worth deploying to production. An example of such efforts, which has been common in machine learning competitions, is model stacking. Model stacking is about using the output of multiple models to train a secondary model, which could increase the cost of inference by orders of magnitude. Python's implementation of stacking of the logistic regression, k-nearest neighbor, random forest, support vector machine, and XGBoost classification models on the breast cancer dataset from `scikit-learn` is shown here. A secondary logistic regression model uses predictions of each of these primary models as input to come up with the final prediction of the stacked model:

```
from sklearn.datasets import load_breast_cancer
from sklearn.preprocessing import StandardScaler
from sklearn.pipeline import make_pipeline
from sklearn.ensemble import StackingClassifier
from sklearn.model_selection import train_test_split

from sklearn.linear_model import LogisticRegression as LR
```

```
from sklearn.neighbors import KNeighborsClassifier as KNN
from sklearn.svm import LinearSVC
from sklearn.ensemble import RandomForestClassifier as RF
from xgboost import XGBClassifier

X, y = load_breast_cancer(return_X_y=True)
X_train, X_test, y_train, y_test = train_test_split(X, y,
    stratify=y, random_state=123)

estimators = [
    ('lr', make_pipeline(StandardScaler(),
    LR(random_state=123))),
    ('knn', make_pipeline(StandardScaler(), KNN())),
    ('svr', make_pipeline(StandardScaler(),
    LinearSVC(random_state=123))),
    ('rf', RF(random_state=123)),
    ('xgb', XGBClassifier(random_state=123))
    ]

stacked_model = StackingClassifier(estimators=estimators,
    final_estimator=LR())

stacked_model.fit(X_train, y_train).score(X_test, y_test)

individual_models = [estimators[iter][1].fit(X_train,
    y_train).score(X_test, y_test) for iter in range(
        0, len(estimators))]
```

In this example, the performance of the stacked model is less than 1% better than the best individual model, while the inference time could be more than 20 times higher, depending on the hardware and software configurations you have. Although inference time could be less important, such as in the case of disease diagnosis or scientific discoveries, it could be of critical importance if your model needs to provide the output in real time, such as in recommending products to consumers. So, you need to consider other factors, such as inference or prediction time, when you're deciding to bring a model into production or planning for new expensive computational experiments or data collection.

Although inference time or other factors need to be considered in your model building and selection, it doesn't mean that you cannot use complex models for real-time output generation. Depending on the application and your budget, you can use better configurations, for example, on your cloud-based system, to eliminate the issues that arise due to higher performance but slower models.

# Summary

In this chapter, we learned about different performance and error metrics for supervised and unsupervised learning models. We discussed the limitations of each metric and the right way of interpreting them. We also reviewed bias and variance analysis and different validation and cross-validation techniques for assessing the generalizability of models. We also presented error analysis as an approach for detecting the components of a model that contribute to model overfitting. We went through Python code examples for these topics to help you practice with them and be able to quickly use them in your projects.

In the next chapter, we will review techniques to improve the generalizability of machine learning models, such as synthetic data addition to training data, removing data inconsistencies, and regularization methods.

# Questions

1. A classifier is designed to identify if patients of a clinic need to go through the rest of the diagnostic steps after the first round of testing. What classification metric would be more or less appropriate? Why?

2. A classifier is designed to assess the risk of investment for different investment options, for a specific amount of money, and is going to be used to suggest investment opportunities to your clients. What classification metric would be more or less appropriate? Why?

3. If the calculated ROC-AUCs of two binary classification models on the same validation set are the same, does it mean that the models are the same?

4. If model A has a lower log-loss compared to model B on the same test set, does it always mean that the MCC of model A is also higher than model B?

5. If model A has a higher $R^2$ on the same number of data points compared to model B, could we claim that model A is better than model B? How does the number of features affect our comparison between the two models?

6. If model A has higher performance than model B, does it mean that choosing model A is the right one to bring into production?

# References

- Rosenberg, Andrew, and Julia Hirschberg. *V-measure: A conditional entropy-based external cluster evaluation measure.* Proceedings of the 2007 joint conference on empirical methods in natural language processing and computational natural language learning (EMNLP-CoNLL). 2007.

- Vinh, Nguyen Xuan, Julien Epps, and James Bailey. *Information theoretic measures for clusterings comparison: is a correction for chance necessary?* Proceedings of the 26th annual international conference on machine learning. 2009.

- Andrew Ng, *Stanford CS229: Machine Learning Course*, Autumn 2018.

- Van der Maaten, Laurens, and Geoffrey Hinton. *Visualizing data using t-SNE.* Journal of machine learning research 9.11 (2008).

- McInnes, Leland, John Healy, and James Melville. *Umap: Uniform manifold approximation and projection for dimension reduction.* arXiv preprint arXiv:1802.03426 (2018).

# 5

# Improving the Performance of Machine Learning Models

In the previous chapter, you learned about different techniques for properly validating and assessing the performance of your machine learning models. The next step is to extend your knowledge of those techniques for improving the performance of your models.

In this chapter, you will learn about techniques to improve the performance and generalizability of your models by working on the data or algorithm you select for machine learning modeling.

In this chapter, we will cover the following topics:

- Options for improving model performance
- Synthetic data generation
- Improving pre-training data processing
- Regularization to improve model generalizability

By the end of this chapter, you will be familiar with different techniques to improve the performance and generalizability of your models and you will know how you can benefit from Python in implementing them for your projects.

## Technical requirements

The following requirements are needed for this chapter as they help you better understand the concepts and enable you to use them in your projects and practice with the provided code:

- Python library requirements:

  - `sklearn` >= 1.2.2

  - `ray` >= 2.3.1

  - `tune_sklearn` >= 0.4.5

  - `bayesian_optimization` >= 1.4.2

  - `numpy` >= 1.22.4

  - `imblearn`

  - `matplotlib` >= 3.7.1

- Knowledge of machine learning validation techniques such as $k$-fold cross-validation

You can find the code files for this chapter on GitHub at `https://github.com/PacktPublishing/ Debugging-Machine-Learning-Models-with-Python/tree/main/Chapter05`.

## Options for improving model performance

The changes we can make to improve the performance of our models could be related to the algorithms we use or the data we feed them to train our models (see *Table 5.1*). Adding more data points could reduce the variance of the model, for example, by adding data close to the decision boundaries of classification models to increase confidence in the identified boundaries and reduce overfitting. Removing outliers could reduce both bias and variance by eliminating the effect of distant data points. Adding more features could help the model to become better at the training stage (that is, lower model bias), but it might result in higher variance. There could also be features that cause overfitting and their removal could help to increase model generalizability.

| Change | Potential effect | Description |
|---|---|---|
| Adding more training data points | Reducing variance | We could add new data points randomly or try to add data points with specific feature values, output values, or labels. |
| Removing outliers with lower stringency | Reducing bias and variance | Removing outliers could reduce errors in the training set but it could also help in training a more generalizable model (that is, a model with lower variance). |
| Adding more features | Reducing bias | We could add features that provide unknown information to the model. For example, adding the crime rate of a neighborhood for house price prediction could improve model performance if that info is not already captured by existing features. |
| Removing features | Reducing variance | Each feature could have a positive effect on training performance but it might add information that is not generalizable to new data points and result in higher variance. |
| Running optimization process for more iterations | Reducing bias | Optimizing for more iteration reduces training error but might result in overfitting. |
| Using more complex models | Reducing bias | Increasing the depth of decision trees is an example of an increase in model complexity that could result in lower model bias but potentially a higher chance of overfitting. |

Table 5.1 – Some of the options to reduce the bias and/or variance of machine learning models

Increasing model complexity could help to reduce bias, as we discussed in the previous chapter, but a model can have many hyperparameters that affect its complexity or result in improving or lowering model bias and generalizability. Some of the hyperparameters that you could start with in the optimization process for the widely used supervised and unsupervised learning methods are provided in *Table 5.2*. These hyperparameters should help you to improve the performance of your models, but you don't need to write new functions or classes for hyperparameter optimization.

| Method | Hyperparameter |
| --- | --- |
| Logistic regression<br><br>`sklearn.linear_model.LogisticRegression()` | • `penalty`: Choosing regularization between `l1`, `l2`, `elasticnet`, and `None`<br>• `class_weight`: Associating weights to classes<br>• `l1_ratio`: The Elastic-Net mixing parameter |
| K-Nearest Neighbors<br><br>`sklearn.neighbors.KNeighborsClassifier()` | • `n_neighbors`: Number of neighbors<br>• `weights`: Choosing between `uniform` or `distance` to use neighbors equally or assign weights to them based on their distance |
| Support Vector Machine (SVM) classifier or regressor<br><br>`sklearn.svm.SVC()`<br><br>`sklearn.svm.SVR()` | • `C`: Inverse strength of regularization with the `l2` penalty<br>• `kernel`: An SVM kernel with prebuilt kernels including `linear`, `poly`, `rbf`, `sigmoid`, and `precomputed`<br>• `degree` (degree of polynomial): Degree of the polynomial kernel function (`poly`)<br>• `class_weight` (only for classification): Associating weights with classes |
| Random forest classifier or regressor<br><br>`sklearn.ensemble.RandomForestClassifier()`<br><br>`sklearn.ensemble.RandomForestRegressor()` | • `n_estimators`: Number of trees in the forest<br>• `max_depth`: Maximum depth of the trees<br>• `class_weight`: Associating weights with classes<br>• `min_samples_split`: The minimum number of samples required to be at a leaf node |
| XGBoost classifier or regressor<br><br><br><br>`xgboost.XGBClassifier()`<br><br>`xgboost.XGBRegressor()` | • `booster` (`gbtree`, `gblinear`, or `dart`)<br>• For a tree booster:<br>    ○ `eta`: Step size shrinkage to prevent overfitting.<br>    ○ `max_depth`: Maximum depth of the trees<br>    ○ `min_child_weight`: The minimum sum of data point weights needed to continue partitioning<br>    ○ `lambda`: L2 regularization factor<br>    ○ `alpha`: L1 regularization factor |

| LightGBM classifier or regressor<br><br>Lightgbm.<br>LGBMClassifier()<br><br>Lightgbm.<br>LGBMRegressor() | • `boosting_type` (`gbdt`, `dart`, or `rf`)<br>• `num_leaves`: Maximum tree leaves<br>• `max_depth`: Maximum tree depth<br>• `n_estimators`: Number of boosted trees<br>• `reg_alpha`: L1 regularization term on weights<br>• `reg_lambda`: L2 regularization term on weights |
|---|---|
| K-Means clustering<br><br>`sklearn.cluster.`<br>`KMeans()` | • `n_clusters`: Number of clusters |
| Agglomerative clustering<br><br>`sklearn.cluster.`<br>`AgglomerativeClustering()` | • `n_clusters`: Number of clusters<br>• `metric`: Distance measures with prebuilt measures including `euclidean`, `l1`, `l2`, `manhattan`, `cosine`, or `precomputed`<br>• `linkage`: Linkage criterion with prebuilt methods including `ward`, `complete`, `average`, and `single` |
| DBSCAN clustering<br><br>`sklearn.cluster.`<br>`DBSCAN()` | • `eps`: Maximum allowed distance between data points for them to be considered neighbors<br>• `min_samples`: The minimum number of neighbors a data point needs to be considered a core point |
| UMAP<br><br>`umap.UMAP()` | • `n_neighbors`: Constraining the size of the local neighborhood for the learning data structure<br>• `min_dist`: Controlling the compactness of groups in low-dimensional space |

Table 5.2 – Some of the most important hyperparameters of widely used supervised and unsupervised machine learning methods to start hyperparameter optimization with

The Python libraries listed in *Table 5.3* have modules dedicated to different hyperparameter optimization techniques such as *grid search*, *random search*, *Bayesian search*, and *successive halving*.

| Library | URL |
|---------|-----|
| scikit-optimize | https://pypi.org/project/scikit-optimize/ |
| Optuna | https://pypi.org/project/optuna/ |
| GpyOpt | https://pypi.org/project/GPyOpt/ |
| Hyperopt | https://hyperopt.github.io/hyperopt/ |
| ray.tune | https://docs.ray.io/en/latest/tune/index.html |

Table 5.3 – Commonly used Python libraries for hyperparameter optimization

Let's talk about each method in detail.

## Grid search

This method is about determining a series of hyperparameter nomination sets to be tested one by one to find the optimum combination. The cost of grid-searching to find an optimal combination is high. Also, considering there would be a specific set of hyperparameters that mattered for each problem, grid search with a predetermined set of hyperparameter combinations for all problems is not an effective approach.

Here is an example of grid search hyperparameter optimization using sklearn.model_selection.GridSearchCV() for a random forest classifier model. 80% of the data is used for hyperparameter optimization and the performance of the model is assessed using stratified 5-fold CV:

```
# determining random state for data split and model initialization
random_state = 42
# loading and splitting digit data to train and test sets
digits = datasets.load_digits()
x = digits.data
y = digits.target
x_train, x_test, y_train, y_test = train_test_split(
    x, y, random_state= random_state, test_size=0.2)
# list of hyperparameters to use for tuning
parameter_grid = {"max_depth": [2, 5, 10, 15, 20],
    "min_samples_split": [2, 5, 7]}
# validating using stratified k-fold (k=5) cross-validation
stratified_kfold_cv = StratifiedKFold(
    n_splits = 5, shuffle=True, random_state=random_state)
# generating the grid search
start_time = time.time()
sklearn_gridsearch = GridSearchCV(
```

```
       estimator = RFC(n_estimators = 10,
           random_state = random_state),
       param_grid = parameter_grid, cv = stratified_kfold_cv,
       n_jobs=-1)
   # fitting the grid search cross-validation
   sklearn_gridsearch.fit(x_train, y_train)
```

In this code, 10 estimators are used and different `min_samples_split` and `max_depth` values are considered for the hyperparameter optimization process. You can specify different performance metrics according to what you learned in the previous chapter using the scoring parameter, as one of the parameters of `sklearn.model_selection.GridSearchCV()`. A combination of `max_depth` of 10 and `min_samples_split` of 7 was identified as the best hyperparameter set in this case, which resulted in 0.948 accuracy using the stratified 5-fold CV. We can extract the best hyperparameter and corresponding score using `sklearn_gridsearch.best_params_` and `sklearn_gridsearch.best_score_`.

## Random search

This method is an alternative to grid search. It randomly tries different combinations of hyperparameter values. For the same high enough computational budget, it is shown that random search can achieve a higher performance model compared to grid search, as it can search a larger space (Bergstra and Bengio, 2012).

Here is an example of random search hyperparameter optimization using `sklearn.model_selection.RandomizedSearchCV()` for the same model and data used in the previous code:

```
   # generating the grid search
   start_time = time.time()
   sklearn_randomsearch = RandomizedSearchCV(
       estimator = RFC(n_estimators = 10,
           random_state = random_state),
       param_distributions = parameter_grid,
       cv = stratified_kfold_cv, random_state = random_state,
       n_iter = 5, n_jobs=-1)
   # fitting the grid search cross-validation
   sklearn_randomsearch.fit(x_train, y_train)
```

With only five iterations, this random search resulted in 0.942 CV accuracy with less than one-third of running time, which could depend on your local or cloud system configuration. In this case, a combination of `max_depth` of 15 and `min_samples_split` of 7 was identified as the best hyperparameter set. Comparing the results of grid search and random search, we can conclude that models with different `max_depth` values could result in similar CV accuracies for this specific case of random forest modeling with 10 estimators using the digit dataset from `scikit-learn`.

## Bayesian search

In Bayesian optimization, instead of randomly selecting hyperparameter combinations without checking the value of previous combination sets, each combination of hyperparameter sets gets selected in an iteration based on the history of previously tested hyperparameter sets. This process helps to reduce the computational cost compared to grid search but it doesn't always beat random search. We want to use Ray Tune (`ray.tune`) here for this approach. You can read more about different functionalities available in Ray Tune such as *logging tune runs*, *how to stop and resume*, *analyzing tune experiment results*, and *deploying tune in the cloud* on the tutorial page: `https://docs.ray.io/en/latest/tune/tutorials/overview.html`.

The following implementation of Bayesian hyperparameter optimization using `ray.tune.sklearn.TuneSearchCV()` for the same random forest model, as explained previously, achieves 0.942 CV accuracy:

```
start_time = time.time()
tune_bayessearch = TuneSearchCV(
    RFC(n_estimators = 10, random_state = random_state),
    parameter_grid,
    search_optimization="bayesian",
    cv = stratified_kfold_cv,
    n_trials=3, # number of sampled parameter settings
    early_stopping=True,
    max_iters=10,
    random_state = random_state)

tune_bayessearch.fit(x_train, y_train)
```

## Successive halving

The idea behind successive having is to not invest in all hyperparameters equally. Candidate hyperparameter sets get evaluated using limited resources, for example, using only a fraction of training data or a limited number of trees in a random forest model in an iteration, and some of them pass to the next iteration. In later iterations, more resources get used until the last iteration in which all resources, for example, all training data, get used to evaluate the remaining hyperparameter sets. You can use `HalvingGridSearchCV()` and `HalvingRandomSearchCV()` as part of `sklearn.model_selection` to try out successive halving. You can read more about these two Python modules at `https://scikit-learn.org/stable/modules/grid_search.html#id3`.

There are other hyperparameter optimization techniques, such as **Hyperband** (Li et al., 2017) and **BOHB** (Falkner et al., 2018) that you can try out, but the general idea behind most advancements in hyperparameter optimization is to minimize the computational resources necessary to achieve an optimum hyperparameter set. There are also techniques and libraries for hyperparameter optimization in deep learning, which we will cover in *Chapter 12*, *Going Beyond ML Debugging with Deep Learning*, and *Chapter 13, Advanced Deep Learning Techniques*. Although hyperparameter optimization helps us to get better models, using the provided data for model training and the selected machine learning method, we can improve model performance with other approaches, such as generating synthetic data for model training, which is our next topic.

# Synthetic data generation

The data we have access to for training and evaluating our machine learning models may be limited. For example, in the case of classification models, we might have classes with a limited number of data points, resulting in lower performance of our models for unseen data points of the same classes. We will go through a few methods here to help you improve the performance of your models in these situations.

## Oversampling for imbalanced data

Imbalanced data classification is challenging due to the dominating effect of majority classes during training as well as in model performance reporting. For model performance reporting, we discussed different performance metrics in the previous chapter and how you can select a reliable metric even in the case of imbalanced data classification. Here, we want to talk about the concept of oversampling to help you improve the performance of your models by synthetically improving your training data. The concept of oversampling is to increase the number of data points in your minority classes using the real data points you have in your dataset. The simplest way of thinking about it is to duplicate some of the data points in minority classes, which is not a good approach as they will not provide complementary information to real data in the training process. There are techniques designed for oversampling processes, such as the **Synthetic Minority Oversampling Technique** (**SMOTE**) and its variations for tabular data, which we will present here.

---

**Undersampling**

In classifying imbalanced data, an alternative to oversampling is to decrease the imbalance by sampling the majority class. This process reduces the ratio of the majority-class to minority-class data points. As not all the data points get included in one set of sampling, multiple models can be built by sampling different subsets of majority-class data points and the output of those models can be combined, for example, through majority voting between the models. This process is called **undersampling**. Oversampling usually results in higher performance improvement compared to undersampling.

---

### *SMOTE*

SMOTE is an old yet widely used approach to oversampling the minority class, for continuous feature sets, using the distribution of neighboring data points (Chawla et al., 2022; see *Figure 5.1*).

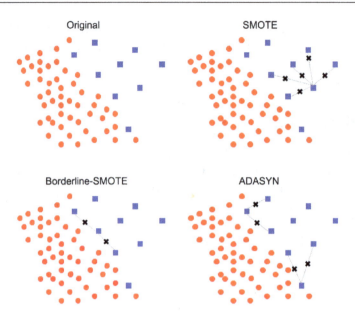

Figure 5.1 – Schematic illustration of synthetic data generation
using SMOTE, Borderline-SMOTE, and ADASYN

The steps in generating any synthetic data point using SMOTE can be summarized as follows:

1.  Choose a random data point from a minority class.

2.  Identify the K-Nearest Neighbors for that data point.

3.  Choose one of the neighbors randomly.

4.  Generate a synthetic data point at a randomly selected point between the two data points in the feature space.

SMOTE and two of its variations, **Borderline-SMOTE** and **Adaptive synthetic** (**ADASYN**), are shown in *Figure 5.1*. *Steps 2* to *4* of SMOTE, Borderline-SMOTE, and ADASYN are similar. However, Borderline-SMOTE focuses on the real data points that divide the classes and ADASYN focuses on the data points of the minority class in regions of the feature space dominated by the majority classes. In this way, Borderline-SMOTE increases the confidence in decision boundary identification to avoid overfitting and ADASYN improves generalizability for minority-class prediction in the parts of the space dominated by majority classes.

You can use the `imblearn` Python library for synthetic data generation using SMOTE, Borderline-SMOTE, and ADASYN. However, before getting into using these functionalities, we need to write a plotting function for later use to show the data before and after the oversampling process:

```
def plot_fun(x_plot: list, y_plot: list, title: str):
    """
```

```
    Plotting a binary classification dataset
    :param x_plot: list of x coordinates (i.e. dimension 1)
    :param y_plot: list of y coordinates (i.e. dimension 2)
    :param title: title of plot
    """
    cmap, norm = mcolors.from_levels_and_colors([0, 1, 2],
        ['black', 'red'])
    plt.scatter([x_plot[iter][0] for iter in range(
        0, len(x_plot))],
        [x_plot[iter][1] for iter in range(
            0, len(x_plot))],
        c=y_plot, cmap=cmap, norm=norm)
    plt.xticks(fontsize = 12)
    plt.yticks(fontsize = 12)
    plt.xlabel('1st dimension', fontsize = 12)
    plt.ylabel('2nd dimension', fontsize = 12)
    plt.title(title)
    plt.show()
```

Then, we generate a synthetic dataset with two classes and only two features (that is, two-dimensional data) and consider it our real dataset. We consider 100 data points in one of the classes as the majority class, and 10 data points in another class as the minority class:

```
np.random.seed(12)
minority_sample_size = 10
majority_sample_size = 100
# generating random set of x coordinates
group_1_X1 = np.repeat(2,majority_sample_size)+\
np.random.normal(loc=0, scale=1,size=majority_sample_size)
group_1_X2 = np.repeat(2,majority_sample_size)+\
np.random.normal(loc=0, scale=1,size=majority_sample_size)
# generating random set of x coordinates
group_2_X1 = np.repeat(4,minority_sample_size)+\
np.random.normal(loc=0, scale=1,size=minority_sample_size)
group_2_X2 = np.repeat(4,minority_sample_size)+\
np.random.normal(loc=0, scale=1,size=minority_sample_size)

X_all = [[group_1_X1[iter], group_1_X2[iter]] for\
            iter in range(0, len(group_1_X1))]+\
            [[group_2_X1[iter], group_2_X2[iter]]\
                for iter in range(0, len(group_2_X1))]
y_all = [0]*majority_sample_size+[1]*minority_sample_size
# plotting the randomly generated data
plot_fun(x_plot = X_all, y_plot = y_all,
    title = 'Original')
```

The resulting data points are shown in the following scatter plot with red and black data points representing the minority and majority classes, respectively. We are using this synthetic data instead of a real dataset to visually show you how different synthetic data generation methods work.

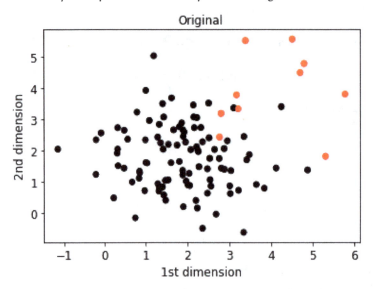

Figure 5.2 – Example dataset with two features (that is, dimensions), generated
synthetically, to use for practicing with SMOTE and its alternatives

We now use SMOTE via `imblearn.over_sampling.SMOTE()`, as shown in the following code snippet, to generate synthetic data points for the minority class only:

```
k_neighbors = 5
# initializing smote
# using 'auto', equivalent to 'not majority',
# sampling_strategy that enforces resampling all classes but the
majority class
smote = SMOTE(sampling_strategy='auto',
                    k_neighbors=k_neighbors)
# fitting smote to oversample the minority class
x_smote, y_smote = smote.fit_resample(X_all, y_all)
# plotting the resulted oversampled data
plot_fun(x_plot = x_smote, y_plot = y_smote,
    title = 'SMOTE')
```

As you can see in the following figure, the new oversampled data points will be within the gaps between the original data points of the minority class (that is, red data points). However, many of these new data points don't help to identify a reliable decision boundary as they are grouped in the very top-right corner, far from the black data points and potential decision boundaries.

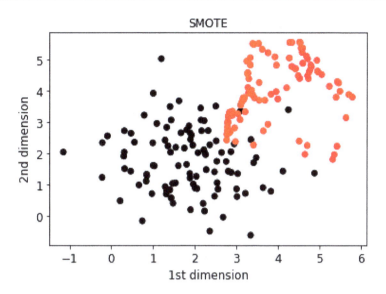

Figure 5.3 – Visualization of the dataset shown in Figure 5.2 after implementing SMOTE

We use Borderline-SMOTE instead via `imblearn.over_sampling.BorderlineSMOTE()` as follows for synthetic data generation:

```
k_neighbors = 5
# using 5 neighbors to determine if a minority sample is in "danger"
m_neighbors = 10
# initializing borderline smote
# using 'auto', equivalent to 'not majority', sampling_strategy that
enforces resampling all classes but the majority class
borderline_smote = BorderlineSMOTE(
    sampling_strategy='auto',
    k_neighbors=k_neighbors,
    m_neighbors=m_neighbors)
# fitting borderline smote to oversample the minority class
x_bordersmote,y_bordersmote =borderline_smote.fit_resample(
    X_all, y_all)
# plotting the resulted oversampled data
plot_fun(x_plot = x_bordersmote, y_plot = y_bordersmote,
    title = 'Borderline-SMOTE')
```

We can see that the new synthetically generated data points are closer to the black data points of the majority class, which helps with identifying a generalizable decision boundary:

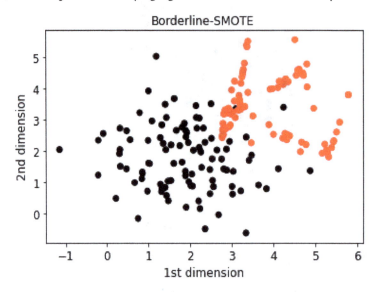

Figure 5.4 – Visualization of the dataset shown in Figure 5.2 after implementing Borderline-SMOTE

We can also use ADASYN via `imblearn.over_sampling.ADASYN()`, which also generates more of the new synthetic data close to the black data points as it focuses on the regions with more majority-class samples:

```
# using 5 neighbors for each datapoint in the oversampling process by
SMOTE
n_neighbors = 5
# initializing ADASYN
# using 'auto', equivalent to 'not majority', sampling_strategy that
enforces resampling all classes but the majority class
adasyn_smote = ADASYN(sampling_strategy = 'auto',n_neighbors
                                    = n_neighbors)
# fitting ADASYN to oversample the minority class
x_adasyn_smote, y_adasyn_smote = adasyn_smote.fit_resample(X_all, y_
all)
# plotting the resulted oversampled data
plot_fun(x_plot = x_adasyn_smote, y_plot = y_adasyn_smote,
    title = "ADASYN")
```

The data including original and synthetically generated data points using ADASYN are shown in *Figure 5.5*.

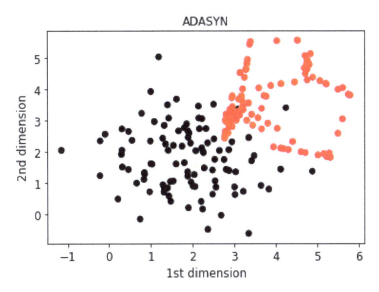

Figure 5.5 – Visualization of the dataset shown in Figure 5.2 after implementing ADASYN

There have been more recent methods built upon SMOTE for synthetic data generation such as **density-based synthetic minority over-sampling technique (DSMOTE)** (Xiaolong et al., 2019) and **k-means SMOTE** (Felix et al., 2017). Both of these methods try to capture groupings of data points either within the target minority class or the whole dataset. In DSMOTE, **Density-based spatial clustering of applications with noise (DBSCAN)** is used to divide data points of the minority class into three groups of core samples, borderline samples, and noise (i.e., outlying) samples, and then the core and borderline samples only get used for oversampling. This approach is shown to work better than SMOTE and Borderline-SMOTE (Xiaolong et al., 2019). K-means SMOTE is another recent alternative to SMOTE (Last et al., 2017) that relies on clustering of the whole dataset using a k-means clustering algorithm before oversampling (see *Figure 5.6*).

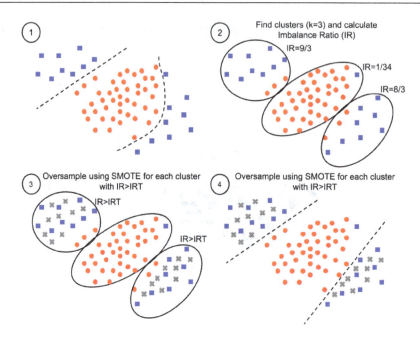

Figure 5.6 – Schematic illustration of the four main steps of k-means SMOTE (Last et al. 2017))

Here are the steps in the k-means SMOTE method for data generation, which you can use via the kmeans-smote Python library:

1.  Identify the decision boundary based on the original data.

2.  Cluster data points into k clusters using k-means clustering.

3.  Oversample using SMOTE for clusters with an **Imbalance Ratio (IR)** greater than the **Imbalance Ratio Threshold (IRT)**.

4.  Repeat the decision boundary identification process. (Note: IRT can be chosen by the user or optimized like a hyperparameter.)

You can practice with different variations of SMOTE and find out which one works best for your datasets, but Borderline-SMOTE and K-means SMOTE could be good starting points.

Next, you will learn about techniques that help you in improving the quality of your data before getting into model training.

# Improving pre-training data processing

Data processing in the early stages of a machine learning life cycle, before model training and evaluation, determines the quality of the data we feed into the training, validation, and testing process, and consequently our success in achieving a high-performance and reliable model.

## Anomaly detection and outlier removal

Anomalies and outliers in your data could decrease the performance and reliability of your models in production. The existence of outliers in training data, the data you use for model evaluation, and unseen data in production could have different impacts:

- **Outliers in model training**: The existence of outliers in the training data for supervised learning models could result in lower model generalizability. It could cause unnecessarily complex decision boundaries in classification or unnecessary nonlinearity in regression models.

- **Outliers in model evaluation**: Outliers in validation and test data could lower the model performance. As the models are not necessarily designed for outlying data points, they cause the model performance assessment to be unreliable by impacting the performance of the models, which cannot predict their labels or continuous values properly. This issue could make the process of model selection unreliable.

- **Outliers in production**: Unseen data points in production could be far from the distribution of training or even test data. Our model may have been designed to identify those anomalies, as in the case of fraud detection, but if that is not the objective, then we should tag those data points as samples, which our model is not confident doing or designed for. For example, if we designed a model to suggest drugs to cancer patients based on the genetic information of their tumors, our model should report low confidence for patients that need to be considered as outlier samples, as wrong medication could have life-threatening consequences.

*Table 5.4* provides a summary of some of the anomaly detection methods you can use to identify anomalies in your data and remove outliers if necessary:

| Method | Article and URL |
|---|---|
| Isolation Forest (iForest) | Liu et al. 2008 <br><br> `https://ieeexplore.ieee.org/abstract/` <br> `document/4781136` |
| Lightweight on-line detector of anomalies (Loda) | Penvy, 2016 <br><br> `https://link.springer.com/` <br> `article/10.1007/s10994-015-5521-0` |
| Local outlier factor (LOF) | Breunig et al., 2000 <br><br> `https://dl.acm.org/doi/` <br> `abs/10.1145/342009.335388` |
| Angle-Based Outlier Detection (ABOD) | Kriegel et al., 2008 <br><br> `https://dl.acm.org/doi/` <br> `abs/10.1145/1401890.1401946` |
| Robust kernel density estimation (RKDE) | Kim and Scott, 2008 <br><br> `https://ieeexplore.ieee.org/` <br> `document/4518376` |
| Support Vector Method for Novelty Detection | Schölkopf et al., 1999 <br><br> `https://proceedings.neurips.cc/` <br> `paper/1999/hash/8725fb777f25776ffa9076e4` <br> `4fcfd776-Abstract.html` |

Table 5.4 – Widely used anomaly detection techniques (Emmott et al., 2013 and 2015)

One of the effective methods for anomaly detection is **iForest** (Emmott et al., 2013 and 2015; Liu et al. 2008), which is available as one of the functionalities of `scikit-learn`. To try it out, we first generate a synthetic training dataset as follows:

```
n_samples, n_outliers = 100, 20
rng = np.random.RandomState(12)
# Generating two synthetic clusters of datapoints sampled from a
univariate "normal" (Gaussian) distribution of mean 0 and variance 1
cluster_1 = 0.2 * rng.randn(n_samples, 2) + np.array(
    [1, 1])
cluster_2 = 0.3 * rng.randn(n_samples, 2) + np.array(
    [5, 5])
# Generating synthetic outliers
```

```
outliers = rng.uniform(low=2, high=4, size=(n_outliers, 2))

X = np.concatenate([cluster_1, cluster_2, outliers])
y = np.concatenate(
    [np.ones((2 * n_samples), dtype=int),
        -np.ones((n_outliers), dtype=int)])
```

Then, we use `IsolationForest()` from `scikit-learn`:

```
# initializing iForest
clf = IsolationForest(n_estimators = 10, random_state=10)
# fitting iForest using training data
clf.fit(X)
# plotting the results
scatter = plt.scatter(X[:, 0], X[:, 1])
handles, labels = scatter.legend_elements()
disp = DecisionBoundaryDisplay.from_estimator(
    clf,
    X,
    plot_method = "contour",
    response_method="predict",
    alpha=1
)
disp.ax_.scatter(X[:, 0], X[:, 1], s = 10)
disp.ax_.set_title("Binary decision boundary of iForest (
    n_estimators = 10)")
plt.xlabel('Dimension 1', fontsize = 12)
plt.ylabel('Dimension 2', fontsize = 12)
plt.show()
```

We used 10 decision trees in the previous code using `n_estimator = 10` when initializing `IsolationForest()`. This is one of the hyperparameters of iForest and we can play with it to get better results. You can see the resulting boundaries for `n_estimator = 10` and `n_estimator = 100` next.

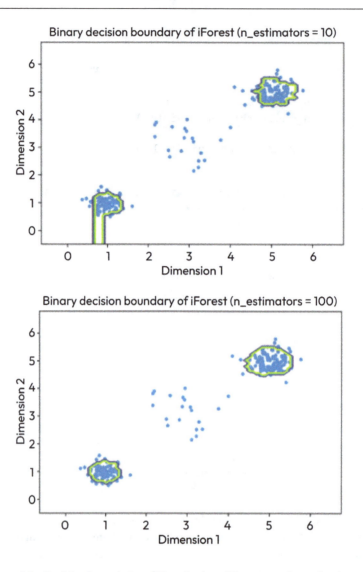

Figure 5.7 – Decision boundaries of iForest using different numbers of estimators

If you accept the result of an anomaly detection method such as iForest without further investigation, you might decide to use only the data within the shown boundaries. However, there could be issues with these techniques, as with any other machine method. Although iForest is not a supervised learning method, the boundaries for identifying anomalies could be prone to overfitting and not generalizable for further evaluation or use on unseen data in production. Also, the choice of hyperparameters could result in considering a large fraction of the data points as outliers mistakenly.

# Benefitting from data of lower quality or relevance

When doing supervised machine learning, we would like to ideally have access to a large quantity of high-quality data. However, features or output values do not have the same level of certainty across the data points we have access to. For example, in the case of classification, labels might not all have the same level of validity. In other words, our confidence in the labels of different data points could be different. Some of the commonly used labeling processes for data points are conducted by averaging experimental measurements (for example, as in biological or chemical contexts), or by using the annotations of multiple experts (or non-experts).

You could also have a problem such as predicting the response of breast cancer patients to specific drugs where you have access to data on patients' response to the same or similar drugs in other cancer types. Then, part of your data has a lower level of relevance to the objective of breast cancer patients' responses to the drug.

We preferably want to rely on high-quality data, or highly confident annotations and labels in these cases. However, we might have access to large quantities of data points that are either of lower quality, or lower relevance to the objective we have in mind. There are a few methods we could use to benefit from these data points of lower quality or relevance, although they are not successful all the time:

- **Assigning weight during optimization**: You can assign a weight to each data point when training machine learning models. For example, in `scikit-learn`, after initializing a random forest model such as `rf_model = RandomForestClassifier(random_state = 42)`, you can specify the weight of each datapoint in the fitting step as `rf_model.fit(X_train,y_train, sample_weight = weights_array)`, where `weights_array` is an array of weights for each data point in the training set. These weights could be the confidence scores you have for each data point according to their relevance to the objective in mind or their quality. For example, if you use 10 different expert annotators for assigning labels to a series of data points, you can use a fraction of them to agree on a class label as the weight of each data point. If there is a data point with a class of 1 but only 7 out of 10 annotators agreed on this class, it will receive a lower weight compared to another class-1 data point for which all 10 annotators agreed on its label.

- **Ensemble learning**: If you consider a distribution of the quality of or confidence score for each data point, then you can build different models using data points of each part of this distribution and then combine the predictions of the models, for example, using their weighted average (see *Figure 5.8*). The weights assigned to each model could be a number, representative of the quality of the data points used for its training.

- **Transfer learning**: In transfer learning, we can train a model on a reference task, typically with many more data points, and then fine-tune it on a smaller task to come up with the task-specific predictions (Weiss et al., 2016, Madani Tonekaboni et al., 2020). This method can be used on data with different levels of confidence (Madani Tonekaboni et al., 2020). You can train a model on a large dataset with different levels of label confidence (see *Figure 5.8*), excluding very low-confidence data and then fine-tune it on the very high-confidence part of your dataset.

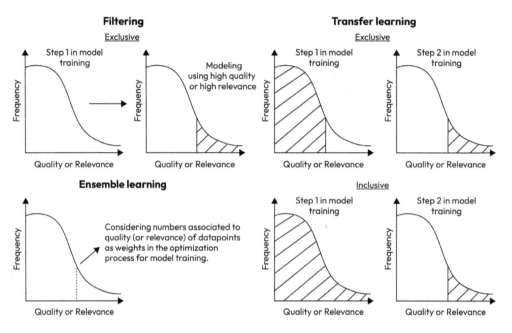

Figure 5.8 – Techniques for using data points of different quality or relevance
to the target problem in training machine learning models

These methods could help you reduce the need to generate more high-quality data. However, having more high-quality and highly relevant data is preferred, if possible.

As the final approach we want to go through in this chapter, we will talk about regularization as a technique to control overfitting and help in generating models with a higher chance of generalizability.

## Regularization to improve model generalizability

We learned in the previous chapter that high model complexity could cause overfitting. One of the approaches to controlling the model complexity and reducing the effect of features that affect model generalizability is **regularization**. In the regularization process, we consider a regularization or penalty term in the loss function to be optimized during the training process. Regularization, in the simple case of linear modeling, can be added as follows to the loss function during the optimization process:

$$L = \sum_{i=1}^{n} \left( y_i - \left( \sum_{j=1}^{p} w_{ij} \ x_j + b \right) \right)^2 + \Omega(W)$$

where the first term is the loss and $\Omega(W)$ is the regularization term as a function of model weights, or parameters, $W$. However, regularization could be used with different machine learning methods such as SVMs or **LightGBM** (refer to *Table 5.2*). Three of the common regularization terms are shown in the following table including **L1 regularization**, **L2 regularization**, and their combination.

| Method | Regularization term | Parameters |
|---|---|---|
| L2 regularization | $$\Omega(W) = \lambda \sum_{j=1}^{p} w_j^{\,2}$$ | $\lambda$: The regularization parameter that determines the strength of regularization |
| L1 regularization | $$\Omega(W) = \lambda \sum_{j=1}^{p} |w_p|$$ | $\lambda$: As in L2 regularization |
| L2 and L1 | $$\Omega(W) = \lambda \left( \frac{1-\alpha}{2} \sum_{j=1}^{p} w_j^{\,2} + \alpha \sum_{j=1}^{p} |w_j| \right)$$ | $\lambda$: As in L1 and L2 regularization <br><br> $\alpha$: A missing parameter to determine the effect of L1 versus L2 in the regularization process |

Table 5.5 – Commonly used regularization methods for machine learning modeling

We can consider the process of optimization with regularization as the process of getting as close as possible to the optimal parameter set $\hat{\beta}$ while keeping the parameters bound to a constrained region, as shown in *Figure 5.9*:

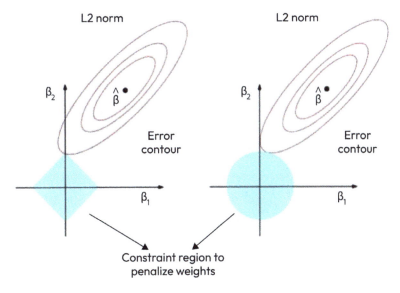

Figure 5.9 – Schematic representation of L1 and L2 norm regularizations
for controlling overfitting in a two-dimensional feature space

Corners in parameter-constrained regions of L1 regularization result in the elimination of some of the parameters, or making their associated weights zero. However, the convexity of the constrained parameter region for L2 regularization only results in lowering the effect of parameters by decreasing their weights. This difference usually results in a higher robustness of L1 regularization to outliers.

Linear classification models with L1 regularization and L2 regularization are called **Lasso** and **Ridge** regression, respectively (Tibshirani, 1996). Elastic-Net was proposed later using a combination of both L1 regularization and L2 regularization terms (Zou et al., 2005). Here, we want to practice using these three methods, but you can use regularization hyperparameters with other methods, such as an SVM or XGBoost classifier (see *Table 5.2*).

We first import the necessary libraries and design a plotting function to visually show the effect of the regularization parameter values. We also load the digit dataset from `scikit-learn` to use for model training and evaluation:

```python
random_state = 42
# loading and splitting digit data to train and test sets
digits = datasets.load_digits()
x = digits.data
y = digits.target
# using stratified k-fold (k=5) cross-validation
stratified_kfold_cv = StratifiedKFold(n_splits = 5,
    shuffle=True, random_state=random_state)
# function for plotting the CV score across different hyperparameter
values
def reg_search_plot(search_fit, parameter: str):
    """

    :param search_fit: hyperparameter search object after model
fitting
    :param parameter: hyperparameter name
    """

    parameters = [search_fit.cv_results_[
        'params'][iter][parameter] for iter in range(
            0,len(search_fit.cv_results_['params']))]
    mean_test_score = search_fit.cv_results_[
        'mean_test_score']
    plt.scatter(parameters, mean_test_score)
    plt.xticks(fontsize = 12)
    plt.yticks(fontsize = 12)
    plt.xlabel(parameter, fontsize = 12)
    plt.ylabel('accuracy', fontsize = 12)
    plt.show()
```

We can use the GridSearchCV() function to assess the effect of different regularization parameter values in the following models. In scikit-learn, the regularization parameter is usually named alpha instead of $\lambda$, and the mixing parameter is called l1_ratio instead of $\alpha$. Here, we first assess the effect of different alpha values on Lasso models, with L1 regularization, trained and evaluated using a digit dataset:

```
# Defining hyperparameter grid
parameter_grid = {"alpha": [0, 0.1, 0.2, 0.3, 0.4, 0.5]}
# generating the grid search
lasso_search = GridSearchCV(Lasso(
    random_state = random_state),
    parameter_grid,cv = stratified_kfold_cv,n_jobs=-1)
# fitting the grid search cross-validation
lasso_search.fit(x, y)

reg_search_plot(search_fit = lasso_search,
    parameter = 'alpha')
```

The optimum alpha is identified to be 0.1, as shown in the following plot, which results in the highest accuracy across the considered values. This means that increasing the effect of regularization after an alpha value of 0.1 increases the model bias, resulting in a model with low performance in training.

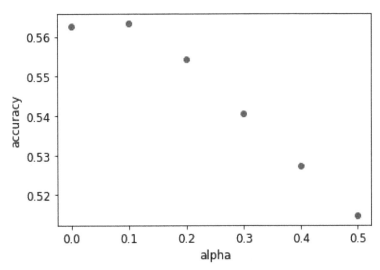

Figure 5.10 – Accuracy versus the regularization parameter alpha for a Lasso model

If we assess the effect of different `alpha` values in a ridge model, with L2 regularization, we can see that the performance increases as we increase the strength of regularization (see *Figure 5.11*).

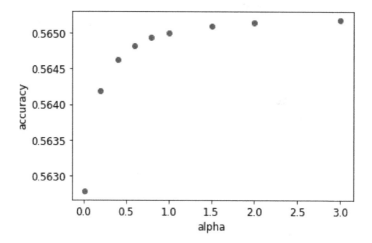

Figure 5.11 – Accuracy versus the regularization parameter alpha for a ridge model

An alternative to these two methods is Elastic-Net, which combines the effect of L1 and L2 regularizations. In this case, the trend of the effect of `alpha` on the model performance is more similar to Lasso; however, the range of accuracy values is narrower in comparison with Lasso, which only relies on L1 regularization (see *Figure 5.12*).

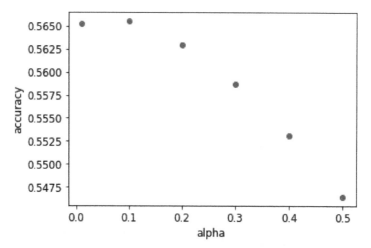

Figure 5.12 – Accuracy versus the regularization parameter alpha for an Elastic-Net model

If your dataset is not very small, more complex models help you to achieve higher performance. It would be only in rare cases that you would consider a linear model your ultimate model. To assess the effect of regularization on more complex models, we chose the SVM classifier and examined the effect of different values of C as the regularization parameter in `sklearn.svm.SVC()`:

```
# Defining hyperparameter grid
parameter_grid = {"C": [0.01, 0.2, 0.4, 0.6, 0.8, 1]}
# generating the grid search
svc_search = GridSearchCV(SVC(kernel = 'poly',
    random_state = random_state),parameter_grid,
    cv = stratified_kfold_cv,n_jobs=-1)
# fitting the grid search cross-validation
svc_search.fit(x, y)

reg_search_plot(search_fit = svc_search, parameter = 'C')
```

As shown next, the range of accuracy for the models is higher, between 0.92 and 0.99, compared to linear models with an accuracy of lower than 0.6, but higher regularization controls overfitting and achieves better performance.

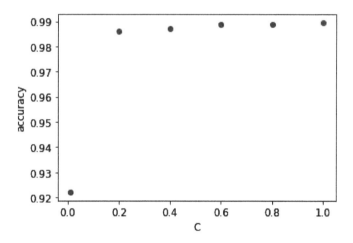

Figure 5.13 – Accuracy versus regularization parameter C for an SVM classification model

In *Chapter 12, Going Beyond ML Debugging with Deep Learning*, you will also learn about regularization techniques in deep neural network models.

# Summary

In this chapter, you learned about techniques to improve the performance of your models and reduce their bias and variance. You learned about the different hyperparameters of widely used machine learning methods, other than deep learning, which will be covered later in the book, and Python libraries to help you in identifying the optimal hyperparameter sets. You learned about regularization as another technique to help you in training generalizable machine learning models. You also learned how to increase the quality of the data to be fed into the training process by methods such as synthetic data generation and outlier detection.

In the next chapter, you will learn about interpretability and explainability in machine learning modeling and how you can use the related techniques and Python tools to identify opportunities for improving your models.

# Questions

1. Does adding more features and training data points reduce model variance?

2. Could you provide examples of methods to use to combine data with different confidence in class labels?

3. How could oversampling improve the generalizability of your supervised machine learning models?

4. What is the difference between DSMOTE and Borderline-SMOTE?

5. Do you need to check the effect of every single value of every hyperparameter of a model during hyperparameter optimization?

6. Could L1 regularization eliminate the contribution of some of the features to supervised model predictions?

7. Could Lasso and Ridge regression models result in the same performance on the same test data if trained using the same training data?

# References

- Bergstra, James, and Yoshua Bengio. *"Random search for hyper-parameter optimization."* *Journal of machine learning research* 13.2 (2012).

- Bergstra, James, et al. *"Algorithms for hyper-parameter optimization."* *Advances in neural information processing systems* 24 (2011).

- Nguyen, Vu. *"Bayesian optimization for accelerating hyper-parameter tuning."* *2019 IEEE second international conference on artificial intelligence and knowledge engineering (AIKE).* IEEE (2019).

- Li, Lisha, et al. *"Hyperband: A novel bandit-based approach to hyperparameter optimization."* *Journal of Machine Learning Research* 18.1 (2017): pp. 6765-6816.

- Falkner, Stefan, Aaron Klein, and Frank Hutter. "*BOHB: Robust and efficient hyperparameter optimization at scale.*" *International Conference on Machine Learning.* PMLR (2018).

- Ng, Andrew, Stanford CS229: Machine Learning Course, Autumn 2018.

- Wong, Sebastien C., et al. "*Understanding data augmentation for classification: when to warp?*" *2016 international conference on digital image computing: techniques and applications (DICTA).* IEEE (2016).

- Mikołajczyk, Agnieszka, and Michał Grochowski. "*Data augmentation for improving deep learning in image classification problem.*" *2018 international interdisciplinary PhD workshop (IIPhDW).* IEEE (2018).

- Shorten, Connor, and Taghi M. Khoshgoftaar. "*A survey on image data augmentation for deep learning.*" *Journal of big data* 6.1 (2019): pp. 1-48.

- Taylor, Luke, and Geoff Nitschke. "*Improving deep learning with generic data augmentation.*" *2018 IEEE Symposium Series on Computational Intelligence (SSCI).* IEEE (2018).

- Shorten, Connor, Taghi M. Khoshgoftaar, and Borko Furht. "*Text data augmentation for deep learning.*" *Journal of big Data* 8.1 (2021): pp. 1-34.

- Perez, Luis, and Jason Wang. "*The effectiveness of data augmentation in image classification using deep learning.*" arXiv preprint arXiv:1712.04621 (2017).

- Ashrapov, Insaf. "*Tabular GANs for uneven distribution.*" arXiv preprint arXiv:2010.00638 (2020).

- Xu, Lei, et al. "*Modeling tabular data using conditional gan.*" *Advances in Neural Information Processing Systems* 32 (2019).

- Chawla, Nitesh V., et al. "*SMOTE: synthetic minority over-sampling technique.*" *Journal of artificial intelligence research* 16 (2002): pp. 321-357.

- Han, H., Wang, WY., Mao, BH. (2005). "*Borderline-SMOTE: A New Over-Sampling Method in Imbalanced Data Sets Learning.*" In: Huang, DS., Zhang, XP., Huang, GB. (eds) *Advances in Intelligent Computing.* ICIC 2005. *Lecture Notes in Computer Science*, vol. 3644. Springer, Berlin, Heidelberg.

- He, Haibo, Yang Bai, E. A. Garcia, and Shutao Li, "*ADASYN: Adaptive synthetic sampling approach for imbalanced learning.*" *2008 IEEE International Joint Conference on Neural Networks (IEEE World Congress on Computational Intelligence)* (2008): pp. 1322-1328, doi: 10.1109/IJCNN.2008.4633969.

- X. Xiaolong, C. Wen, and S. Yanfei, "*Over-sampling algorithm for imbalanced data classification,*" in *Journal of Systems Engineering and Electronics*, vol. 30, no. 6, pp. 1182-1191, Dec. 2019, doi: 10.21629/JSEE.2019.06.12.

- Last, Felix, Georgios Douzas, and Fernando Bacao. "*Oversampling for imbalanced learning based on k-means and smote.*" arXiv preprint arXiv:1711.00837 (2017).

- Emmott, Andrew F., et al. "*Systematic construction of anomaly detection benchmarks from real data.*" *Proceedings of the ACM SIGKDD workshop on outlier detection and description.* 2013.

- Emmott, Andrew, et al. "*A meta-analysis of the anomaly detection problem.*" arXiv preprint arXiv:1503.01158 (2015).

- Liu, Fei Tony, Kai Ming Ting, and Zhi-Hua Zhou. "*Isolation forest.*" *2008 eighth IEEE international conference on data mining.* IEEE (2008).

- Pevný, Tomáš. "*Loda: Lightweight on-line detector of anomalies.*" *Machine Learning 102* (2016): pp. 275-304.

- Breunig, Markus M., et al. "*LOF: identifying density-based local outliers.*" *Proceedings of the 2000 ACM SIGMOD international conference on Management of data* (2000).

- Kriegel, Hans-Peter, Matthias Schubert, and Arthur Zimek. "*Angle-based outlier detection in high-dimensional data.*" *Proceedings of the 14th ACM SIGKDD international conference on Knowledge discovery and data mining* (2008).

- Joo Seuk Kim and C. Scott, "*Robust kernel density estimation.*" *2008 IEEE International Conference on Acoustics, Speech and Signal Processing*, Las Vegas, NV, USA (2008): pp. 3381-3384, doi: 10.1109/ICASSP.2008.4518376.

- Schölkopf, Bernhard, et al. "*Support vector method for novelty detection.*" *Advances in neural information processing systems 12* (1999).

- Weiss, Karl, Taghi M. Khoshgoftaar, and DingDing Wang. "*A survey of transfer learning.*" *Journal of Big data* 3.1 (2016): pp. 1-40.

- Tonekaboni, Seyed Ali Madani, et al. "*Learning across label confidence distributions using Filtered Transfer Learning.*" *2020 19th IEEE International Conference on Machine Learning and Applications (ICMLA).* IEEE (2020).

- Tibshirani, Robert. "*Regression shrinkage and selection via the lasso.*" *Journal of the Royal Statistical Society: Series B (Methodological)* 58.1 (1996): pp. 267-288.

- Hastie, Trevor, et al. *The elements of statistical learning: data mining, inference, and prediction.* vol. 2. New York: Springer, 2009.

- Zou, Hui, and Trevor Hastie. "*Regularization and variable selection via the elastic net.*" *Journal of the Royal Statistical Society: Series B (Statistical Methodology)* 67.2 (2005): pp. 301-320.

# 6

# Interpretability and Explainability in Machine Learning Modeling

The majority of the machine learning models we use or develop are complex and require the use of explainability techniques to identify opportunities for improving their performance, reducing their bias, and increasing their reliability.

We will look at the following topics in this chapter:

- Interpretable versus black-box machine learning
- Explainability methods in machine learning
- Practicing machine learning explainability in Python
- Reviewing why having explainability is not enough

By the end of this chapter, you will have learned about the importance of explainability in machine learning modeling and practiced using some of the explainability techniques in Python.

## Technical requirements

The following requirements should be considered for this chapter as they help you better understand the mentioned concepts, use them in your projects, and practice with the provided code:

- Python library requirements:
  - `sklearn` >= 1.2.2
  - `numpy` >= 1.22.4
  - `matplotlib` >= 3.7.1

You can find the code files for this chapter on GitHub at `https://github.com/PacktPublishing/Debugging-Machine-Learning-Models-with-Python/tree/main/Chapter06`.

# Interpretable versus black-box machine learning

Interpretable and simple models such as linear regression make it easy to assess the possibility of improving them, finding issues with them such as biases that need to be detected and removed, and building trust in using such models. However, to achieve higher performance, we usually don't stop with these simple models and rely on complex or so-called black-box models. In this section, we will review some of the interpretable models and then introduce techniques you can use to explain your black-box models.

## Interpretable machine learning models

Linear models such as linear and logistic regression, shallow decision trees, and Naive Bayes classifiers are examples of simple and interpretable methods (*Figure 6.1*). We can easily extract the contribution of features in predictions of outputs for these models and identify opportunities for improving their performance, such as by adding or removing features or changing feature normalization. We can also easily identify if there are biases in our models – for example, for a specific race or gender group. However, these models are very simple, and having access to large datasets of thousands or millions of samples allows us to train high-performance but complex models:

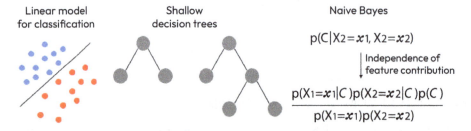

Figure 6.1 – Examples of interpretable classification methods

Complex models, such as random forest models with many deep decision trees or deep neural networks, help us in achieving higher performance, although they work almost like black-box systems. To be able to understand these models and explain how they come up with their predictions, and to build trust in their utility, we can use machine learning explainability techniques.

## Explainability for complex models

Explainability techniques work like bridges between complex machine learning models and users. They are supposed to provide explainabilities that are faithful to how the models work. And on the other side, they are supposed to provide explanations that are useful and understandable for the users. These explanations can be used to identify opportunities for improving model performance, reducing the sensitivity of models to small feature value changes, increasing data efficiency in model training, trying to help in proper reasoning in the model and avoid spurious correlations, and helping in achieving fairness (Weber et al., 2022; *Figure 6.2*):

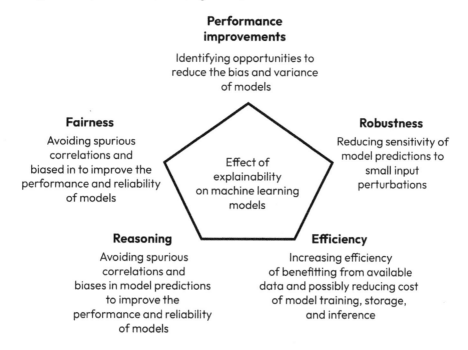

Figure 6.2 – Effects of using explainability on machine learning models

Now that you have a better understanding of the importance of explainability in machine learning modeling, we are ready to get into the details of explainability techniques.

# Explainability methods in machine learning

We need to keep the following considerations in mind when using or developing explainability techniques for machine learning modeling (Ribeiro et al., 2016):

- **Interpretability**: The explanations need to be understandable to users. One of the main objectives of machine learning explanation is to make complex models understandable for users and, if possible, provide actionable information.

- **Local fidelity (faithfulness)**: Capturing the complexity of models so that they are completely faithful and meet global faithfulness criteria can't be achieved by all techniques. However, an explanation should be at least locally faithful to the model. In other words, an explanation needs to properly explain how the model behaves in the close neighborhood of the data point under investigation.

- **Being model-agnostic**: Although there are techniques that are designed for specific machine learning methods, such as random forest, they are supposed to be agnostic to models that are built with different hyperparameters or for different datasets. An explainability technique needs to consider the model as a black box and provide explanations for the model either globally or locally.

Explainability techniques can be categorized into **local explainability** and **global explainability** methods. Local explainability methods aim to meet the previously listed criteria, while global explainability techniques try to go beyond local explainability and provide global explanations to the models.

## Local explainability techniques

Local explainability helps us understand the behavior of a model close to a data point in a feature space. Although these models meet local fidelity criteria, features identified to be locally important might not be globally important, and vice versa (Ribeiro et al., 2016). This means that we cannot infer local explanations from global explanations, and vice versa, easily. In this section, we will discuss five local explanation techniques:

- Feature importance
- Counterfactuals
- Sample-based explainability
- Rule-based explainability
- Saliency maps

We will also go through a few global explainability techniques after.

## *Feature importance*

One of the primary approaches to local explainability is explaining the contribution of each feature *locally* in predicting the outcome of the target data points in a neighborhood. Widely used examples of such methods include **SHapley Additive exPlanations (SHAP)** (Lundberg et al., 2017) and **Local Interpretable Model-agnostic Explanations (LIME)** (Ribeiro et al., 2016). Let's briefly discuss the theory behind these two methods and practice them in Python.

## Local explanation using SHAP

SHAP is a Python framework that was introduced by Scott Lundberg and Su-In Lee (Lundberg and Lee, 2017). The idea of this framework is based on using the Shapely value, a known concept named after Lloyd Shapley, an American game theorist and Nobel Prize winner (Winter, 2022). SHAP can determine the contribution of each feature to a model's prediction. As features work cooperatively in determining the decision boundaries of classification models and eventually affecting model predictions, SHAP tries to first identify the marginal contribution of each feature and then provide Shapely values as an estimate of the contribution of each feature in cooperation with the whole feature set regarding the predictions of a model. From a theoretical perspective, these marginal contributions can be calculated by removing features individually and in different combinations, calculating the effect of each feature set removal, and then normalizing the contributions. This process can't be repeated for all possible feature combinations as the number of possible combinations could grow exponentially to billions, even for a model with 40 features. Instead, this process is used a limited number of times to come up with an approximation of Shapely values. Also, since removing features is not possible in most machine learning models, feature values get replaced by alternative values either from a random distribution or from a background set of meaningful and possible values for each feature. We don't want to get into the theoretical details of this process but we will practice using this approach in the next section.

## Local explanation using LIME

LIME is an alternative to SHAP for local explainability that explains the predictions of any classifier or regressor, in a model-agnostic way, by approximating a model locally with an interpretable model (*Figure 6.3*; Ribeiro et al., 2016):

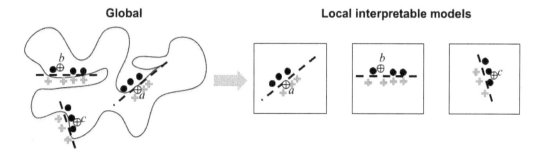

Figure 6.3 – Schematic representation of local interpretable modeling in LIME

Some of the advantages of this technique, which were also mentioned in the original paper by Ribeiro et al., 2016, include the following:

- The theory and the provided explanations are intuitive and easy to understand
- Sparse explanations are provided to increase interpretability
- Works with different types of structured and unstructured data, such as texts and images

### Counterfactuals

Counterfactual examples, or explanations, help us identify what needs to be changed in an instance to change the outcome of a classification model. These counterfactuals could help in identifying actionable paths in many applications, such as finance, retail, marketing, recruiting, and healthcare. One example is when suggesting to a bank customer how they can change the rejection to their loan application (Guidotti, 2022). Counterfactuals could also help in identifying biases in models that help us improve model performance or eliminate fairness issues in our models. We need to keep the following considerations in mind while generating and using counterfactual explanations (Guidotti, 2022):

- **Validity**: A counterfactual example is valid if and only if its classification outcome would be different from the original sample.
- **Similarity**: A counterfactual example should be as similar as possible to the original data point.
- **Diversity**: Although counterfactual examples should be similar to the original samples they are derived from, they need to be diverse among each other to provide different options (that is, different possible feature changes).
- **Actionability**: Not all the feature value changes are actionable. The actionability of the counterfactuals that are suggested by a counterfactual method is an important factor in benefitting from them in practice.
- **Plausibility**: The feature values of a counterfactual example should be plausible. The plausibility of the counterfactuals increases trust in deriving explanations from them.

We also have to note that counterfactual explainers need to be efficient and fast enough in generating the counterfactuals and stable in generating counterfactuals for similar data points (Guidotti, 2022).

### Sample-based explainability

Another approach to explainability is to rely on the feature values and results of real or synthetic data points to help in local model explainability. In this category of explainability techniques, we aim to find out which samples are misclassified and what feature sets result in an increasing chance of misclassification to help us explain our models. We can also assess which training data points result in a change in the decision boundary so that we can predict the output of test or production data points. There are statistical methods such as the **Influence function** (Koh and Liang 2017), a classical approach for assessing the influence of samples on model parameters, that we can use to identify the sample's contribution to the decision-making process of models.

### Rule-based explainability

Rule-based methods such as **Anchor explanations** aim to find the conditions of feature values that result in a high probability of getting the same output (Ribeiro et al., 2018). For example, in the case of predicting the salary of individuals in a dataset to be less than or equal to 50k or above 50k, "Education <= high school to result in <=50k salary" could be considered a rule in rule-based explanation. These explanations need to be locally faithful.

### Saliency maps

The objective of saliency maps is to explain which features contribute more or less to the predicted outputs for a data point. These methods are commonly used in machine learning or deep learning models that have been trained on image data (Simonyan et al., 2013). For example, we can use saliency maps to figure out if a classification model uses a background forest to identify if it is an image of a bear rather than a teddy bear or uses the components of the bear's body for it.

## Global explanation

Despite the difficulty in achieving a reliable global explanation for machine learning models, it could increase trust in them (Ribeiro et al., 2016). Performance is not the only aspect of building trust when developing and deploying machine learning models. And local explanations, although very helpful in investigating individual samples and providing actionable information, might not be enough for this trust building. Here, we will discuss three approaches for going beyond local explanation, including collecting local explanations, knowledge distillation, and summaries of counterfactuals.

### Collecting local explanations

**Submodular pick LIME (SP-LIME)** is a global explanation technique that uses local explanations of LIME to come up with a global perspective of a model's behavior (Riberio et al., 2016). As it might not be feasible to use the local explanations of all data points, SP-LIME picks a representative diverse set of samples capable of representing the global behavior of the model.

### Knowledge distillation

The idea of **knowledge distillation** is to approximate the behavior of complex models, which was initially proposed for neural network models, using simpler interpretable models such as decision trees (Hinton et al., 2015; Frosst and Hinton, 2017). In other words, we aim to build simpler models, such as decision trees, that approximate the predictions of complex models for a given set of samples.

### Summaries of counterfactuals

We can use a summary of counterfactuals that's been generated for multiple data points with correct and incorrect predicted outcomes to figure out the contribution of features in output prediction and the sensitivity of a prediction to feature perturbation. We will practice using counterfactuals later in this chapter, where you will see that not all counterfactuals are acceptable and they need to be chosen according to the meaning behind features and their values.

## Practicing machine learning explainability in Python

There are several Python libraries you can use to extract local and global explanations for your machine learning models (*Table 6.1*). Here, we want to practice with a few of the ones that focus on local model explainability:

| Library | Library Name for Importing and Installation | URL |
|---|---|---|
| SHAP | Shap | https://pypi.org/project/shap/ |
| LIME | Lime | https://pypi.org/project/lime/ |
| Shapash | shapash | https://pypi.org/project/shapash/ |
| ELI5 | eli5 | https://pypi.org/project/eli5/ |
| Explainer dashboard | explainer dashboard | https://pypi.org/project/explainerdashboard/ |
| Dalex | dalex | https://pypi.org/project/dalex/ |
| OmniXAI | omnixai | https://pypi.org/project/omnixai/ |
| CARLA | carla | https://carla-counterfactual-and-recourse-library.readthedocs.io/en/latest/ |
| **Diverse Counterfactual Explanations (DiCE)** | dice-ml | https://pypi.org/project/dice-ml/ |
| Machine Learning Library Extensions | mlxtend | https://pypi.org/project/mlxtend/ |
| Anchor | anchor | https://github.com/marcotcr/anchor |

Table 6.1 – Python libraries or repositories with available functionalities
for machine learning model explainability

First, we will practice with SHAP, a widely used technique for machine learning explainability.

## Explanations in SHAP

We'll first look at performing local explanation with SHAP, followed by global explanation later.

### *Local explanation*

In this section, we will practice with SHAP to extract feature importance from our machine learning models. We will use the **University of California Irvine** (**UCI**) adult dataset to predict if people made over $50k in the 90s; this is also available as the adult income dataset as part of the SHAP library. You can read about the definition of the features and other information about this dataset at https://archive.ics.uci.edu/ml/datasets/adult.

First, we need to build a supervised machine learning model using this dataset before using any explainability method. We will use **XGBoost** as a high-performance machine learning method for tabular data to practice with SHAP:

```
# loading UCI adult income dataset
# classification task to predict if people made over $50k in the 90s
or not
X,y = shap.datasets.adult()
# split the data to train and test sets
X_train, X_test, y_train, y_test = train_test_split(
    X, y, test_size = 0.3, random_state=10)
# initializing a XGboost model
xgb_model = xgboost.XGBClassifier(random_state=42)
# fitting the XGboost model with training data
xgb_model.fit(X_train, y_train)
# generating predictions for the test set
y_pred = xgb_model.predict(X_test)
# identifying misclassified datapoints in the test set
misclassified_index = np.where(y_test != y_pred)[0]
# calculating roc-auc of predictions
print("ROC-AUC of predictions: {}".format(
    roc_auc_score(y_test, xgb_model.predict_proba(
        X_test)[:, 1])))

print("First 5 misclassified test set datapoints:
    {}".format(misclassified_index[0:5]))
```

There are different methods to approximate feature importance that are available in the SHAP library, such as shap.LinearExplainer(), shap.KernelExplainer(), shap.TreeExplainer(), and shap.DeepExplainer(). You can use shap.TreeExplainer() in the case of tree-based methods such as random forest and XGBoost. Let's build an explainer object using the trained model and then extract Shapely values:

```
# generate the Tree explainer
explainer = shap.TreeExplainer(xgb_model)
# extract SHAP values from the explainer object
shap_values = explainer.shap_values(X_test)
```

There are multiple plotting functions in the SHAP library to provide us with visual illustrations of feature importance using Shapely values. For example, we can use `shap.dependence_plot()` to identify the Shapely value for the *Education-Num* feature:

```
# If interaction_index of "auto" is chosen then
# the strongest interaction is used to color the dots.
shap.dependence_plot("Education-Num", shap_values, X_test)
```

The following dependence plot clearly shows that a higher *Education-Num* value results in a higher Shapely value or a greater contribution in predicting a positive outcome (that is, >50k salary):

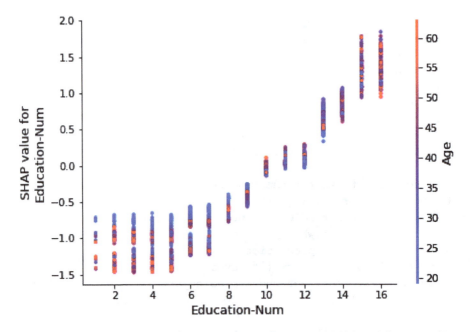

Figure 6.4 – SHAP values for the Education-Num feature in the test set of the adult income dataset

We can repeat this process with other features, such as *Age*, which results in a similar explanation as *Education-Num*. The only difference in using `shap.dependence_plot()` for *Education-Num* and *Age* is `interaction_index`, which is specified as None for *Age*:

```
# generate dependence plot for "Age" feature
shap.dependence_plot("Age", shap_values, X_test,
    interaction_index=None)
```

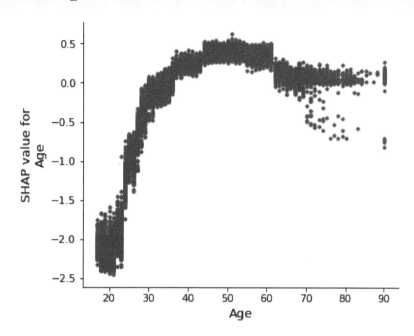

Figure 6.5 – SHAP values for the Age feature in the test set of the adult income dataset

If we need to extract an explanation of our model on a specific subset of our dataset, we can use the same functions but use the subset of data we want to investigate instead of the whole dataset. We can also use training and test sets to identify explanations in the data that's used for model training and unseen data we want to use to evaluate the performance of our model. To showcase this, we will investigate the importance of *Age* on a subset of the test set that's been misclassified using the following code:

```
# generate dependence plot for "Age" feature
shap.dependence_plot("Age",
    shap_values[misclassified_index],
    X_test.iloc[misclassified_index,:],
    interaction_index=None)
```

As you can see, the SHAP values have similar trends for misclassified data points (*Figure 6.6*) and the whole dataset (*Figure 6.5*):

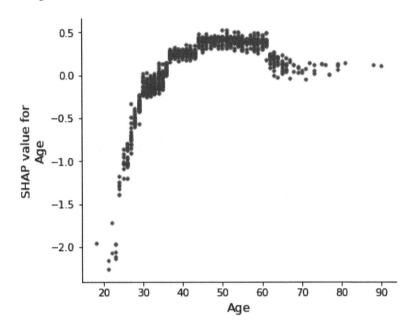

Figure 6.6 – SHAP values for the Age feature for the misclassified
data points in the test set of the adult income dataset

In addition to extracting Shapely values across a series of data points, we also need to investigate how features contributed to the correct or wrong prediction for a data point. Here, we chose two samples: `sample 12`, with the actual label being False or 0 (that is, low income) and the predicted label being True or 1 (that is, high income), and `sample 24`, with the actual and predicted labels of True and False, respectively. Here, we can use `shap.plots._waterfall.waterfall_legacy()` and extract the expected values of the input features, as shown in *Figure 6.7*. In this kind of plotting in SHAP, for each feature, $X$, $f(X)$ is the predicted value given $X$, and $E[f(X)]$ is the expected value of the target variable (that is, the mean of all predictions, *mean(model.predict(X))*). This plot shows us how much a single feature affected the prediction:

```
# extracting expected values
expected_value = explainer.expected_value
# generate waterfall plot for observation 12
shap.plots._waterfall.waterfall_legacy(expected_value,
    shap_values[12], features=X_test.iloc[12,:],
    feature_names=X.columns, max_display=15, show=True)
```

```
# generate waterfall plot for observation 24
shap.plots._waterfall.waterfall_legacy(expected_value,
    shap_values[24],features=X_test.iloc[24,:],
    feature_names=X.columns,max_display=15, show=True)
```

*Figure 6.7*, which is for `sample 12`, shows us that *Relationship* and *Education-Num* are the features with the most effect, and *Race* and *Country* are the ones with the least effect on the outcome of this sample:

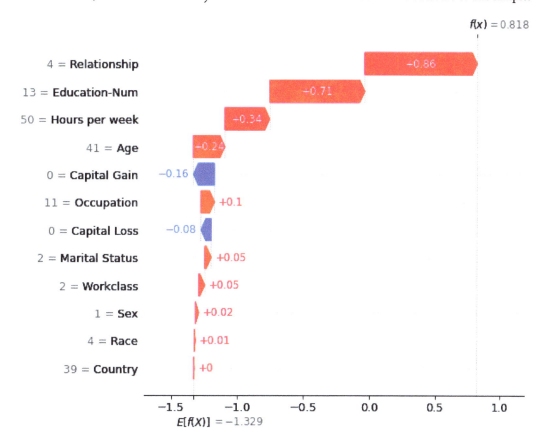

Figure 6.7 – SHAP waterfall plot of sample 12 in the adult income dataset

*Relationship* and *Education-Num* are also the features with the most effect for `sample 24` (*Figure 6.8*). However, the third most contribution in `sample 12` is from *Hours per week*, which has a low effect on the outcome of `sample 24`. This is the type of analysis we can do to compare some of the incorrect predictions and identify potentially actionable suggestions for improving model performance. Alternatively, we can extract actionable suggestions to improve the future income of individuals in this dataset:

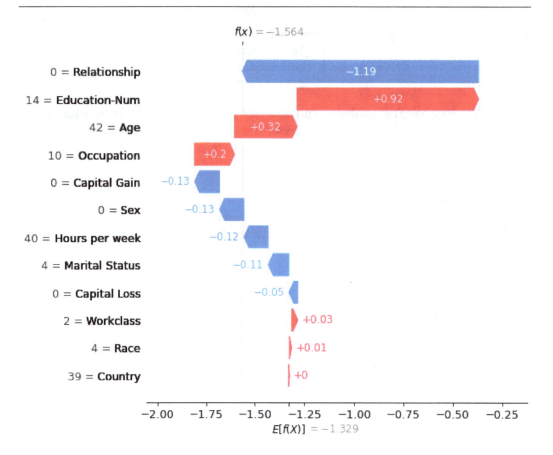

Figure 6.8 – SHAP waterfall plot of sample 24 in the adult income dataset

Despite the easy-to-understand insights provided by SHAP, we need to make sure feature dependencies in our models don't lead to confusion when we interpret Shapely values.

## Global explanation

Although shap.dependence_plot() might seem to provide a global explanation, as it shows the effect of a feature across all or a subset of data points, we need explanations across model features and data points to build trust for our models. shap.summary_plot() is an example of such a global explanation that summarizes the Shapely values of features across the specified set of data points. These kinds of summary plots and results are important for identifying the most effective features and understanding if there are biases, such as concerning race or sex, in our model. With the following summary plot (*Figure 6.9*), we can easily see that *Sex* and *Race* are not among the features with the most effect, although their effect is not necessarily negligible and might need further investigation. We will talk about model bias and fairness in the next chapter:

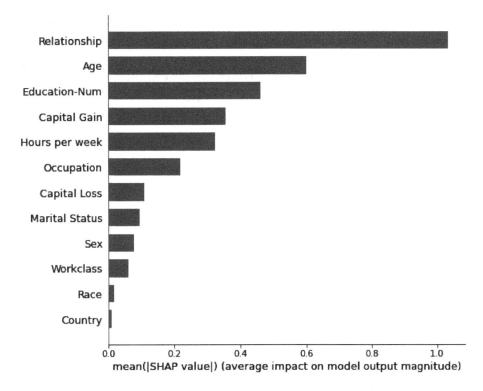

Figure 6.9 – SHAP summary plot for the adult income dataset

Here is the code to generate the previous summary plot:

```
# create a SHAP beeswarm plot (i.e. SHAP summary plot)
shap.summary_plot(shap_values, X_test,plot_type="bar")
```

## Explanations using LIME

Having learned how to perform explanations using SHAP, we will now turn our attention to LIME. We will start with local explanation first.

### Local explanation

LIME is another way to get an easy-to-understand local explanation for individual data points. We can use the lime Python library to build an explainer object and then use it to identify local explanations for samples of interest. Here, once again, we will use the XGBoost model we trained for SHAP and generate explanations for sample 12 and sample 24 to show that their outcomes were incorrectly predicted.

By default, lime uses *ridge regression* as the interpretable model for generating local explanations. We can change this method in the lime.lime_tabular.LimeTabularExplainer() class by changing feature_selection to none for linear modeling without any feature selection, or lasso_path, which uses lasso_path() from scikit-learn, as another form of supervised linear modeling with regularization.

> **Note**
>
> The mode fitting line for fitting the XGBoost model for the UCI adult dataset, which was presented in a previous code snippet, needs to be changed since xgb_model.fit(np.array(X_train), y_train) makes the model usable for the lime library:

```
# create explainer
explainer = lime.lime_tabular.LimeTabularExplainer(
    np.array(X_train), feature_names=X_train.columns,
    #X_train.to_numpy()
    class_names=['Lower income','Higher income'],
    verbose=True)
# visualizing explanation by LIME
print('actual label of sample 12: {}'.format(y_test[12]))
print('prediction for sample 12: {}'.format(y_pred[12]))
exp = explainer.explain_instance(
    data_row = X_test.iloc[12],
    predict_fn = xgb_model.predict_proba)
exp.show_in_notebook(show_table=True)
```

You can interpret the middle plot in *Figure 6.10* for sample 12 as the local contribution of features in predicting the outcome as *Higher income* or *Lower income*. Similar to SHAP, the *Education-Num* and *Relationship* features contribute the most to the sample being incorrectly predicted as *Higher income*. On the other hand, *Capital Gain* and *Capital Loss* have the maximum contribution in pushing the prediction of the sample's output as the other class. But we also have to pay attention to feature values as both *Capital Gain* and *Capital Loss* are zero for this sample:

```
actual label of sample 12: False
prediction for sample 12: True
Intercept 0.6782841844012466
Prediction_local [0.4516226]
Right: 0.69382423
```

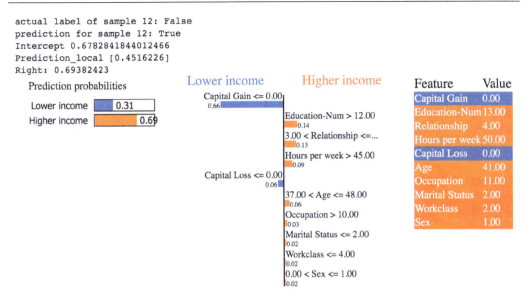

Figure 6.10 – LIME local explanation for sample 12 in the adult income dataset

Similarly, we can investigate the result of LIME for `sample 24`, as shown in *Figure 6.11*:

```
actual label of sample 24: True
prediction for sample 24: False
Intercept 0.87248362152509
Prediction_local [0.14014471]
Right: 0.17307502
```

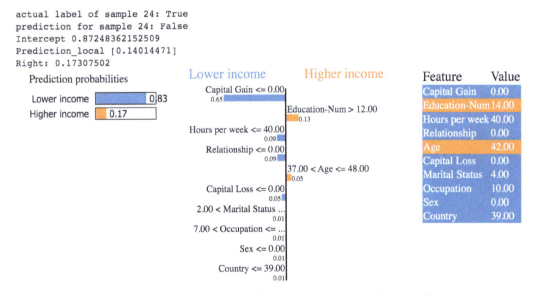

Figure 6.11 – LIME local explanation for sample 24 in the adult income dataset

*Capital Gain*, *Education-Num*, and *Hours per week* contribute the most to predicting the output in positive or negative directions. However, *Capital Gain* doesn't affect this specific data point as its value is zero.

### Global explanation

**Submodular pick LIME (SP_LIME)** is a global explanation method in which a subset of samples get selected as candidates, and then we can use the explanation of these candidates via LIME so that they're representative of the global explanation of the model. We can use `lime.submodular_pick.SubmodularPick()` to pick these samples. Here are the parameters of this class that could help you explain your global regression or classification models:

- `predict_fn` (prediction function): For `ScikitClassifiers`, this is `classifier.predict_proba()`, while for `ScikitRegressors`, this is `regressor.predict()`

- `sample_size`: The number of data points to explain if `method == 'sample'` is chosen

- `num_exps_desired`: The number of explanation objects returned

- `num_features`: The maximum number of features present in the explanation:

```
sp_obj = submodular_pick.SubmodularPick(explainer,
    np.array(X_train), xgb_model.predict_proba,
    method='sample', sample_size=3, num_features=8,
    num_exps_desired=5)


# showing explanation for the picked instances for explanation if you
are using Jupyter or Colab notebook
[exp.show_in_notebook() for exp in sp_obj.explanations]
```

*Figure 6.12* shows the three data points that were picked by SP-LIME:

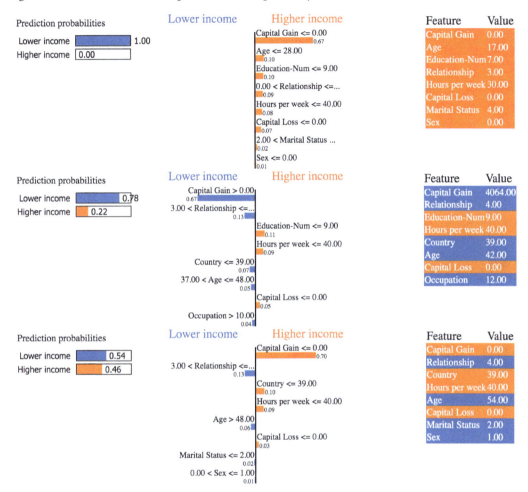

Figure 6.12 – Data points selected by SPI-LIME for global explainability

But instead of visualizing the picked instances, you can use the `as_map()` parameter instead of `show_in_notebook()` for each explanation object, as part of the explanation objects in `sp_obj`. `explanations`, and then summarize the information for a bigger set of data points instead of investigating a handful of samples. For such analysis, you can use a small percentage of data points, such as 1% or lower in the case of very large datasets with tens of thousands of data points or more.

## Counterfactual generation using Diverse Counterfactual Explanations (DiCE)

You can use the `dice_ml` Python library (Mothilal et al., 2020) to generate counterfactuals and understand how a model can switch from one prediction to another, as explained earlier in this chapter. First, we must train a model and then make an explanation object using the `dice_ml.Dice()` Python class, after installing and importing the `dice_ml` library, as follows:

```
### This example is taken from https://github.com/interpretml/DiCE ###
dataset = helpers.load_adult_income_dataset()
target = dataset["income"] # outcome variable
train_dataset, test_dataset, _, _ = train_test_split(
    dataset,target,test_size=0.2,random_state=0,
    stratify=target)
# Dataset for training an ML model
d = dice_ml.Data(dataframe=train_dataset,
    continuous_features=['age','hours_per_week'],
    outcome_name='income')
# Pre-trained ML model
m = dice_ml.Model(
    model_path=dice_ml.utils.helpers.get_adult_income_modelpath(),
    backend='TF2', func="ohe-min-max")
# DiCE explanation instance
exp = dice_ml.Dice(d,m)
```

Then, we can use the generated explanation object to generate counterfactuals for one or multiple samples. Here, we are generating 10 counterfactuals for `sample 1`:

```
query_instance = test_dataset.drop(columns="income")[0:1]
dice_exp = exp.generate_counterfactuals(query_instance,
    total_CFs=10, desired_class="opposite",
    random_seed = 42)
# Visualize counterfactual explanation
dice_exp.visualize_as_dataframe()
```

*Figure 6.13* shows both the feature values of the target sample and 10 corresponding counterfactuals:

| | age | workclass | education | marital_status | occupation | race | gender | hours_per_week | income |
|---|---|---|---|---|---|---|---|---|---|
| 0 | 29 | Private | HS-grad | Married | Blue-Collar | White | Female | 38 | 0 |

Diverse Counterfactual set (new outcome: 1.0)

| | age | workclass | education | marital_status | occupation | race | gender | hours_per_week | income |
|---|---|---|---|---|---|---|---|---|---|
| 0 | 80.0 | Private | HS-grad | Married | Service | White | Female | 38 | 1 |
| 1 | 29.0 | Private | HS-grad | Married | Blue-Collar | White | Female | 97.0 | 1 |
| 2 | 29 | Private | HS-grad | Married | Service | White | Female | 92.0 | 1 |
| 3 | 29 | Private | HS-grad | Married | Blue-Collar | White | Female | 93.0 | 1 |
| 4 | 29 | Private | Assoc | Married | Blue-Collar | White | Female | 59.0 | 1 |
| 5 | 49.0 | Private | HS-grad | Married | Blue-Collar | White | Female | 72.0 | 1 |
| 6 | 29 | Private | Assoc | Married | Service | White | Female | 38 | 1 |
| 7 | 29 | Private | HS-grad | Married | Blue-Collar | Other | Female | 97.0 | 1 |
| 8 | 90.0 | Private | Doctorate | Married | Blue-Collar | White | Female | 38 | 1 |
| 9 | 58.0 | Private | HS-grad | Married | Blue-Collar | White | Female | 76.0 | 1 |

Figure 6.13 – A selected data point and the generated counterfactuals from the adult income dataset

Although all counterfactuals meet the objective of switching the outcome of the target sample (that is, `sample 1`), not all counterfactuals are feasible according to the definition and meaning of each feature. For example, if we want to suggest to a 29-year-old individual that they change their outcome from low to high salary, suggesting that they will earn a high salary when they are 80 years old is not an effective and actionable suggestion. Also, suggesting a change of *hours_per_week* of work from 38 to >90 is not feasible. You need to use such considerations in rejecting counterfactuals so that you can identify opportunities for model performance and provide actionable suggestions to users. Also, you can switch between different techniques to generate more meaningful counterfactuals for your models and applications.

There are more recent Python libraries such as `Dalex` (Baniecki et al., 2021) and `OmniXA` (Yang et al., 2022) that you can use for model explainability. We will also discuss how these methods and Python libraries can be used to decrease bias and help us move toward fairness in developing new or revising our already trained machine learning models.

# Reviewing why having explainability is not enough

Explainability helps us build trust for the users of our models. As you learned in this chapter, you can use explainability techniques to understand how your models generate the outputs for one or multiple instances in a dataset. These explanations could help in improving our models from a performance and fairness perspective. However, we cannot achieve such improvements by simply using these techniques blindly and generating some results in Python. For example, as we discussed in the *Counterfactual generation using Diverse Counterfactual Explanations (DiCE)* section, some of the generated counterfactuals might not be reasonable and meaningful and we cannot rely on them. Or, when generating local explanations for one or multiple data points using SHAP or LIME, we need to pay attention to the meaning of features, the range of values for each feature and the meaning behind them, and the characteristics of each data point we investigate. One aspect of decision-making using explainability is to distinguish the issues with the model and the specific data points in training, testing, or production that we are investigating. A data point could be an outlier that makes our model less reliable for it but doesn't necessarily make our model less reliable as a whole. In the next chapter, *Chapter 7, Decreasing Bias and Achieving Fairness*, we will discuss that bias detection is not simply about identifying if there are features such as *age*, *race*, or *skin color* that our models rely on.

Altogether, these considerations tell us that running a few Python classes to use explainability for our models is not enough to achieve trust and generate meaningful explanations. There is more to it.

## Summary

In this chapter, you learned about interpretable machine learning models and how explainability techniques could help you in improving the performance and reliability of your models. You learned about different local and global explainability techniques, such as SHAP and LIME, and practiced with them in Python. You also had the chance to practice with the provided Python code to learn how to use machine learning explainability techniques in your projects.

In the next chapter, you will learn about the approaches to detect and decrease biases in your models and how you can use the available functionalities in Python to meet the necessary fairness criteria when developing machine learning models.

## Questions

1. How could explainability help you improve your model's performance?
2. What is the difference between local and global explainability?
3. Is it better to use linear models because of their interpretability?
4. Does explainability analysis make a machine learning model more reliable?
5. Could you explain the difference between SHAP and LIME for machine learning explainability?
6. How could you benefit from counterfactuals in developing machine learning models?

7.  Assume a machine learning model is used for loan approval in a bank. Are all suggested counterfactuals useful in suggesting ways a person could improve their chance of getting approval?

# References

- Weber, Leander, et al. *Beyond explaining: Opportunities and challenges of XAI-based model improvement*. Information Fusion (2022).

- Linardatos, Pantelis, Vasilis Papastefanopoulos, and Sotiris Kotsiantis. *Explainable AI: A review of machine learning interpretability methods*. Entropy 23.1 (2020): 18.

- Gilpin, Leilani H., et al. *Explaining explanations: An overview of interpretability of machine learning*. 2018 IEEE 5th International Conference on data science and advanced analytics (DSAA). IEEE, 2018.

- Carvalho, Diogo V., Eduardo M. Pereira, and Jaime S. Cardoso. *Machine learning interpretability: A survey on methods and metrics*. Electronics 8.8 (2019): 832.

- Winter, Eyal. *The Shapley value*. Handbook of game theory with economic applications 3 (2002): 2025-2054.

- *A Guide to Explainable AI Using Python*: https://www.thepythoncode.com/article/explainable-ai-model-python

- Burkart, Nadia, and Marco F. Huber. *A survey on the explainability of supervised machine learning*. Journal of Artificial Intelligence Research 70 (2021): 245-317.

- Guidotti, Riccardo. *Counterfactual explanations and how to find them: literature review and benchmarking*. Data Mining and Knowledge Discovery (2022): 1-55.

- Ribeiro, Marco Tulio, Sameer Singh, and Carlos Guestrin. *Anchors: High-precision model-agnostic explanations*. Proceedings of the AAAI conference on artificial intelligence. Vol. 32. No. 1. 2018.

- Hinton, Geoffrey, Oriol Vinyals, and Jeff Dean. *Distilling the knowledge in a neural network*. arXiv preprint arXiv:1503.02531 (2015).

- Simonyan, Karen, Andrea Vedaldi, and Andrew Zisserman. *Deep inside convolutional networks: Visualising image classification models and saliency maps*. arXiv preprint arXiv:1312.6034 (2013).

- Frosst, Nicholas, and Geoffrey Hinton. *Distilling a neural network into a soft decision tree*. arXiv preprint arXiv:1711.09784 (2017).

- Lundberg, Scott M., and Su-In Lee. *A unified approach to interpreting model predictions*. Advances in neural information processing systems 30 (2017).

- Ribeiro, Marco Tulio, Sameer Singh, and Carlos Guestrin. *"Why should I trust you?" Explaining the predictions of any classifier*. Proceedings of the 22nd ACM SIGKDD international conference on knowledge discovery and data mining. 2016.

- Baniecki, Hubert, et al. *Dalex: responsible machine learning with interactive explainability and fairness in Python.* The Journal of Machine Learning Research 22.1 (2021): 9759-9765.

- Yang, Wenzhuo, et al. *OmniXAI: A Library for Explainable AI.* arXiv preprint arXiv:2206.01612 (2022).

- Hima Lakkaraju, Julius Adebayo, Sameer Singh, *AAAI 2021 Tutorial on Explaining Machine Learning Predictions.*

- Mothilal, Ramaravind K., Amit Sharma, and Chenhao Tan. *Explaining machine learning classifiers through diverse counterfactual explanations.* Proceedings of the 2020 conference on fairness, accountability, and transparency. 2020.

# 7
# Decreasing Bias and Achieving Fairness

Fairness is an important topic when it comes to using machine learning across different industries, as we discussed in *Chapter 3*, *Debugging toward Responsible AI*. In this chapter, we will provide you with some widely used notions and definitions of fairness in machine learning settings, as well as how to use fairness and explainability Python libraries that are designed to not only help you in assessing fairness in your models but also improve them in this regard.

This chapter includes many figures and code examples to help you better understand these concepts and start benefiting from them in your projects. Note that one chapter is far from enough to make you an expert on the topic of fairness, but this chapter will provide you with the necessary knowledge and tools to start practicing this subject in your projects. You can learn more about this topic using more advanced resources dedicated to machine learning fairness.

We will cover the following topics in this chapter:

- Fairness in machine learning modeling
- Sources of bias
- Using explainability techniques
- Fairness assessment and improvement in Python

By the end of this chapter, you will have learned about some technical details and Python tools that you can use to assess fairness and reduce biases in your models. You will also learn how to benefit from the machine learning explainability techniques you learned about in *Chapter 6*, *Interpretability and Explainability in Machine Learning Modeling*.

# Technical requirements

The following requirements should be considered for this chapter as they will help you better understand the concepts, use them in your projects, and practice with the provided code:

- Python library requirements:

  - `sklearn` >= 1.2.2

  - `numpy` >= 1.22.4

  - `pytest` >= 7.2.2

  - `shap` >= 0.41.0

  - `aif360` >= 0.5.0

  - `fairlearn` >= 0.8.0

- Basic knowledge of the machine learning explainability concepts discussed in the previous chapter

You can find the code files for this chapter on GitHub at `https://github.com/PacktPublishing/Debugging-Machine-Learning-Models-with-Python/tree/main/Chapter07`.

# Fairness in machine learning modeling

To assess fairness, we need to have specific considerations in mind and then use proper metrics to quantify fairness in our models. *Table 7.1* provides you with some of the considerations, definitions, and approaches to either evaluate or achieve fairness in machine learning modeling. We will go through the mathematical definitions of **demographic parity**, **equality of odds** or **equalized odds**, and **equality of opportunity** here as different group fairness definitions. Group fairness definitions ensure the fairness of groups of people with common attributes and characteristics instead of individuals:

| Topics in Machine Learning Fairness | Description |
| --- | --- |
| Demographic parity | Ensures predictions are not dependent on a given sensitive attribute, such as ethnicity, sex, or race |
| Equality of odds | Ensures the independence of predictions to a given sensitive attribute, such as ethnicity, sex, or race given a true output |
| Equality of opportunity | Ensures the equality of opportunities provided for individuals or groups of people |
| Individual fairness | Ensures fairness for individuals rather than groups of people with common attributes |
| Consistency | Provides consistency in decision-making not only between similar data points or users but also across time |
| Fairness through unawareness | Achieves fairness if you're unaware of sensitive attributes in decision making |
| Fairness through transparency | Improves fairness through transparency and trust building through explainability |

Table 7.1 – Some important topics and considerations in fairness
in machine learning and artificial intelligence

Demographic parity is a group fairness definition that ensures that a model's predictions are not dependent on a given sensitive attribute, such as ethnicity or sex. Mathematically, we can define it as the equality of probability of predicting a class, such as $C_i$, for different groups of a given attribute, as follows:

$$P(C = C_i | G = g_1) = P(C = C_i | G = g_2)$$

To better understand the meaning of demographic parity, we can consider the following examples, which meet fairness according to demographic parity:

- The same percentage of bail denial in each race group in COMPAS. We covered COMPAS in *Chapter 3, Debugging toward Responsible AI*.

- The same acceptance rate for loan applications between men and women.

- The same likelihood of hospitalization between poor and rich neighborhoods. We covered more about this problem in *Chapter 3, Debugging toward Responsible AI*.

**Disparate impact ratio** (**DIR**) is a metric that quantifies the deviation from equality based on demographic parity:

$$DIR = \frac{P(C = 1|G = g_1)}{P(C = 1|G = g_2)}$$

The DIR value's range is $[0, \infty)$, where a value of 1 satisfies demographic parity while deviation toward higher or lower values translates to deviation from fairness based on this definition. DIR values of greater and less than 1 are referred to as negative and positive bias, respectively, considering the group we use in the numerator.

Despite the importance of demographic parity in fairness, it has its limitations. For example, in the case of DIR in the data itself (that is, the difference in class prevalence between different groups), a perfect model will not meet demographic parity criteria. Also, it doesn't reflect the quality of predictions for each group. Other definitions help us improve our fairness assessment. Equality of odds or equalized odds is one such definition. Equalized odds is satisfied when a given prediction is independent of the group of a given sensitive attribute and the real output:

$$P(\hat{y}|y, G = g_1) = P(\hat{y}|y, G = g_2) = P(\hat{y}|y)$$

The definition of equality of opportunity is very similar to equalized odds, which assesses the independence of a prediction concerning groups for a given real output. But equality of opportunity focuses on a particular label of true values. Usually, the positive class is considered the target class and is representative of providing an opportunity for individuals, such as admission to school or having a high salary. Here is a formula for equality of opportunity:

$$P(\hat{y}|y = 1, G = g_1) = P(\hat{y}|y = 1, G = g_2) = P(\hat{y}|y = 1)$$

According to these notions of fairness, each could give you a different result. You need to consider the differences between different notions so that you don't generalize fairness based on one definition or another.

## Proxies for sensitive variables

One of the challenges in assessing fairness in machine learning models is the existence of proxies for sensitive attributes such as sex and race. These proxies could be among the major contributors in generating model outputs and could result in bias in our models to specific groups. However, we cannot simply remove them as this could have a significant effect on performance. *Table 7.2* provides some examples of these proxies for different sensitive attributes:

| Sensitive Variable | Example Proxies |
|---|---|
| Sex | Level of education, salary and income (in some countries), occupation, history of a felony charge, keywords in user-generated content (for example, in a resume or social media), being a university faculty |
| Race | History of a felony charge, keywords in user-generated content (for example, in a resume or social media), ZIP or postal code |
| Disabilities | Speed of walking, eye movement, body posture |
| Marital status | Level of education, salary and income (in some countries), and house size and number of bedrooms |
| Age | Posture and keywords in user-generated content (for example, in a resume or social media) |

Table 7.2 – Examples of proxies for some of the important sensitive variables, in the context of fairness (Caton and Haas, 2020)

Now that you've learned about the importance of fairness and some important definitions under this topic, let's review some of the possible sources of bias that play against your goal of achieving fairness in your models.

# Sources of bias

There are different sources of bias in a machine learning life cycle. Bias could exist in the collected data, introduced in the data subsampling, cleaning and filtering, or model training and selection. Here, we will review examples of such sources to help you better understand how to avoid or detect such biases throughout the life cycle of a machine learning project.

## Biases introduced in data generation and collection

The data that we feed into our models could be biased by default, even before the modeling starts. The first source of such biases we want to review here is the issue of dataset size. Consider a dataset as a sample of a bigger population – for example, a survey of 100 students or the loan application information of 200 customers of a bank. The small size of these datasets could increase the chance of bias. Let's simulate this with a simple random data generation. We will write a function that generates two vectors of random binary values using `np.random.randint()` and then calculates *DIR* between the two groups of 0 and 1:

```
np.random.seed(42)
def disparate_impact_randomsample(sample_size,
    sampling_num = 100): disparate_impact = []
    for sam_iter in range(0, sampling_num):
```

```
        # generating random array of 0 and 1 as two groups with
different priviledges (e.g. male versus female)
        group_category = np.random.randint(2,
            size=sample_size)
    # generating random array of 0 and 1 as the output labels (e.g.
accepted for loan or not)
    output_labels = np.random.randint(2, size=sample_size)
    group0_label1 = [iter for iter in range(0, len(
        group_category)) if group_category[iter] == 0
        and output_labels[iter] == 1]
    group1_label1 = [iter for iter in range(0, len(
        group_category)) if group_category[iter] == 1 and
        output_labels[iter] == 1]
    # calculating disparate impact
    disparate_impact.append(len
        (group1_label1)/len(group0_label1))
    return disparate_impact
```

Now, let's use this function to calculate DIR for 1,000 different groups of different sizes, including 50, 100, 1000, 10000, and 1000000 data points:

```
sample_size_list = [50, 100, 1000, 10000, 1000000]
disparate_impact_list = []
for sample_size_iter in sample_size_list:
    disparate_impact_list.append(
        disparate_impact_randomsample(
            sample_size = sample_size_iter,
            sampling_num = 1000))
```

The following boxplots show the distributions of *DIR* across different sample sizes. You can see that lower sample sizes have wider distributions covering very low or high *DIR* values, distant from the ideal case of 1:

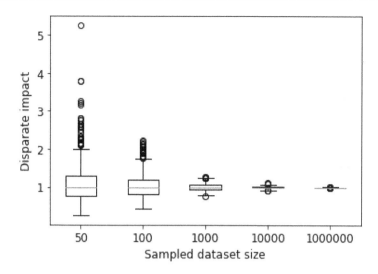

Figure 7.1 – Distributions of DIR across different sampling sizes

We can also calculate the percentage of sampled groups of different sizes that don't pass a specific threshold, such as >=0.8 and <=1.2. *Figure 7.2* shows that higher dataset sizes result in a lower chance of having datasets that have positive or negative bias given a sensitive attribute:

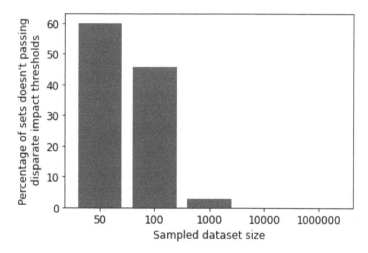

Figure 7.2 – Percentage of sets of samples that don't pass DIR thresholds

The source of existing bias in datasets might not just be an artifact of a small sample size. For example, if you were to train a model to predict if an individual will end up in STEM, which is an acronym for fields of science, technology, engineering, and math, then you must consider the reality of the existence of it being imbalanced toward men over women in the corresponding data in fields, such as engineering, even up until recently (*Figure 7.3*):

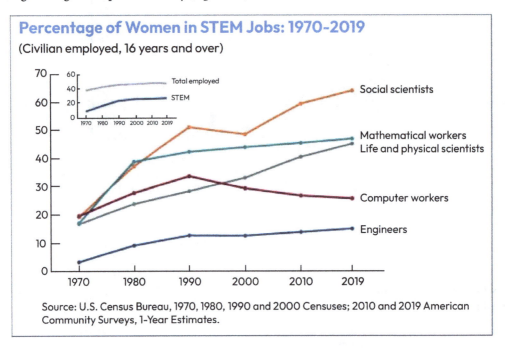

Figure 7.3 – Percentage of women in STEM jobs between 1970 and 2019

Having less than 20% of engineers being women over the years, because of their lower interest, bias in hiring processes, or stereotypes in society, has resulted in bias in the data on workers in this field. If this is not rectified with fairness in your data processing and modeling tasks, it could result in predicting a higher chance for men getting into STEM compared to women, despite their talents, knowledge, and experience.

There is another category of intrinsic bias in the data, although it needs to be considered when developing machine learning models. For example, less than 1% of breast cancer cases occur in men (www.breastcancer.org). This prevalence difference between men and women is not caused by any sort of bias in data generation or collection or biases that have existed in societies. It is the natural difference between the prevalence of breast cancer occurrence between men and women. But if you were responsible for developing a machine learning model to diagnose breast cancer, there could be a high chance of false negatives (that is, not diagnosing breast cancer) in men. If your model doesn't consider the high prevalence of women over men, it will not be a fair model in breast cancer diagnosis for men. This was a high-level example to clarify this kind of bias. There are many other considerations in building a machine learning tool for cancer diagnosis.

## Bias in model training and testing

If a dataset has a high imbalance toward men or women, different ethnicities, or any sort of bias considering different sensitive attributes, our models could have biases due to the way the corresponding machine learning algorithms use the features in predicting the outcome of data points. For example, our models could be highly reliant on sensitive attributes or their proxies (*Table 7.2*). This is an important consideration in model selection. In the model selection process, we need to select a model among the trained models, with different methods or hyperparameters of the same method, to be pushed for further testing or production. If we base our decision-making solely on performance, then we might select a model that is not fair. We need to consider both fairness and performance in our model selection process if we have sensitive attributes and those models will directly or indirectly affect individuals of different groups.

## Bias in production

Bias and unfairness in production could happen because of differences in the distribution of data between training, testing, and production. For example, women and men could have some differences in the production stage that don't exist in your training and test data. This situation could result in biases in production that might not have been detectable in previous stages of the life cycle. We will talk about such kinds of differences in more detail in *Chapter 11, Avoiding and Detecting Data and Concept Drifts*.

The next step in this chapter is to start practicing with techniques and Python libraries that help you in detecting and eliminating model biases. First, will practice using the explainability techniques that were introduced in *Chapter 6, Interpretability and Explainability in Machine Learning Modeling*.

# Using explainability techniques

We can use explainability techniques to identify potential biases in our models and then plan to improve them toward fairness. Here, we want to practice this concept with SHAP and identify fairness issues between male and female groups in the adult income dataset we practiced with in the previous chapter. Using the same SHAP explainer object we built for the XGBoost model we trained on adult income data in the previous chapter, in the following bar plots, we can see that there is a low, but non-negligible, dependency on *sex* regarding the whole dataset or only the incorrectly predicted data points:

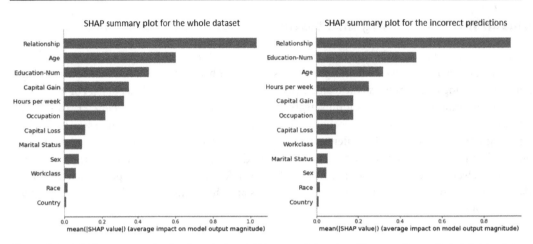

Figure 7.4 – SHAP summary plot for the whole adult income dataset and incorrectly predicted data points

Now, we can extract the fraction of misclassified data points in each sex group, as follows:

```
X_WithPred.groupby(['Sex', 'Correct Prediction']).size().unstack(fill_
value=0)
```

This will produce the following result:

| Correct Prediction | False | True |
| --- | --- | --- |
| **Sex** | | |
| 0 | 689 | 10082 |
| 1 | 3644 | 18146 |

Figure 7.5 – Number of males and females among correct and incorrect predictions

Here, we have 6.83% and 20.08% misclassification percentages for female and male groups, respectively. The ROC-AUC of the predictions of the model for only male and female groups in the test set are 0.90 and 0.94, respectively.

You might consider identifying the correlation between features as an approach to identifying proxies and potential ways of removing biases in your models. The following code and heatmap (*Figure 7.6*) show a correlation between the features of this dataset:

```
corr_features = X.corr()
corr_features.style.background_gradient(cmap='coolwarm')
```

The output will be as follows:

| | Age | Workclass | Education-Num | Marital Status | Occupation | Relationship | Race | Sex | Capital Gain | Capital Loss | Hours per week | Country |
|---|---|---|---|---|---|---|---|---|---|---|---|---|
| Age | 1.000000 | 0.003787 | 0.036527 | -0.266288 | -0.020947 | 0.092767 | 0.028718 | 0.088832 | 0.077674 | 0.057775 | 0.068756 | -0.001151 |
| Workclass | 0.003787 | 1.000000 | 0.052085 | -0.064731 | 0.254892 | 0.038873 | 0.049742 | 0.095981 | 0.033835 | 0.012216 | 0.138962 | -0.007690 |
| Education-Num | 0.036527 | 0.052085 | 1.000000 | -0.069304 | 0.109697 | 0.019554 | 0.031838 | 0.012280 | 0.122630 | 0.079923 | 0.148123 | 0.050840 |
| Marital Status | -0.266288 | -0.064731 | -0.069304 | 1.000000 | -0.009654 | -0.223729 | -0.068013 | -0.129314 | -0.043393 | -0.034187 | -0.190519 | -0.023819 |
| Occupation | -0.020947 | 0.254892 | 0.109697 | -0.009654 | 1.000000 | 0.020417 | 0.006763 | 0.080296 | 0.025505 | 0.017987 | 0.080383 | -0.012543 |
| Relationship | 0.092767 | 0.038873 | 0.019554 | -0.223729 | 0.020417 | 1.000000 | 0.063248 | 0.326166 | 0.058407 | 0.053343 | 0.065066 | 0.004677 |
| Race | 0.028718 | 0.049742 | 0.031838 | -0.068013 | 0.006763 | 0.063248 | 1.000000 | 0.087204 | 0.011145 | 0.018899 | 0.041910 | 0.137852 |
| Sex | 0.088832 | 0.095981 | 0.012280 | -0.129314 | 0.080296 | 0.326166 | 0.087204 | 1.000000 | 0.048480 | 0.045567 | 0.229309 | -0.008119 |
| Capital Gain | 0.077674 | 0.033835 | 0.122630 | -0.043393 | 0.025505 | 0.058407 | 0.011145 | 0.048480 | 1.000000 | -0.031615 | 0.078409 | -0.001982 |
| Capital Loss | 0.057775 | 0.012216 | 0.079923 | -0.034187 | 0.017987 | 0.053343 | 0.018899 | 0.045567 | -0.031615 | 1.000000 | 0.054256 | 0.000419 |
| Hours per week | 0.068756 | 0.138962 | 0.148123 | -0.190519 | 0.080383 | 0.065066 | 0.041910 | 0.229309 | 0.078409 | 0.054256 | 1.000000 | -0.002671 |
| Country | -0.001151 | -0.007690 | 0.050840 | -0.023819 | -0.012543 | 0.004677 | 0.137852 | -0.008119 | -0.001982 | 0.000419 | -0.002671 | 1.000000 |

Figure 7.6 – Correlation DataFrame between the features of the adult income dataset

However, there are disadvantages to using such correlation analysis as the way of approaching the problem of proxy identification or even for filtering features toward improving performance. Here are two of these disadvantages:

- You need to consider proper correlation measures for each pair of features. For example, *Pearson* correlation cannot be used for all feature pairs as the distribution of data for each pair has to satisfy the assumptions for this method. Both variables need to follow normal distributions and data should not have any outliers as two of the assumptions for proper use of *Pearson* correlation. This means that to have a proper use of the feature correlation analysis approach, you need to use proper correlation measures to compare the features. Non-parametric statistical measures such as *Spearman* rank correlation could be more suitable as there are fewer assumptions behind its use across different variable pairs.

- Not all numerical values have the same meaning. Some of the features are categorical and, through different methods, are transformed into numerical features. Sex is one of those features. Values of 0 and 1 can be used to show female and male groups but they don't have any numerical meaning that you can find in numerical features such as age or salary.

Explainability techniques such as SHAP tell you about dependencies to sensitive attributes and their contributions to the outcome of data points. However, by default, they don't offer a way to improve the models in terms of fairness. In this example, we can try to split the data into male and female groups for training and testing. The following code shows this approach for the female group. Similarly, you can repeat this for the male group by separating the train and test input and output data with the Sex feature of 1. The models that were built separately for male and female groups resulted in 0.90 and

0.93 ROC-AUCs, respectively, which is almost the same as the performance without the separation of the groups:

```
X_train = X_train.reset_index(drop=True)
X_test = X_test.reset_index(drop=True)

# training a model only for female category (Sex category of 0 in this
dataset)
X_train_only0 = X_train[X_train['Sex'] == 0]
X_test_only0 = X_test[X_test['Sex'] == 0]
X_only0 = X[X['Sex'] == 0]
y_train_only0 = [y_train[iter] for iter in X_train.index[
    X_train['Sex'] == 0].tolist()]
y_test_only0 = [y_test[iter] for iter in X_test.index[
    X_test['Sex'] == 0].tolist()]
# initializing an XGboost model
xgb_model = xgboost.XGBClassifier(random_state=42)
# fitting the XGboost model with training data
xgb_model.fit(X_train_only0, y_train_only0)
# calculating roc-auc of predictions
print("ROC-AUC of predictions:
    {}".format(roc_auc_score(y_test_only0,
        xgb_model.predict_proba(X_test_only0)[:, 1])))
# generate the Tree explainer
explainer_xgb = shap.TreeExplainer(xgb_model)
# extract SHAP values from the explainer object
shap_values_xgb = explainer_xgb.shap_values(X_only0)
# create a SHAP beeswarm plot (i.e. SHAP summary plot)
shap.summary_plot(shap_values_xgb, X_only0,
    plot_type="bar")
```

We didn't remove the Sex feature from the models. This feature cannot contribute to the model's performance as there is no difference between the values of this feature across the data points of each model. This is also shown by zero Shapely values in the bar plots:

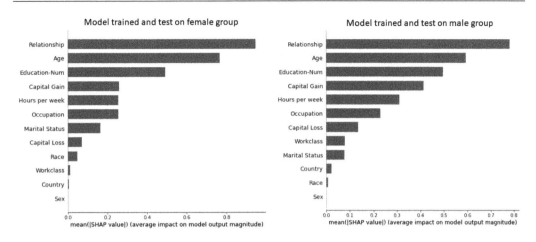

Figure 7.7 – SHAP summary plot for models trained and tested on female and male groups separately

This approach of separating groups according to a sensitive attribute, although sometimes seen as taken, is not an ideal way of dealing with the issue of fairness. It might not be an effective approach as the model could be highly reliant on other sensitive features. Also, we cannot split the data into small chunks according to all combinations of all sensitive attributes in our dataset. There are fairness tools that could help you not only assess fairness and detect biases but select a model that better satisfies fairness notions.

In addition to libraries for explainability, there are Python libraries that are designed specifically for fairness detection and improvement in machine learning modeling, which we will cover next.

## Fairness assessment and improvement in Python

There are few widely used Python libraries to assess fairness in your models (*Table 7.3*). You can use these libraries to identify if the model satisfies fairness definitions according to the different sensitive attributes in a dataset you want to or have used for modeling:

| Library | Library Name for Importing and Installation | URL |
|---|---|---|
| IBM AI Fairness 360 | `aif360` | `https://pypi.org/project/aif360/` |
| Fairlearn | `fairlearn` | `https://pypi.org/project/fairlearn/` |
| Black Box Auditing | `BlackBoxAuditing` | `https://pypi.org/project/BlackBoxAuditing/` |
| Aequitas | `aequitas` | `https://pypi.org/project/aequitas/` |
| Responsible AI Toolbox | `responsibleai` | `https://pypi.org/project/responsibleai/` |
| Responsibly | `responsibly` | `https://pypi.org/project/responsibly/` |
| Amazon Sagemaker Clarify | `smclarify` | `https://pypi.org/project/smclarify/` |
| Fairness-aware machine learning | `fairness` | `https://pypi.org/project/fairness/` |
| Bias correction | `biascorrection` | `https://pypi.org/project/biascorrection/` |

Table 7.3 – Python libraries or repositories with available functionalities for machine learning fairness

First, let's load the adult income dataset, after importing the required libraries, and prepare the training and test sets, as follows:

```
# loading UCI adult income dataset
# classification task to predict if people made over $50k in the 90s
or not
X,y = shap.datasets.adult()
# split the data to train and test sets
X_train, X_test, y_train, y_test = train_test_split(
    X, y, test_size = 0.3, random_state=10)
# making a dataframe out of y values with "Sex" being their indices
y_train = pd.DataFrame({'label': y_train},
    index = X_train['Sex'])
y_test = pd.DataFrame({'label': y_test},
    index = X_test['Sex'])
```

Now, we can train and test an XGBoost model:

```
xgb_model = xgboost.XGBClassifier(random_state=42)
# fitting the XGboost model with training data
xgb_model.fit(X_train, y_train)
# calculating roc-auc of predictions
print("ROC-AUC of predictions:
    {}".format(roc_auc_score(y_test,
        xgb_model.predict_proba(X_test)[:, 1])))
# generating predictions for the test set
y_pred_train = xgb_model.predict(X_train)
y_pred_test = xgb_model.predict(X_test)
```

Here, we want to use `aif360` to calculate the *DIR* of real and predicted outcomes in the training and test data according to the `Sex` attribute:

```
# calculating disparate impact ratio
di_train_orig = disparate_impact_ratio(y_train,
    prot_attr='Sex', priv_group=1, pos_label=True)
di_test_orig = disparate_impact_ratio(y_test,
    prot_attr='Sex', priv_group=1, pos_label=True)
di_train = disparate_impact_ratio(y_train, y_pred_train,
    prot_attr='Sex', priv_group=1, pos_label=True)
di_test = disparate_impact_ratio(y_test, y_pred_test,
    prot_attr='Sex', priv_group=1, pos_label=True)
```

The following group bar plot shows that the predictions make the *DIR* even worse in both the training and test sets:

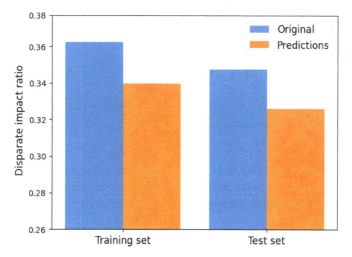

Figure 7.8 – Comparison of DIR in the original data and predicted outputs

We can use **reject option classification** as an available class in `aif360` to improve our models toward fairness. Reject option classification is a postprocessing technique that gives favorable outcomes to unprivileged groups and unfavorable outcomes to privileged groups in a confidence band around the decision boundary with the highest uncertainty (`https://aif360.readthedocs.io/`, Kamira et al., 2012). First, let's import all the necessary libraries and functionalities we need for doing so in Python:

```
# importing Reject option classification, a post processing technique
that gives favorable outcomes to unprivileged groups and unfavourable
outcomes to
# privileged groups in a confidence band around the decision boundary
# with the highest uncertainty
from aif360.sklearn.postprocessing import RejectOptionClassifierCV
# importing PostProcessingMeta, a meta-estimator which wraps a given
# estimator with a post-processing step.

# fetching adult dataset from aif360 library
X, y, sample_weight = fetch_adult()
X.index = pd.MultiIndex.from_arrays(X.index.codes,
    names=X.index.names)
y.index = pd.MultiIndex.from_arrays(y.index.codes,
    names=y.index.names)
y = pd.Series(y.factorize(sort=True)[0], index=y.index)
X = pd.get_dummies(X)
```

Then, we can use `RejectOptionClassifierCV()` to train and validate a random forest classifier on the adult dataset available in `aif360`. We switched from XGBoost to random forest solely for the sake of practicing with different models. We need to fit a `PostProcessingMeta()` object with an initial random forest model and `RejectOptionClassifierCV()`. `'sex'` is considered the sensitive feature in the process:

```
metric = 'disparate_impact'
ppm = PostProcessingMeta(RF(n_estimators = 10,
    random_state = 42),
    RejectOptionClassifierCV('sex', scoring=metric,
        step=0.02, n_jobs=-1))
ppm.fit(X, y)
```

We can then plot the balanced accuracy and *DIR* across different attempts in the grid search to show the best-chosen parameters, which is the starred point in the scatter plot in *Figure 7.9*. The points in cyan show you the Pareto front for the tradeoff between balanced accuracy and *DIR*:

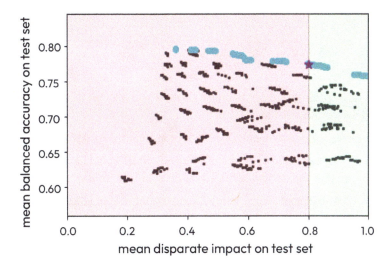

Figure 7.9 – Balanced accuracy versus DIR in a grid search

As you can see, there is a compromise between performance and fairness in this case. But in this case, a less than 4% decrease in performance results in improving *DIR* from lower than 0.4 to 0.8.

As you saw in this example, we can use `aif360` to assess fairness and improve our model's fairness with little loss in performance. You can use other libraries in Python similarly. And each one has its functionality for the two objectives of fairness assessment and improvement in machine learning modeling.

What we provided in this chapter was only the tip of the iceberg of fairness in machine learning. But at this point, you are ready to try different libraries and techniques and learn about them with the help of the practices we went through.

## Summary

In this chapter, you learned more about the concept of fairness in the machine learning era, as well as the metrics, definitions, and challenges for assessing fairness. We talked about example proxies for sensitive attributes such as *sex* and *race*. We also talked about possible sources of bias, such as in data collection or model training. You also learned how you can use Python libraries for model explainability and fairness to assess fairness or improve it in your models, as well as avoid biases that not only would be unethical but could have legal and financial consequences for your organization.

In the next chapter, you will learn about test-driven development and concepts such as unit and differential testing. We will also talk about machine learning experiment tracking and how it helps us avoid issues in our models in the model training, testing, and selection processes.

## Questions

1. Does fairness depend only on observable features?

2. What are examples of proxy features for `'sex'`?

3. If one model is fair according to demographic parity, would it be fair according to other notions of fairness such as equalized odds?

4. What is the difference between demographic parity and equalized odds as two fairness metrics?

5. If you have a `'sex'` feature in your model and your model would have a low dependency on that, does it mean that your model is fair across different sex groups?

6. How could you use explainability techniques to assess fairness in your models?

## References

- Barocas, Solon, Moritz Hardt, and Arvind Narayanan. *Fairness in machine learning*. Nips tutorial 1 (2017): 2017.

- Mehrabi, Ninareh, et al. *A survey on bias and fairness in machine learning*. ACM Computing Surveys (CSUR) 54.6 (2021): 1-35.

- Caton, Simon, and Christian Haas. *Fairness in machine learning: A survey*. arXiv preprint arXiv:2010.04053 (2020).

- Pessach, Dana, and Erez Shmueli. *A review on fairness in machine learning*. ACM Computing Surveys (CSUR) 55.3 (2022): 1-44.

- Lechner, Tosca, et al. *Impossibility results for fair representations*. arXiv preprint arXiv:2107.03483 (2021).

- McCalman, Lachlan, et al. *Assessing AI fairness in finance*. Computer 55.1 (2022): 94-97.

- F. Kamiran, A. Karim, and X. Zhang, *Decision Theory for Discrimination-Aware Classification*. IEEE International Conference on Data Mining, 2012.

# Part 3:
# Low-Bug Machine Learning Development and Deployment

With this part of the book, we will provide the essential practices to ensure the robustness and reliability of machine learning models, especially in production. We will start with the adoption of Test-Driven Development, illustrating its crucial role in mitigating risks during model development. Subsequently, we will delve into the testing techniques and the significance of model monitoring, ensuring that our models remain dependable when deployed. We will then explain techniques and challenges in achieving reproducibility in machine learning through code, data, and model versioning. We will conclude this part by addressing the challenges of data and concept drifts to have reliable models in production.

This part has the following chapters:

- *Chapter 8, Controlling Risks Using Test-Driven Development*
- *Chapter 9, Testing and Debugging for Production*
- *Chapter 10, Versioning and Reproducible Machine Learning Modeling*
- *Chapter 11, Avoiding and Detecting Data and Concept Drifts*

# 8

# Controlling Risks Using Test-Driven Development

There are risks, such as selecting unreliable models, associated with creating models and technologies built on top of our models. The question is, could we avoid them and better manage the risks associated with machine learning modeling? In this chapter, we will talk about programming strategies such as unit testing, which could help us not only in developing and selecting better models but also in reducing risks associated with modeling.

In this chapter, we will cover the following topics:

- Test-driven development
- Machine learning differential testing
- Tracking machine learning experiments

By the end of this chapter, you will have learned how to reduce the risk of unreliable modeling and software development using unit and differential testing and how to reliably build upon previous attempts in model training and evaluation using machine learning experiment tracking.

## Technical requirements

The following requirements should be considered for this chapter as they will help you better understand the concepts, use them in your projects, and practice with the provided code:

- Python library requirements:
  - pytest >= 7.2.2
  - ipytest >= 0.13.0
  - mlflow >= 2.1.1
  - aif360 >= 0.5.0

- shap >= 0.41.0

- sklearn >= 1.2.2

- numpy >= 1.22.4

- pandas >= 1.4.4

- You will also require basic knowledge of model bias and the definition of bias measures such as the **disparate impact ratio (DIR)**

You can find the code files for this chapter on GitHub at `https://github.com/PacktPublishing/Debugging-Machine-Learning-Models-with-Python/tree/main/Chapter08`.

# Test-driven development for machine learning modeling

One approach to reducing the risks of developing unreliable models and pushing them to production is test-driven development. We aim to design unit tests (that is, tests designed to test individual components of software) that reduce the risks of code revision either within the same or in different life cycles. To better understand this concept, we need to understand what unit tests are and how we can design and use them in Python.

## Unit testing

Unit tests are designed to test the smallest components, or units, in the code and software we design. In machine learning modeling, we might have many modules taking care of different steps of a machine learning life cycle, such as data curation and wrangling or model evaluation. Unit tests help us avoid errors and mistakes, and design our code without the need to worry about whether we made a mistake that will not be detected early on. Detecting issues in our code early has lower costs and helps us to avoid error pile-ups, which makes the debugging process easier. Pytest is a Python testing framework that helps us in designing different tests, including unit tests, in machine learning programming.

### Using Pytest

Pytest is a simple-to-use Python library that we can use to design unit tests by performing the following steps:

1. Identify the component we want to design the unit test for.

2. Define a small operation to be used for testing that component. For example, if the module is part of data processing, the test can be designed using a very small toy dataset, either real or synthetic.

3. Design a function starting with `"test_"` for the corresponding component.

4. Repeat *Steps 1* to *3* for all the components of the code for which we want to design unit tests. It is better to cover as many components as possible.

The designed tests can then be used to test changes in your code. We will practice unit test design here, using Pytest, for a function that calculates the DIR and returns "unbiased data" or "biased data" using the input thresholds for DIR for bias detection:

```python
import pandas as pd
from aif360.sklearn.metrics import disparate_impact_ratio

def dir_grouping(data_df: pd.DataFrame,
    sensitive_attr: str, priviledge_group,
    dir_threshold = {'high': 1.2, 'low': 0.8}):
        """

        Categorizing data as fair or unfair according to DIR

        :param data_df: Dataframe of dataset
        :param sensitive_attr: Sensitive attribute under investigation
        :priviledge_group: The category in the sensitive attribute
    that needs to be considered as priviledged
        :param dir_threshold:
        """
    dir = disparate_impact_ratio(data_df,
        prot_attr=sensitive_attr,
        priv_group=priviledge_group, pos_label=True)
    if dir < dir_threshold['high'] and dir > dir_threshold[
        'low']:
        assessment = "unbiased data"
    else:
        assessment = "biased data"

    return assessment
```

Now that we've defined an example usage of this function to use for our unit test design, we can select the first 100 rows of the dataset and calculate the DIR:

```python
# calculating DIR for a subset of adult income data in shap library
import shap
X,y = shap.datasets.adult()
X = X.set_index('Sex')
X_subset = X.iloc[0:100,]
```

According to the calculated DIR, this subset of the data is biased concerning the 'Sex' attribute. To design the unit tests, we need to import the pytest library. But if you are using Jupyter or Colab notebooks for prototyping, you can use ipytest to test your code:

```python
import pytest
# you can use ipytest if you are using Jupyter or Colab notebook
```

```
import ipytest
ipytest.autoconfig()
```

We must add `%%ipytest -qq` if we're using `pytest` in a Jupyter or Colab notebook and want to run the tests using `ipytest`. Then, we can define our unit test function, `test_dir_grouping()`, as follows:

```
%%ipytest -qq

def test_dir_grouping():
    bias_assessment = dir_grouping(data_df = X_subset,
        sensitive_attr = 'Sex',priviledge_group = 1,
        dir_threshold = {'high':1.2, 'low': 0.8})

    assert bias_assessment == "biased data"
```

The `assert` command checks whether the result of the `dir_grouping()` function is "biased data," as it is supposed to be according to our previous analysis, for the first 100 rows of the dataset. If the result is different, then the test fails.

When you have all the unit tests ready for the components of your software, you can run `pytest` in the **command-line interface (CLI)** for a specific module, directory, or all of your tests (source: `https://docs.pytest.org/en/7.1.x/how-to/usage.html`). For example, if you wrote `test_dir_grouping`, as shown in the preceding code, within a Python script called `test_script.py`, you can only test that script as follows:

```
pytest test_script.py
```

Alternatively, you can run `pytest` in a specific directory. If you have a code base that contains many different modules, you can organize your tests according to the grouping of your main functions and classes and then test each directory, as follows:

```
# "testdir" could be a directory containing test scripts
pytest testdir/
```

Instead, if you simply run `pytest`, it will execute all the tests in all the files named `test_*.py` or `\*_test.py` in the current directory and its subdirectories:

```
pytest
```

You can also use a Python interpreter to execute the tests using `pytest`:

```
python -m pytest
```

If you are using Jupyter or Colab Notebook and used `ipytest`, you can run Pytest as follows:

```
ipytest.run()
```

Now, imagine we execute the designed `test_dir_grouping()` function in one of these ways. When the test is passed, we will see a message like the following, which tells us 100% of the tests passed. This is because we are only testing one test and the test passed (*Figure 8.1*):

```
.                                                         [100%]
1 passed in 0.02s
<ExitCode.OK: 0>
```

Figure 8.1 – The output of Pytest when the designed test passed

If we mistakenly change `assessment = "biased data"` to `assessment = "unbiased data"` in the `dir_grouping()` function, we get the following result instead, which tells us 100% of the tests failed. This is because we only have one test, which failed in this case (*Figure 8.2*):

```
F                                                                          [100%]
=========================================== FAILURES ===========================================
_____ test_dir_grouping _____

    def test_dir_grouping():

        bias_assessment = dir_grouping(data_df = X_subset,
                                       sensitive_attr = 'Sex',
                                       priviledge_group = 1,
                                       dir_threshold = {'high': 1.2, 'low': 0.8})
>       assert bias_assessment == "biased data"
E       AssertionError: assert 'unbiased data' == 'biased data'
E         - biased data
E         + unbiased data
E         ? ++

<ipython-input-6-5ca48f4fae8d>:8: AssertionError
================================= short test summary info =====================================
FAILED t_9e92c882a9524464809ba00d9adb50e5.py::test_dir_grouping - AssertionError: assert 'unbiased data' == 'biased data'
1 failed in 0.04s
<ExitCode.TESTS_FAILED: 1>
```

Figure 8.2 – Failure message after running Pytest

The failure message in `pytest` contains some complementary information that we can use to debug our code. In this case, it is telling us that in `test_dir_grouping()`, it tried to assert the output of `test_dir_grouping()`, which was "unbiased data," with "biased data."

## Pytest fixtures

When programming for data analysis and machine learning modeling, we need to use data that is in different variables or data objects, comes from a file in our local machine or the cloud, is queried from a database, or comes from a URL in our tests. Fixtures help us in these processes by removing the need to repeat the same code across our tests. Attaching a fixture function to a test will run it and return data to the test before each test runs. Here, we have used examples provided on the Pytest documentation page for fixtures (source: `https://docs.pytest.org/en/7.1.x/how-to/fixtures.html`). First, let's define two very simple classes called `Fruit` and `FruitSalad`:

```
# Example of using Pytest fixtures available in
https://docs.pytest.org/en/7.1.x/how-to/fixtures.html
class Fruit:
```

```
    def __init__(self, name):
        self.name = name
        self.cubed = False

    def cube(self):
        self.cubed = True

class FruitSalad:
    def __init__(self, *fruit_bowl):
        self.fruit = fruit_bowl
        self._cube_fruit()

    def _cube_fruit(self):
        for fruit in self.fruit:
            fruit.cube()
```

When we use `pytest`, it looks at the parameters in the test function signature and looks for fixtures with the same names as those parameters. Pytest then runs those fixtures, captures what they return, and passes those objects as arguments to the test function. We inform Pytest that a function is a fixture by decorating it with `@pytest.fixture`. In the following example, when we run the tests, `test_fruit_salad` requests `fruit_bowl`, and Pytest executes `fruit_bowl` and passes the returned object into `test_fruit_salad`:

```
# Arrange
@pytest.fixture
def fruit_bowl():
    return [Fruit("apple"), Fruit("banana")]

def test_fruit_salad(fruit_bowl):
    # Act
    fruit_salad = FruitSalad(*fruit_bowl)

    # Assert
    assert all(fruit.cubed for fruit in fruit_salad.fruit)
```

Here are some of the features of fixtures that can help us in designing our tests:

- Fixtures can request other fixtures. This helps us in designing smaller fixtures that can be even used as part of other fixtures to make more complex tests.

- Fixtures can be reused in different tests. They work like functions to be used in different tests with their own returned results.

- A test or fixture can request more than one fixture at a time.

- Fixtures can be requested more than once per test.

In test-driven development, we aim to write production-ready code that passes the designed unit tests. Higher coverage of the modules and components in your code by the designed unit test could help you in revising your code that's related to any component of a machine learning life cycle with peace of mind.

In this section, you learned about unit testing, but other techniques can help us in reliable programming and machine learning model development, such as differential testing. We will introduce this next.

## Machine learning differential testing

Differential testing attempts to check two versions of a piece of software, considered as base and test versions, on the same input and then compare the outputs. This process helps us identify whether the outputs are the same and identify unexpected differences (Gulzar et al., 2019; *Figure 8.3*):

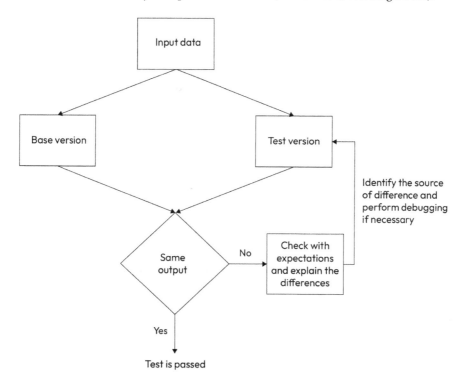

Figure 8.3 – Simplified flowchart of differential testing as a process to test the outputs of two implementations of the same process on the same data

In differential testing, the base version is already verified and considered the approved version, while the test version needs to be checked in comparison with the base version in producing the correct output. In differential testing, we can also aim to assess whether the observed differences between the outputs of the base and test versions are expected or can be explained.

In machine learning modeling, we can also benefit from differential testing when comparing two different implementations of the same algorithms on the same data. For example, we can use it to compare models built using `scikit-learn` and Spark MLlib as two different libraries for machine learning modeling. If we need to recreate a model using `scikit-learn` and add it to our pipeline while the original model is built in Spark MLlib, we can use differential testing to assess the outputs and make sure either there is no difference or the differences are expected (Herbold and Tunkel, 2023). *Table 8.1* provides some examples of algorithms with available classes in both `scikit-learn` and Spark MLlib. This approach has been used more extensively to compare models between different deep learning frameworks, such as TensorFlow and PyTorch:

| Method | scikit-learn | Spark MLlib |
| --- | --- | --- |
| Logistic regression | `LogisticRegression` | `LogisticRegression` |
| Naive Bayes | `GaussianNB, MultinomialNB` | `NaiveBayes` |
| Decision tree | `DecisionTree Classifier` | `DecisionTreeClassifier` |
| Random forest | `RandomForest Classifier` | `RandomForestClassifier` |
| Support vector machine | `LinearSVC` | `LinearSVC` |
| Multilayer perceptron | `MLPClassifier` | `MultilayerPerceptron Classifier` |
| Gradient boosting | `GradientBoosting Classifier` | `GBTClassifier` |

Table 8.1 – Some of the overlapping algorithms and their class names in scikit-learn and Spark MLlib

Experiment tracking is another technique that we can benefit from besides unit and differential testing in our machine learning projects.

## Tracking machine learning experiments

Keeping track of our machine learning experiments will help us reduce the risks of invalid conclusions and selecting unreliable models. Experiment tracking in machine learning is about saving the information about the experiments – for instance, the data that has been used – the testing performance and the metric used for performance assessment, and the algorithms and the hyperparameters used for modeling. Here are some of the important considerations for using a machine learning experiment tracking tool:

- Can you integrate the tool with your **continuous integration/continuous development** (**CI/CD**) pipeline and machine learning modeling frameworks?

- Can you reproduce your experiments?

- Can you easily search through the experiments to find the best models or models with bad or unexpected behaviors?

- Does it cause any security or privacy issues?

- Does the tool help you better collaborate in your machine learning projects?

- Does the tool let you track hardware (for example, memory) consumption?

Some of the commonly used machine learning experiment tracking tools and their URLs are provided in *Table 8.2*:

| Tool | URL |
|---|---|
| MLflow Tracking | `https://mlflow.org/docs/latest/tracking.html` |
| DVC | `https://dvc.org/doc/use-cases/experiment-tracking` |
| Weights & Biases | `https://wandb.ai/site/experiment-tracking` |
| Comet ML | `https://www.comet.com/site/products/ml-experiment-tracking/` |
| ClearML | `https://clear.ml/clearml-experiment/` |
| Polyaxon | `https://polyaxon.com/product/#tracking` |
| TensorBoard | `https://www.tensorflow.org/tensorboard` |
| Neptune AI | `https://neptune.ai/product/experiment-tracking` |
| SageMaker | `https://aws.amazon.com/sagemaker/experiments/` |

Table 8.2 – Examples of tools for teaching machine learning experiments

Here, we want to practice **MLflow Tracking** in Python. First, we need to import the required libraries:

```
import pandas as pd
import numpy as np
from sklearn.metrics import mean_squared_error, roc_auc_score
from sklearn.model_selection import train_test_split
from sklearn.ensemble import RandomForestClassifier as RF
from sklearn.datasets import load_breast_cancer
import mlflow
import mlflow.sklearn
np.random.seed(42)
```

Then, we must define a function for evaluating the results of the models we would like to test:

```
def eval_metrics(actual, pred, pred_proba):
    rmse = np.sqrt(mean_squared_error(actual, pred))
    roc_auc = roc_auc_score(actual, pred_proba)
    return rmse, roc_auc
```

Next, we must load the breast cancer dataset from `scikit-learn` for modeling:

```
X, y = load_breast_cancer(return_X_y=True)
# split the data into training and test sets. (0.7, 0.3) split
X_train, X_test, y_train, y_test = train_test_split(X, y,
    test_size = 0.3, random_state=42)
```

Now, we are ready to define an experiment using `mlflow`:

```
experiment_name = "mlflow-randomforest-cancer"
existing_exp = mlflow.get_experiment_by_name(
    experiment_name)
if not existing_exp:
    experiment_id = mlflow.create_experiment(
        experiment_name, artifact_location="...")
else:
    experiment_id = dict(existing_exp)['experiment_id']
mlflow.set_experiment(experiment_name)
```

Now, we must go over three different numbers of decision trees, or three different numbers of estimators, to build, train, and test three different random forest models on the loaded breast cancer dataset. All the information from these three runs will be stored within the specified experiment but as different runs. As you can see in the following code, we use different functionalities in `mlflow`:

- `mlflow.start_run`: To start a run as part of an experiment

- `mlflow.log_param`: To log the number of estimators as a hyperparameter of the model

- `mlflow.log_metric`: To log the calculated metric for the performance of the model on the defined test set

- `mlflow.sklearn.log_model`: To log the model:

```
for idx, n_estimators in enumerate([5, 10, 20]):
    rf = RF(n_estimators = n_estimators, random_state = 42)
    rf.fit(X_train, y_train)

    pred_probs = rf.predict_proba(X_test)
    pred_labels = rf.predict(X_test)
```

```
# calculating rmse and roc-auc for the randorm forest
# model predictions on the test set
rmse, roc_auc = eval_metrics(actual = y_test,
    pred = pred_labels,pred_proba = [
        iter[1]for iter in pred_probs])
# start mlflow
RUN_NAME = f"run_{idx}"
with mlflow.start_run(experiment_id=experiment_id,
    run_name=RUN_NAME) as run:
        # retrieve run id
        RUN_ID = run.info.run_id
    # track parameters
    mlflow.log_param("n_estimators", n_estimators)
    # track metrics
    mlflow.log_metric("rmse", rmse)
    # track metrics
    mlflow.log_metric("roc_auc", roc_auc)
    # track model
    mlflow.sklearn.log_model(rf, "model")
```

We can also retrieve an already stored experiment, as follows:

```
from mlflow.tracking import MlflowClient
esperiment_name = "mlflow-randomforest-cancer"
client = MlflowClient()
# retrieve experiment information
experiment_id = client.get_experiment_by_name(
    esperiment_name).experiment_id
```

Then, we can get information on different runs in that experiment:

```
# retrieve runs information (parameter: 'n_estimators',
    metric: 'roc_auc')
experiment_info = mlflow.search_runs([experiment_id])
# extracting run ids for the specified experiment
runs_id = experiment_info.run_id.values
# extracting parameters of different runs
runs_param = [client.get_run(run_id).data.params[
    "n_estimators"] for run_id in runs_id]
# extracting roc-auc across different runs
runs_metric = [client.get_run(run_id).data.metrics[
    "roc_auc"] for run_id in runs_id]
```

We can also identify the best runs according to a metric used for model testing, which is ROC-AUC in this example:

```
df = mlflow.search_runs([experiment_id],
    order_by=["metrics.roc_auc"])
best_run_id = df.loc[0,'run_id']
best_model_path = client.download_artifacts(best_run_id,
    "model")
best_model = mlflow.sklearn.load_model(best_model_path)
print("Best model: {}".format(best_model))
```

This results in the following output:

```
Best mode: RandomForestClassifier(n_estimators=5,
    random_state=42)
```

We can also delete runs of a run or an experiment altogether if needed, as follows. But you need to make sure you wish to delete such information:

```
# delete runs (make sure you are certain about deleting the runs)
for run_id in runs_id:
    client.delete_run(run_id)
# delete experiment (make sure you are certain about deleting the
experiment)
client.delete_experiment(experiment_id)
```

In this section, you learned about experiment tracking in a machine learning setting. You will learn more about the techniques you can use for risk control in your machine learning projects in the next two chapters.

## Summary

In this chapter, you learned about test-driven development using unit testing to control risks in your machine learning development projects. You learned about unit testing in Python using the pytest library. We also briefly reviewed the concept of differential testing, which helps you in comparing different versions of your machine learning modules and software. Later, you learned about model experiment tracking as an important tool that not only facilitates your model experimentations and selection but also helps you in risk control in your machine learning projects. You practiced using mlflow in Python as one of the widely used machine learning experiment tracking tools. Now, you know how to develop reliable models and programming modules through test-driven development and experiment tracking.

In the next chapter, you will learn about strategies to test models, assess their qualities, and monitor their performance in production. You will learn about practical methods for model monitoring, integration testing, and model pipeline and infrastructure testing.

# Questions

1.  How does `pytest` help you in developing code modules in your machine learning projects?

2.  How do `pytest` fixtures help you in using `pytest`?

3.  What is differential testing and when do you need it?

4.  What is `mlflow` and how does it help you in your machine learning modeling projects?

# References

- Herbold, Steffen, and Steffen Tunkel. *Differential testing for machine learning: an analysis for classification algorithms beyond deep learning.* Empirical Software Engineering 28.2 (2023): 34.

- Lichman, M. (2013). *UCI Machine Learning Repository* [`https://archive.ics.uci.edu/ml`]. Irvine, CA: University of California, School of Information and Computer Science.

- Gulzar, Muhammad Ali, Yongkang Zhu, and Xiaofeng Han. *Perception and practices of differential testing.* 2019 IEEE/ACM 41st International Conference on Software Engineering: Software Engineering in Practice (ICSE-SEIP). IEEE, 2019.

# 9
# Testing and Debugging for Production

You might have gotten excited about training and testing a machine learning model without thinking about the unexpected behavior of your model in production and how your model fits into a bigger technology. Most academic courses don't go through details of strategies to test models, assess their qualities, and monitor their performance pre-deployment and in production. There are important concepts and techniques in testing and debugging models for production that we will review in this chapter.

In this chapter, we will cover the following topics:

- Infrastructure testing
- Integration testing of machine learning pipelines
- Monitoring and validating live performance
- Model assertion

By the end of this chapter, you will have learned about the importance of infrastructure and integration testing, as well as model monitoring and assertion. You will have also learned how to use Python libraries so that you can benefit from them in your projects.

# Technical requirements

The following requirements should be considered for this chapter as they will help you better understand the concepts, use them in your projects, and practice with the provided code:

- Python library requirements:

  - `sklearn` >= 1.2.2

  - `numpy` >= 1.22.4

  - `pytest` >= 7.2.2

- You must also have basic knowledge of the machine learning life cycle

You can find the code files for this chapter on GitHub at `https://github.com/PacktPublishing/Debugging-Machine-Learning-Models-with-Python/tree/main/Chapter09`.

# Infrastructure testing

Infrastructure testing refers to the process of verifying and validating the various components and systems involved in deploying, managing, and scaling machine learning models. This includes testing software, hardware, and other resources that make up the infrastructure that supports machine learning workflows. Infrastructure testing in machine learning helps you ensure that models are trained, deployed, and maintained effectively. It provides you with reliable models in a production environment. Regular infrastructure testing can help you detect and fix issues early and reduce the risk of failures during deployment and in the production stage.

Here are some of the important aspects of infrastructure testing in machine learning:

- **Data pipeline testing**: This ensures that the data pipelines responsible for data collection, selection, and wrangling are working correctly and efficiently. This helps maintain data quality and consistency for training, testing, and deploying your machine learning models.

- **Model training and evaluation**: This validates the functionality of the model training process, such as hyperparameter tuning and model evaluation. This process eliminates unexpected issues in training and evaluation to achieve a reliable and responsible model.

- **Model deployment and serving**: This tests the process of deploying the trained model in a production environment, ensuring that the serving infrastructure, such as API endpoints, is working correctly and can handle the expected request load.

- **Monitoring and observability**: This tests the monitoring and logging systems that provide insights into the performance and behavior of the machine learning infrastructure.

- **Integration testing**: This verifies that all components of the machine learning infrastructure, such as data pipelines, model training systems, and deployment platforms, are working together seamlessly and without conflicts.

- **Scalability testing**: This evaluates the ability of the infrastructure to scale up or down in response to changing requirements, such as increased data volume, higher user traffic, or more complex models.

- **Security and compliance testing**: This ensures that the machine learning infrastructure meets necessary security requirements, data protection regulations, and privacy standards.

Now that you understand the importance and benefits of infrastructure testing, you are ready to learn about the related tools that can help you in model deployment and infrastructure management.

## Infrastructure as Code tools

**Infrastructure as Code** (**IaC**) and configuration management tools such as **Chef**, **Puppet**, and **Ansible** can be used to automate the deployment, configuration, and management of software and hardware infrastructures. These tools could help us ensure consistency and reliability across different environments. Let's understand how Chef, Puppet, and Ansible work, and how they can help you in your projects:

- **Chef** (`https://www.chef.io/products/chef-infrastructure-management`): Chef is an open source configuration management tool that relies on a client-server model, where the Chef server stores the desired configuration, and the Chef client applies it to the nodes.

- **Puppet** (`https://www.puppet.com/`): Puppet is another open source configuration management tool that works in a client-server model or as a standalone application. Puppet enforces desired configurations across nodes by periodically pulling them from the Puppet master server.

- **Ansible** (`https://www.ansible.com/`): Ansible is an open source and easy-to-use configuration management, orchestration, and automation tool that communicates and applies configurations to nodes.

These tools primarily focus on infrastructure management and automation, but they also have modules or plugins to perform basic testing and validation of the infrastructure.

## Infrastructure testing tools

Test Kitchen, ServerSpec, and InSpec are infrastructure testing tools we can use to verify and validate the desired configuration and behavior of our infrastructures:

- **Test Kitchen** (`https://github.com/test-kitchen/test-kitchen`): Test Kitchen is an integration testing framework mainly used with Chef but can also work with other IaC tools such as Ansible and Puppet. It allows you to test your infrastructure code on different platforms and configurations. Test Kitchen creates temporary instances on various platforms (using drivers such as Docker or cloud providers), converges your infrastructure code, and runs tests against the configured instances. You can use Test Kitchen with different testing frameworks, such as ServerSpec or InSpec, to define your tests.

- **ServerSpec** (`https://serverspec.org/`): ServerSpec is a **behavior-driven development (BDD)** testing framework for infrastructure. It allows you to write tests in a human-readable language. ServerSpec tests the desired state of your infrastructure by executing commands on the target system and checking the output against the expected results. You can use ServerSpec with Test Kitchen or other IaC tools to ensure that your infrastructure is configured correctly.

- **InSpec** (`https://github.com/inspec/inspec`): InSpec, developed by Chef, is an open source infrastructure testing framework. It defines tests and compliance rules in a human-readable language. You can run InSpec tests independently or in conjunction with tools such as Test Kitchen, Chef, or other IaC platforms.

These tools ensure that our IaC and configuration management setups work as expected before deployment to achieve consistency and reliability across different environments.

## Infrastructure testing using Pytest

We can also use Pytest, which we used for unit testing in the previous chapter for infrastructure testing. Let's assume we write test functions that should start with the `test_` prefix in a Python file called `test_infrastructure.py`. We can use Python libraries such as `paramiko`, `requests`, or `socket` to interact with our infrastructure (for example, making API calls, connecting to servers, and so on). For example, we can test whether a web server is responding with status code 200:

```
import requests
def test_web_server_response():
    url = "http://your-web-server-url.com"
    response = requests.get(url)
    assert response.status_code == 200,
        f"Expected status code 200,
        but got {response.status_code}"
```

Then, we can run the tests that we explained in the previous chapter.

Other techniques besides infrastructure testing can help you in preparing your models for a successful deployment, such as integration testing, which we will cover next.

# Integration testing of machine learning pipelines

When we train a machine learning model, we need to evaluate how well it interacts with the other components of a larger system it belongs to. Integration testing helps us in validating that the model works correctly within the overall application or infrastructure and meets the desired performance criteria. Some of the important components of integration testing to rely on in our machine learning projects are as follows:

- **Testing data pipelines**: We need to evaluate that the data preprocessing components before model training, such as data wrangling, are consistent between the training and deployment stages.

- **Testing APIs**: If our machine learning model is exposed through an API, we can test the API endpoints to ensure it handles requests and responses correctly.

- **Testing model deployment**: We can use integration testing to assess the model's deployment process, whether it's deployed as a standalone service, within a container, or embedded in an application. This process helps us ensure that the deployment environment provides the necessary resources, such as CPU, memory, and storage, and that the model can be updated if needed.

- **Testing interactions with other components**: We need to verify that our machine learning model works seamlessly with databases, user interfaces, or third-party services. This may include testing how the model's predictions are stored, displayed, or used within the application.

- **Testing end-to-end functionality**: We can use end-to-end tests that simulate real-world scenarios and user interactions to validate that the model's predictions are accurate, reliable, and useful in the context of the overall application.

We can benefit from integration testing to ensure a smooth deployment and reliable operation in real-world applications. There are several tools and libraries we can use to create robust integration tests for our machine learning models in Python. *Table 9.1* shows some of the popular tools for integration testing:

| Tool | Brief Description | URL |
|---|---|---|
| Pytest | A framework widely used for unit and integration testing in Python | `https://docs.pytest.org/en/7.2.x/` |
| Postman | An API testing tool that's used for testing the interaction between machine learning models and RESTful APIs | `https://www.postman.com/` |
| Requests | A Python library that tests APIs and services by sending HTTP requests | `https://requests.readthedocs.io/en/latest/` |
| Locust | A load testing tool that allows you to simulate user behavior and test the performance and scalability of your machine learning models under various load conditions | `https://locust.io/` |
| Selenium | A browser automation tool you can use to test the end-to-end functionality of web applications that utilize machine learning models | `https://www.selenium.dev/` |

Table 9.1 – Popular tools for integration testing

## Integration testing using pytest

Here, we want to practice integration testing using pytest for a simple Python application with two components: a database and a service, both of which retrieve data from the database. Let's assume we have the database.py and service.py script files:

### database.py:

```
class Database:
    def __init__(self):
        self.data = {"users": [{"id": 1,
            "name": "John Doe"},
            {"id": 2, "name": "Jane Doe"}]}

    def get_user(self, user_id):
        for user in self.data["users"]:
            if user["id"] == user_id:
                return user
            return None
```

### service.py:

```
from database import Database

class UserService:
    def __init__(self, db):
        self.db = db

    def get_user_name(self, user_id):
        user = self.db.get_user(user_id)
        if user:
            return user["name"]
        return None
```

Now, we will write an integration test using pytest to ensure that the UserService component works correctly with the Database component. First, we need to write our tests in a test script file, called test_integration.py, as follows:

```
import pytest
from database import Database
from service import UserService

@pytest.fixture
def db():
```

```
    return Database()

@pytest.fixture
def user_service(db):
    return UserService(db)

def test_get_user_name(user_service):
    assert user_service.get_user_name(1) == "John Doe"
    assert user_service.get_user_name(2) == "Jane Doe"
    assert user_service.get_user_name(3) is None
```

The defined `test_get_user_name` function tests the interaction between the `UserService` and `Database` components by checking whether the `get_user_name` method returns the correct usernames for different user IDs.

To run the test, we can execute the following command in the Terminal:

```
pytest test_integration.py
```

### Integration testing using pytest and requests

We can combine the `requests` and `pytest` Python libraries to perform integration testing on our machine learning APIs. We can use the `requests` library to send HTTP requests and the `pytest` library to write test cases. Let's suppose we have a machine learning API with the following endpoint:

```
POST http://mldebugging.com/api/v1/predict
```

Here, the API accepts a JSON payload with input data:

```
{
    "rooms": 3,
    "square_footage": 1500,
    "location": "suburban"
}
```

This returns a JSON response with the predicted price:

```
{
    "predicted_price": 700000
}
```

Now, we need to create a test script file called `test_integration.py`:

```
import requests
import pytest
API_URL = "http://mldebugging.com/api/v1/predict"
```

```
def test_predict_house_price():
    payload = {
        "rooms": 3,
        "square_footage": 1500,
        "location": "suburban"
    }

    response = requests.post(API_URL, json=payload)
    assert response.status_code == 200
    assert response.headers["Content-Type"] == "application/json"

    json_data = response.json()
    assert "predicted_price" in json_data
    assert isinstance(json_data["predicted_price"],
        (int, float))
```

To run the test, we can execute the following command in the Terminal:

```
pytest test_integration.py
```

In this example, we defined a test function called `test_predict_house_price` that sends a POST request (that is, an HTTP method used to submit data to a server to create or update a resource) to the API with the input data as a JSON payload. The test function then checks the API response's status code, content type, and predicted price value. If you want to try this with a real API you have, replace the example URL with the actual API endpoint.

In addition to the testing strategies we covered in this chapter, you can benefit from model monitoring and assertion to have successful deployments and reliable models in production environments.

## Monitoring and validating live performance

We can use monitoring and logging mechanisms during deployment to track the model's performance and detect potential issues. We can regularly evaluate the deployed model to ensure it continues to meet performance criteria, or other criteria, such as being unbiased, that we defined for it. We can also benefit from the information coming from model monitoring to update or retrain the model as needed. Here are three important concepts in this subject regarding differences between modeling before deployment and in production:

- **Data variance:** The data that is used in model training and testing goes through the steps of data wrangling and all the cleaning and reformatting needed. However, the data that is given to the deployed model – that is, the data coming from the user to the model – might not go through the same data processes, which then causes variations in the model results in production.

- **Data drift**: Data drift happens if the characteristics and meaning of features or independent variables in production differ from those in the modeling stage. Imagine you used a third-party tool to generate a score for the health or financial situation of people. The algorithm behind that tool could change over time, and its range and meaning will not be the same when your model gets used in production. If you have not updated your model accordingly, then your model will not work as expected as the meaning of the value of the features will not be the same between the data used for training and the user data after deployment.

- **Concept drift**: Concept drift is about any change in the definition of output variables. For example, real decision boundaries between training data and production could be different because of concept drift, meaning the effort made in training might result in a decision boundary far from reality in production.

In addition to MLflow, which was introduced in the previous chapter, there are Python and libraries tools (as listed in *Table 9.2*) that you can use to monitor the performance, I/O data, and infrastructure of machine learning models, helping you maintain model quality and reliability in production environments:

| Tool | Brief Description | URL |
|------|-------------------|-----|
| Alibi Detect | An open source Python library that focuses on outlier, adversarial, and drift detection | `https://github.com/SeldonIO/alibi-detect` |
| Evidently | An open source Python library for analyzing and monitoring machine learning models that offers various model evaluation techniques, such as data drift detection and model performance monitoring | `https://github.com/evidentlyai/evidently` |
| ELK Stack | **Elasticsearch**, **Logstash**, and **Kibana** (**ELK**) is a popular stack for collecting, processing, and visualizing logs and metrics from various sources, including machine learning models | `https://www.elastic.co/elk-stack` |
| WhyLabs | A platform that provides observability and monitoring for machine learning models | `https://whylabs.ai/` |

Table 9.2 – Popular tools for machine learning model monitoring and drift detection

We can also benefit from some statistical and visualization techniques for detecting and addressing data and concept drifts. Here are some examples of such methods for data drift evaluation:

- **Statistical tests**: We can use hypothesis tests, such as the *Kolmogorov-Smirnov test*, *Chi-squared test*, or *Mann-Whitney U test*, to determine whether the distribution of input data has changed significantly over time.

- **Distribution metrics**: We can use distribution metrics, such as mean, standard deviation, quantiles, and other summary statistics, to compare training data and the new data in production. Significant differences in these metrics may indicate data drift.

- **Visualization**: We can use visualization techniques such as histograms, boxplots, or scatter plots for the input features of the training data and the new data in production to help identify changes in the data distributions.

- **Feature importance**: We can monitor changes in feature importance values. If feature importance in the new data differs significantly from those in the training data, it may indicate data drift.

- **Distance metrics**: We can measure the difference between the training data and the new data distributions using distance metrics such as *Kullback-Leibler divergence* or *Jensen-Shannon divergence*.

Model assertion is another technique, as you will learn next, that helps you in building and deploying reliable machine learning models.

## Model assertion

We can use traditional programming assertion in machine learning modeling to ensure that the model is behaving as expected. Model assertions can help us detect issues early on, such as input data drift or other unexpected behaviors that might affect the model's performance. We can consider model assertions as a set of rules that get checked during the model's training, validation, or even during deployment to ensure that the model's predictions meet the predefined conditions. Model assertions can help us in many ways, such as detecting issues with the model or input data, allowing us to address them before they impact the model's performance. They can also help us maintain the model's performance. Here are two examples of model assertions:

- **Input data assertions**: These can check that the input features fall within an expected range or have the correct data type. For example, if a model predicts house prices based on the number of rooms, you might assert that the number of rooms is always a positive integer.

- **Output data assertions**: These can check that the model's predictions meet certain conditions or constraints. For example, in a binary classification problem, you might assert that the predicted probability is between 0 and 1.

Let's go through a simple example of model assertion in Python. In this example, we will use a simple linear regression model from `scikit-learn` to predict house prices based on the number of rooms, using a toy dataset. First, let's create a toy dataset and train the linear regression model:

```
import numpy as np
from sklearn.linear_model import LinearRegression

# Toy dataset with number of rooms and corresponding house prices
```

```
X = np.array([1, 2, 3, 4, 5]).reshape(-1, 1)
y = np.array([100000, 150000, 200000, 250000, 300000])

# Train the linear regression model
model = LinearRegression()
model.fit(X, y)
```

Now, let's define our model assertions so that they do the following:

1. Check that the input (number of rooms) is a positive integer.

2. Check that the predicted house price is within the expected range.

Here's the code that does these things:

```
def assert_input(input_data):
    assert isinstance(input_data, int),
        "Input data must be an integer"
    assert input_data > 0, "Number of rooms must be positive"

def assert_output(predicted_price, min_price, max_price):
    assert min_price <= predicted_price <= max_price,
        f"Predicted price should be between {min_price} and
        {max_price}"
```

Now, we can use the defined model assertion functions, as follows:

```
# Test the assertions with example input and output data
input_data = 3
assert_input(input_data)
predicted_price = model.predict([[input_data]])[0]
assert_output(predicted_price, 50000, 350000)
```

The `assert_input` function checks whether the input data (that is, the number of rooms) is an integer and is positive. The `assert_output` function checks whether the predicted house price is within a specified range (for example, between 50,000 and 350,000 in this example). The previous code doesn't give any `AssertionError` assertion as it meets the criteria defined in the model assertion functions. Let's say that, instead of 3, which is an integer, we use a string, as follows:

```
input_data = '3'
assert_input(input_data)
```

Here, we get the following `AssertionError`:

```
AssertionError: Input data must be an integer
```

Let's say we define the output range for `assert_output` so that it's between `50000` and `150000` and use the model predictions for a house with 3 bedrooms, as follows:

```
input_data = 3
predicted_price = model.predict([[input_data]])[0]
assert_output(predicted_price, 50000, 150000)
```

We will get the following `AssertionError`:

```
AssertionError: Predicted price should be between 50000 and 150000
```

Model assertion is another technique, side by side with model monitoring, that helps ensure the reliability of our models.

With this, we have come to the end of this chapter.

## Summary

In this chapter, you learned about important concepts for test-driven development, including infrastructure and integration testing. You learned about the available tools and libraries to implement these two types of testing. We also went through examples in which you learned how to use the `pytest` library for both infrastructure and integration testing. You also learned about model monitoring and model assertion as two other important topics for assessing the behavior of our models before and in production. These techniques and tools help you in designing strategies so that you have a successful deployment and reliable models in production environments.

In the next chapter, you will learn about reproducibility, an important concept in proper machine learning modeling, and how you can use data and model versioning to achieve reproducibility.

## Questions

1. Can you explain the difference between data and concept drifts?
2. How can model assertions help you in developing reliable machine learning models?
3. What are some examples of components of integration testing?
4. How can we use Chef, Puppet, and Ansible?

## References

- Kang, Daniel, et al. *Model assertions for monitoring and improving ML models*. Proceedings of Machine Learning and Systems 2 (2020): 481-496.

# 10

# Versioning and Reproducible Machine Learning Modeling

Reproducibility is an important topic to help machine learning developers go back to different stages of the machine learning life cycle and identify opportunities for model improvement. Having access to different versions of the data and models generated through the machine learning life cycles could help us in improving the reproducibility of our projects.

In this chapter, you will learn about the meaning and importance of reproducibility in machine learning modeling. You will learn about tools for incorporating data versioning in machine learning pipelines to help you attain more effective collaboration in your projects and achieve reproducibility in your models. You will also learn about different aspects of model versioning and tools for incorporating it into your pipelines.

We will cover the following topics:

- Reproducibility in machine learning
- Data versioning
- Model versioning

By the end of this chapter, you'll have learned how to use data and model versioning for your modeling projects in Python to achieve reproducibility.

# Technical requirements

The following are the requirements for this chapter and will help you better understand the concepts, use them in your projects, and practice with the provided code:

- Python library requirements:

  - `pandas` >= 1.4.4

  - `sklearn` >= 1.2.2

- DVC >= 1.10.0

- You should also have basic knowledge of the machine learning life cycle

You can find the code files for this chapter on GitHub at `https://github.com/PacktPublishing/Debugging-Machine-Learning-Models-with-Python/tree/main/Chapter10`.

# Reproducibility in machine learning

Lack of *reproducibility* in your machine learning projects could be a waste of resources and decrease the credibility of your models and findings in your research projects. *Reproducibility* is not the only term used in this context; there are also two other key terms: *repeatability* and *replicability*. We don't want to get into the details of these differences. Instead, we want to have a definition of reproducibility to use in this book. We define reproducibility in machine learning as the ability of different individuals or teams of scientists and developers to achieve the same results using the same dataset, methodology, and development environment as reported in an original report or study. We can ensure reproducibility through the proper sharing of code, data, model parameters and hyperparameters, and other relevant information, which allows others to validate and build upon our findings. Let's better understand the importance of reproducibility by going through two examples.

Scientists from a biotechnology company tried to reproduce the findings of 53 cancer studies (Begley et al., 2012). But they were only able to reproduce the results of 6 out of the 53 studies. These were not necessarily in the context of reproducibility in machine learning, but it highlights the importance of reproducibility in scientific research and the potential consequences of basing decisions or further research and development on irreproducible findings.

Another example of highlighting the importance of reproducibility in the context of data analysis and data-driven discovery is what is known as the *Reinhart-Rogoff Excel Error* (Reinhart, C., and Rogoff, K., 2010). In 2010, the economists Carmen Reinhart and Kenneth Rogoff published a paper suggesting a negative correlation between high public debt and economic growth. This paper influenced economic policies worldwide. However, in 2013, other researchers discovered an error in their Excel calculations, which significantly impacted the results. But later, it was argued that the error was not the driver behind the conclusions (Maziarz, 2017). Here, we don't want to focus on their findings but want to emphasize that the reproducibility of the analysis could eliminate any further argument regardless of whether or not there was an error or not in the original analysis.

The following three concepts can help you achieve reproducibility in your machine learning modeling projects:

- **Code versioning**: Having access to the version of the code used in any given stage of a machine learning life cycle is fundamentally important to repeat an analysis or training and evaluation processes

- **Data versioning**: To achieve reproducibility, we need to have access to the version of the data that's used in any given stage of the machine learning life cycle, such as training and testing

- **Model versioning**: Having a version of your model with frozen parameters and no randomness in initializing, evaluating, or other processes in modeling, helps you eliminate risks of irreproducibility

We briefly talked about code versioning in *Chapter 1*, *Beyond Code Debugging*. Here, we will focus on data and model versioning to help you in designing reproducible machine learning models.

## Data versioning

We have different stages in the machine learning life cycle, from data collection and selection to data wrangling and transformation, in which the data gets prepared step by step for model training and evaluation. Data versioning helps us maintain data integrity and reproducibility throughout these processes. Data versioning is the process of tracking and managing changes in datasets. It involves keeping a record of different versions or iterations of the data, allowing us to access and compare previous states or recover earlier versions when needed. We can reduce the risk of data loss or inconsistencies by ensuring that changes are properly documented and versioned.

There are data versioning tools that can help us in managing and tracking changes in the data we want to use for machine learning modeling or processes to assess the reliability and fairness of our models. Here are some popular data-versioning tools:

- **MLflow**: We introduced MLflow for experiment tracking and model monitoring in previous chapters, but you can also use it for data versioning (`https://mlflow.org/`)

- **Data Version Control** (**DVC**): This is an open source version control system for managing data, code, and ML models. It is designed to handle large datasets and integrates with Git (`https://dvc.org/`)

- **Pachyderm**: This is a data-versioning platform that provides reproducibility, provenance, and scalability in machine learning workflows (`https://www.pachyderm.com/`)

- **Delta Lake**: This is an open source storage layer for Apache Spark and big data workloads that provides data versioning (`https://delta.io/`)

- **Git Large File Storage** (**Git-LFS**): This is an extension of Git that allows the versioning of large files, such as data files or models, alongside code (`https://git-lfs.github.com/`)

Each of these tools provides you with different data-versioning capabilities. You can choose the one that meets your needs considering the size of the data, the nature of the project, and the desired level of integration with other tools.

Here is an example of using DVC with Python for data versioning. After installing DVC, you can initialize it by writing the following command in the Terminal:

```
dvc init
```

This will create a .dvc directory and set up the necessary configuration. Now, let's create a small DataFrame and save it as a CSV file in Python:

```
import pandas as pd

# create a sample dataset
data_df = pd.DataFrame({'feature 1': [0.5, 1.2, 0.4, 0.8],
    'feature 2': [1.1, 1.3, 0.6, 0.1]})

# save the dataset to a CSV file
data_df.to_csv('dataset.csv', index=False)
```

Now, we can add the dataset.csv file to DVC and commit the changes, similar to committing code changes using Git:

```
dvc add dataset.csv
git add dataset.csv.dvc .gitignore
git commit -m "add initial dataset"
```

This creates a data.csv.dvc file that tracks the dataset's version, and it adds data.csv to .gitignore so that Git doesn't track the actual data file. Now, we can modify the dataset as follows and save it with the same name:

```
# Add a new column to the dataset
data_df['feature 3'] = [0.05, 0.6, 0.4, 0.9]

# Save the modified dataset to the same CSV file
data_df.to_csv('dataset.csv', index=False)
```

We can also commit the changes and save it as a different version:

```
dvc add dataset.csv
git add dataset.csv.dvc
git commit -m "update dataset with new feature column"
```

Now that we have two versions of the dataset.csv file, we can switch to the previous version or the latest version of the datasets when needed by using the following commands in the Terminal:

```
# go back to the previous version of the dataset
git checkout HEAD^
dvc checkout

# return to the latest version of the dataset
git checkout master
dvc checkout
```

But if you have many versions of the same file or data, you can use other simple commands available as part of DVC.

In addition to versioning our data, we need to track and manage different versions of our models throughout the development life cycle. We will cover this next.

# Model versioning

A model that goes to production is the eventual result of a series of experimentation and model modifications with different versions of training and test data, and different machine learning methods and their corresponding hyperparameters. Model versioning helps us ensure that changes that are made to models are traceable, helping to establish reproducibility in our machine learning projects. It ensures that every version of a model can be easily reproduced by providing a complete snapshot of the model's parameters, hyperparameters, and training data at a given point in time. It allows us to easily roll back to a previous version in case of issues with a newly deployed model or to recover an older version that may have been unintentionally modified or deleted.

Let's go through a very simple example to better understand the need for model versioning. *Figure 10.1* shows the performance of a random forest model with five estimators, or decision trees, and the different maximum depths allowed for these decision trees. If we simply change the random states that are used to split the data into train and test sets, using train_test_split() from scikit-learn, and perform model initialization for a RandomForestClassifier() model, we get different log-loss values and dependencies on the maximum depth of the trees in the random forest model:

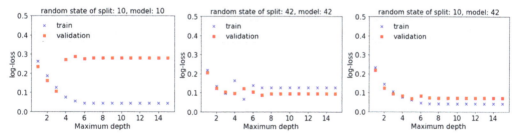

Figure 10.1 – Log-loss in training and validation sets separated from the breast cancer dataset using different random states for modeling and data split

This was a small example to show how such simple changes, which can happen if our models are not versioned, can have drastic effects on our machine learning modeling. When we use experiment tracking tools such as MLflow, we have access to all the tracked information for a selected model.

To version our model, we need to make sure of the following:

- We have access to a saved version of the parameters of the corresponding model

- Other necessary information such as model hyperparameters are documented or saved for model retraining

- The code that needs to be used with the model parameters for inference or even retraining and testing is versioned

- Processes with randomization, such as model initialization and data split for training and testing, have specified random states, or seeds

There are different ways of storing your models and their related documentation. For example, you can store your model using serialization libraries such as `pickle` alone or in combination with DVC (`https://dvc.org/doc/api-reference/open`), as follows:

```
with dvc.api.open(model_path, mode='w', remote=remote_url) as f:
    pickle.dump(model, f)
```

For this, you need to specify a local path on which to save the model using `pickle.dump` and a remote path for model versioning using DVC.

## Summary

In this chapter, you learned about the meaning and importance of reproducibility in machine learning modeling. You also learned about data and model versioning, which help us to develop more reliable and reproducible models and data analysis results. Next, you learned about the different tools and Python libraries you can use to version your data and models. With the concepts and practices introduced in this chapter, you are ready to ensure reproducibility in your machine learning projects.

In the next chapter, you will learn about techniques you can use to avoid and eliminate data drift and concept drift, which constitute two differences between the behavior of models before and after deployment.

## Questions

1. What are three examples of tools that you can use for data versioning?

2. When you generate different versions of the same data, such as by using DVC, do you need to save it with different names?

3. Can you provide an example where you would use the same method and training and evaluation data but get different training and evaluation performance?

# References

- Reinhart, C., & Rogoff, K. (2010b). *Debt and growth revisited*. VOX. CEPRs Policy Portal. Retrieved September 18, 2015.

- Reinhart, C., & Rogoff, K. (2010a). *Growth in a time of debt*. American Economic Review, 100, 573–578.10.1257/aer.100.2.573.

- Maziarz, Mariusz. *The Reinhart-Rogoff controversy as an instance of the 'emerging contrary result' phenomenon*. Journal of Economic Methodology 24.3 (2017): 213-225.

- Begley, C. G., & Ellis, L. M. (2012). *Drug development: Raise standards for preclinical cancer research*. Nature, 483(7391), 531-533.

- Association for Computing Machinery (2016). *Artifact Review and Badging*. Available online at `https://www.acm.org/publications/policies/artifact-review-badging` (Accessed November 24, 2017).

- Plesser, Hans E. *Reproducibility vs. replicability: a brief history of a confused terminology*. Frontiers in neuroinformatics 11 (2018): 76.

- Pineau, J., Vincent, M., Larochelle, H., & Bengio, Y. (2020). *Improving reproducibility in machine learning research (A report from the NeurIPS 2019 reproducibility program)*. arXiv preprint arXiv:2003.12206.

- Raff, E., Lemire, D., & Nicholas, C. (2019). *A new measure of algorithmic stability for machine learning*. Journal of Machine Learning Research, 20(168), 1-32.

- Gundersen, O. E., & Kjensmo, S. (2018). *State of the art: Reproducibility in artificial intelligence*. In Thirty-Second AAAI Conference on Artificial Intelligence.

- Jo, T., & Bengio, Y. (2017). *Measuring the tendency of CNNs to Learn Surface Statistical Regularities*. arXiv preprint arXiv:1711.11561.

- Haibe-Kains, B., Adam, G. A., Hosny, A., Khodakarami, F., & Waldron, L. (2020). *Transparency and reproducibility in artificial intelligence*. Nature, 586(7829), E14-E16.

# 11

# Avoiding and Detecting Data and Concept Drifts

We talked about the effect of data and concept drifts in machine learning modeling in *Chapter 9, Testing and Debugging for Production*. In this chapter, we want to go deeper into these concepts and practice detecting drifts in Python.

Here, you will learn about the importance of concepts we introduced earlier, such as model versioning and model monitoring, to avoid drifts and practice with some of the Python libraries for drift detection.

In this chapter, we will cover the following topics:

- Avoiding drifts in your models
- Detecting drifts

By the end of this chapter, you will be able to detect drifts in your machine learning models in Python and have reliable models in production.

## Technical requirements

The following requirements apply to this chapter as they help you better understand the concepts, allow you to use them in your projects, and to practice with the provided code:

- Python library requirements are as follows:

    - `sklearn >= 1.2.2`
    - `numpy >= 1.22.4`
    - `pandas >= 1.4.4`

- `alibi_detect` >= 0.11.1

- `lightgbm` >= 3.3.5

- `evidently` >= 0.2.8

- Understanding of the following is required:

  - Data and concept drift

  - Data and model versioning

You can find the code files for this chapter on GitHub at `https://github.com/PacktPublishing/ Debugging-Machine-Learning-Models-with-Python/tree/main/Chapter11`.

# Avoiding drifts in your models

Data and concept drifts challenge the reliability of machine learning models in production. Drifts in our machine learning projects can have different characteristics. Some of these characteristics that could help you to detect drifts in your projects and plan to resolve them are as follows:

- **Magnitude**: We might face magnitudes of difference across the data distribution that result in drift in our machine learning models. Small changes in the data distribution may be difficult to detect, while large changes may be more noticeable.

- **Frequency**: Drifts might occur in different frequencies.

- **Gradual versus sudden**: Data drift can occur gradually where changes in the data distribution happen slowly over time, or it can occur suddenly where changes happen quickly and unexpectedly.

- **Predictability**: Some types of drift may be predictable, such as changes that occur seasonally or due to external events. Other types of drift may be unpredictable, such as sudden changes in consumer behavior or market trends.

- **Intentionality**: Drift can be intentional, such as changes made to the data generation process, or unintentional, such as changes that occur naturally over time.

We need to use techniques and practices that help us avoid the occurrence and pile-up of drifts in our machine learning modeling projects.

## Avoiding data drift

Having access to different versions of the data in different stages of the machine learning life cycle of our models can help us to better detect drift by comparing the data in training and production, assessing data processing pre-training, or identifying data selection criteria that could have caused drift. Model monitoring also helps us to identify drifts early on and avoid pile-up.

Let's practice drift monitoring by simply checking the mean of the distribution of features between versions of data used for model training, and the new data in production. We will first define a class to monitor for data drift. Here, we consider drift in a feature if the difference between the mean of the distributions between the two versions of the data is bigger than 0.1:

```python
class DataDriftMonitor:
    def __init__(self, baseline_data: np.array,
        threshold_mean: float = 0.1):
            self.baseline = self.calculate_statistics(
                baseline_data)
            self.threshold_mean = threshold_mean

    def calculate_statistics(self, data: np.array):
        return np.mean(data, axis=0)

    def assess_drift(self, current_data: np.array):
        current_stats = self.calculate_statistics(
            current_data)

        drift_detected = False
        for feature in range(0, len(current_stats)):
            baseline_stat = self.baseline[feature]
            current_stat = current_stats[feature]
            if np.abs(current_stat - baseline_stat) > self.threshold_
mean:
                drift_detected = True
                print('Feature id with drift:
                    {}'.format(feature))
                print('Mean of original distribution:
                    {}'.format(baseline_stat))
                print('Mean of new distribution:
                    {}'.format(current_stat))
                break

        return drift_detected
```

Then, we use it to identify drift between two synthetic datasets:

```python
np.random.seed(23)
# Generating a synthetic dataset, as the original data, with 100
datapoints and 5 features
# from a normal distribution centered around 0 with std of 1
baseline_data = np.random.normal(loc=0, scale=1,
    size=(100, 5))
# Create a DataDriftMonitor instance
```

```
monitor = DataDriftMonitor(baseline_data,
    threshold_mean=0.1)

# Generating a synthetic dataset, as the original data, with 100
datapoints and 5 features from a normal distribution #centered around
0.2 with std of 1
current_data = np.random.normal(loc=0.15, scale=1,
    size=(100, 5))

# Assess data drift
drift_detected = monitor.assess_drift(current_data)
if drift_detected:
    print("Data drift detected.")
else:
    print("No data drift detected.")
```

This generates the following:

```
Feature id with drift: 1
Mean of original distribution: -0.09990597519469419
Mean of new distribution: 0.09662442557421645
Data drift detected.
```

## Addressing concept drift

We can similarly define classes and functions with criteria to detect concept drift, as we practiced for data drift detection. But we can also check, either programmatically or as part of quality assurance when bringing our machine learning models into production, for external factors that might cause concept drift such as environmental factors, changes in institutional or governmental policies, et cetera. In addition to monitoring the data, we can benefit from feature engineering to select features that are more robust to concept drift or ensemble models to be adapted dynamically in case of concept drift.

Although avoiding drift in our models is ideal, we need to be ready to detect and eliminate it in practice. Next, you will learn techniques to detect drift in your model. From a practical perspective, avoiding and detecting drifts in your model are very similar. But there are better techniques than simply checking the mean of feature distributions (as we used for avoiding data drift in this section) that we will practice in the next section.

## Detecting drifts

Avoiding drifts altogether in all our models is not possible, but we can aim to detect them early on and eliminate them. Here, we are going to practice drift detection with `alibi_detect` and `evidently` in Python.

## Practicing with alibi_detect for drift detection

One of the widely-used Python libraries for drift detection that we want to practice with is alibi_
detect. We will first import the necessary Python functions and classes and generate a synthetic
dataset with 10 features and 10,000 samples using make_classification from scikit-learn:

```
import numpy as np
import pandas as pd
import lightgbm as lgb
from alibi_detect.cd import KSDrift
from sklearn.datasets import make_classification
from sklearn.model_selection import train_test_split
from sklearn.metrics import balanced_accuracy_score as bacc

# Generate synthetic data
X, y = make_classification(n_samples=10000, n_features=10,
    n_classes=2, random_state=42)
```

Then, we split the data into train and test sets:

```
# Split into train and test sets
X_train, X_test, y_train, y_test = train_test_split(X, y,
    test_size=0.2, random_state=42)
```

Then, we train a LightGBM classifier on the training data:

```
train_data = lgb.Dataset(X_train, label=y_train)
params = {
    "objective": "binary",
    "metric": "binary_logloss",
    "boosting_type": "gbdt"
}
clf = lgb.train(train_set = train_data, params = params,
    num_boost_round=100)
```

We now evaluate the performance of the model on the test set and define a test label DataFrame to
use for drift detection:

```
# Predict on the test set
y_pred = clf.predict(X_test)
y_pred = [1 if iter > 0.5 else 0 for iter in y_pred]

# Calculate the balanced accuracy of the predictions
balanced_accuracy = bacc(y_test, y_pred)
print('Balanced accuracy on the synthetic test set:
```

```
    {}'.format(balanced_accuracy))

# Create a DataFrame from the test data and predictions
df = pd.DataFrame(X_test,
    columns=[f"feature_{i}" for i in range(10)])
df["actual"] = y_test
df["predicted"] = y_pred
```

Now, we use the defined DataFrame of predictions and actual labels of the test data points to detect drift. We initialize the KSDrift detector from the alibi_detect package and fit it onto the training data. We use the predict method of the detector to calculate the drift scores and p-values on the test data. The drift scores indicate the level of drift for each feature, while the p-values indicate the statistical significance of the drift. If any of the drift scores or p-values are above a certain threshold, we may consider the model to be experiencing drift and take appropriate action, such as retraining the model with updated data:

```
# Initialize the KSDrift detector
drift_detector = KSDrift(X_train)

# Calculate the drift scores and p-values
drift_scores = drift_detector.predict(X_test)
p_values = drift_detector.predict(X_test,
    return_p_val=True)

# Print the drift scores and p-values
print("Drift scores:")
print(drift_scores)
print("P-values:")
print(p_values)
```

Here are the resulting drift scores and p-values. As all the p-values are greater than 0.1, and considering the threshold is 0.005, we can say that no drift is detected in this case:

```
Drift scores:
{'data': {'is_drift': 0, 'distance': array([0.02825 , 0.024625,
0.0225   , 0.01275 , 0.014    , 0.017125,0.01775 , 0.015125, 0.021375,
0.014625], dtype=float32), 'p_val': array([0.15258548, 0.28180763,
0.38703775, 0.95421314, 0.907967 ,0.72927415, 0.68762517, 0.8520056 ,
0.45154762, 0.87837887],dtype=float32), 'threshold': 0.005}, 'meta':
{'name': 'KSDrift', 'online': False, 'data_type': None, 'version':
'0.11.1', 'detector_type': 'drift'}}
P-values:
{'data': {'is_drift': 0, 'distance': array([0.02825 , 0.024625,
0.0225   , 0.01275 , 0.014    , 0.017125,0.01775 , 0.015125, 0.021375,
0.014625], dtype=float32), 'p_val': array([0.15258548, 0.28180763,
0.38703775, 0.95421314, 0.907967 ,0.72927415, 0.68762517, 0.8520056 ,
```

```
0.45154762, 0.87837887],dtype=float32), 'threshold': 0.005}, 'meta':
{'name': 'KSDrift', 'online': False, 'data_type': None, 'version':
'0.11.1', 'detector_type': 'drift'}}
```

## Practicing with evidently for drift detection

Another widely-used Python library for drift detection that we will practice with here is evidently. After importing the necessary libraries, we load the diabetes dataset from scikit-learn:

```
import pandas as pd
import numpy as np
from sklearn import datasets
from evidently.report import Report
from evidently.metrics import DataDriftTable
from evidently.metrics import DatasetDriftMetric

diabetes_data = datasets.fetch_openml(name='diabetes',
    version=1, as_frame='auto')
diabetes = diabetes_data.frame
diabetes = diabetes.drop(['class', 'pres'], axis = 1)
```

The following table shows the features we want to work on from the diabetes dataset for drift detection and their meanings:

| Feature | Description |
| --- | --- |
| preg | Number of times pregnant |
| plas | Plasma glucose concentration after 2 hours in an oral glucose tolerance test |
| skin | Triceps skinfold thickness (mm) |
| insu | 2-hour serum insulin (mu U/ml) |
| mass | Body mass index (weight in kg/(height in m)^2) |
| pedi | Diabetes pedigree function |
| Age | Age (years) |

Table 11.1 – Feature names and their description in diabetes
dataset used for drift detection (Efron et al., 2004)

We separate two sets of datapoints called reference and current sets, then generate a drift report using `Report()` from the `evidently.report.Reference` set to include all individuals aged less than or equal to 40 years, and the current set to include others in the dataset aged more than 40 years:

```
diabetes_reference = diabetes[diabetes.age <= 40]
diabetes_current = diabetes[diabetes.age > 40]
data_drift_dataset_report = Report(metrics=[
    DatasetDriftMetric(),
    DataDriftTable(),
])
data_drift_dataset_report.run(
    reference_data=diabetes_reference,
    current_data=diabetes_current)
Data_drift_dataset_report
```

The following illustration is of the report we generated for the diabetes dataset, considering the selected features and separated reference and current sets:

**Drift is detected for 71.429% of columns (5 out of 7).**

| Column | Type | Reference Distribution | Current Distribution | Data Drift | Stat Test | Drift Score |
|--------|------|------------------------|----------------------|------------|-----------|-------------|
| > pedi | num | | | Not Detected | K-S p_value | 0.519676 |
| > mass | num | | | Not Detected | K-S p_value | 0.058103 |
| > skin | num | | | Detected | K-S p_value | 0.000063 |
| > insu | num | | | Detected | K-S p_value | 0.000009 |
| > plas | num | | | Detected | K-S p_value | 0 |
| > preg | num | | | Detected | K-S p_value | 0 |
| > age | num | | | Detected | K-S p_value | 0 |

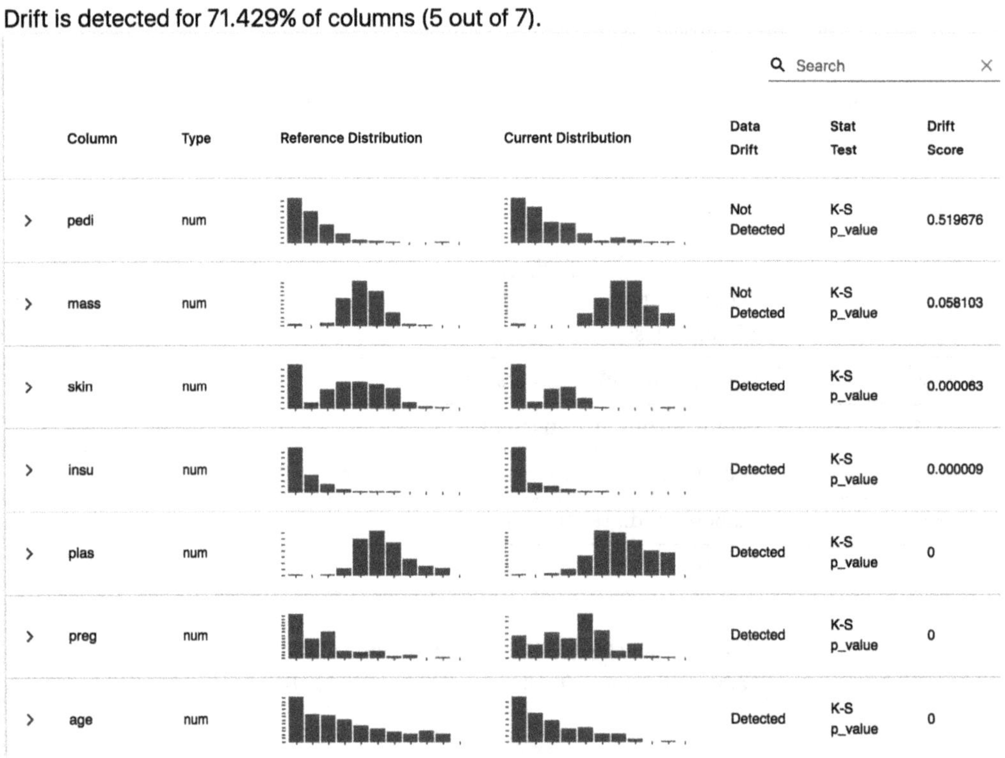

Figure 11.1 – Drift report for the separated reference and current data from the diabetes dataset

We can see that `age`, `preg`, `plas`, `insu`, and `skin` are the features with significant differences in their distributions between the reference and current sets, which are specified as features with detected drift in the report shown in *Figure 11.1*. In spite of the significance of the difference between the distributions, having complementary statistics such as difference of mean could be helpful to develop a more reliable drift detection strategy. We can also get the distribution of the features from the report, such as the distributions of `age` and `preg` in the reference and current sets in *Figures 11.2* and *11.3*, respectively:

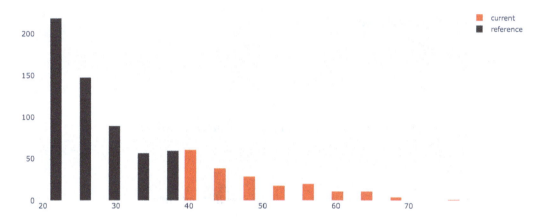

Figure 11.2 – Distribution of the age feature in both current and reference data

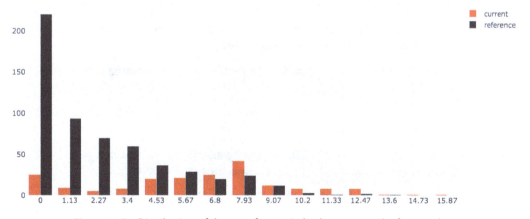

Figure 11.3 – Distribution of the preg feature in both current and reference data

When we detect drifts in our models, we might need to retrain them by ingesting new data or by filtering part of the data that might be the source of the drift. We might also need to change model training if concept drift is detected.

## Summary

In this chapter, you learned about the importance of avoiding drift in your machine learning models, and how you can benefit from the concepts you learned in previous chapters such as model versioning and monitoring to do so. You also practiced with two libraries for drift detection in Python: `alibi_detect` and `evidently`. Using these or similar libraries will help you to eliminate drift in your models and have reliable models in production.

In the next chapter, you will learn about different types of deep neural network models and how to use PyTorch to develop reliable deep learning models.

## Questions

1. Could you explain the difference between magnitude and frequency as two characteristics of drift in machine learning modeling?

2. What is an example of a statistical test we can use for data drift detection?

## References

- Ackerman, Samuel, et al. "*Detection of data drift and outliers affecting machine learning model performance over time.*" arXiv preprint arXiv:2012.09258 (2020).

- Ackerman, Samuel, et al. "*Automatically detecting data drift in machine learning classifiers.*" arXiv preprint arXiv:2111.05672 (2021).

- Efron, Bradley, Trevor Hastie, Iain Johnstone, and Robert Tibshirani (2004) "*Least Angle Regression,*" Annals of Statistics (with discussion), 407-499

- Gama, João, et al. "*A survey on concept drift adaptation.*" ACM computing surveys (CSUR) 46.4 (2014): 1-37.

- Lu, Jie, et al. "*Learning under concept drift: A review.*" IEEE transactions on knowledge and data engineering 31.12 (2018): 2346-2363.

- Mallick, Ankur, et al. "*Matchmaker: Data drift mitigation in machine learning for large-scale systems.*" Proceedings of Machine Learning and Systems 4 (2022): 77-94.

- Zenisek, Jan, Florian Holzinger, and Michael Affenzeller. "*Machine learning based concept drift detection for predictive maintenance.*" Computers & Industrial Engineering 137 (2019): 106031.

# Part 4:
# Deep Learning Modeling

In this part of the book, we will lay the foundation with an introduction to the underlying theories of deep learning, and then transition to hands-on exploration of fully connected neural networks. We will then learn about more advanced techniques including convolutional neural networks, transformers, and graph neural networks. Concluding this part, we will spotlight the cutting-edge advancements in machine learning, with a keen focus on generative modeling and an introduction to reinforcement and self-supervised learning. Throughout these chapters, practical examples are provided using Python and PyTorch, ensuring that we gain both theoretical knowledge as well as hands-on experience.

This part has the following chapters:

- *Chapter 12, Going Beyond ML Debugging with Deep Learning*
- *Chapter 13, Advanced Deep Learning Techniques*
- *Chapter 14, Introduction to Recent Advancements in Machine Learning*

# 12

# Going Beyond ML Debugging with Deep Learning

The most recent advancements in machine learning have been achieved through deep learning modeling. In this chapter, we will introduce deep learning and PyTorch as a framework to use for deep learning modeling. As the focus of this book is not on introducing different machine learning and deep learning algorithms in detail, we will focus on opportunities that deep learning provides for you to develop high-performance models, or use available ones, that can be built on top of the techniques reviewed in this chapter and the next two.

In this chapter, we will cover the following topics:

- Introduction to artificial neural networks
- Frameworks for neural network modeling

By the end of this chapter, you will have learned about some theoretical aspects of deep learning focusing on fully connected neural networks. You will have also practiced with PyTorch, a widely used deep learning framework.

## Technical requirements

The following requirements should be considered for this chapter as they will help you better understand the concepts, use them in your projects, and practice with the provided code:

- Python library requirements:
  - `torch >= 2.0.0`
  - `torchvision >= 0.15.1`

- You will also require basic knowledge of the difference between different types of machine learning models, such as classification, regression, and clustering

You can find the code files for this chapter on GitHub at `https://github.com/PacktPublishing/Debugging-Machine-Learning-Models-with-Python/tree/main/Chapter12`.

# Introduction to artificial neural networks

Our natural networks of neurons work as decision-making systems with information processing units called neurons that help us with, for example, recognizing the faces of our friends. **Artificial neural networks (ANNs)** work similarly. Dissimilar to having a giant network of neurons, as in our bodies, that take care of all decision-making, active or reactive, ANNs are designed to be problem-specific. For example, we have ANNs for image classification, credit risk estimation, object detection, and more. We will use neural networks instead of ANNs for simplicity in this book.

First, we want to focus on **fully connected neural networks (FCNNs)**, which work on tabular data (*Figure 12.1*). FCNNs and **multi-layer perceptrons (MLPs)** are used interchangeably in many resources. To be able to better compare different types of neural networks, we will use FCNNs instead of MLPs in this book:

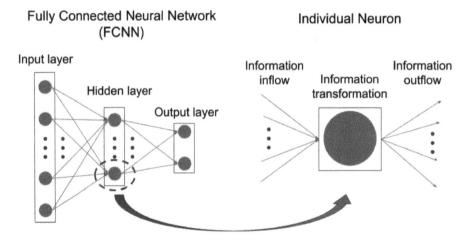

Figure 12.1 – Schematic illustration of an FCNN and an individual neuron

FCNNs for supervised learning have one input, one output, and one or multiple hidden (middle) layers. A neural network with more than three layers, inclusive of the input and the output layers in supervised models, is called a deep neural network, and deep learning refers to modeling with such networks (Hinton and Salakhutdinov, 2006).

The input layer is nothing other than the features of data points used for modeling. The number of neurons in the output layer is also determined based on the problem at hand. For example, in the case of binary classification, two neurons in the output layer represent two classes. The number and size of hidden layers are among the hyperparameters of an FCNN and can be optimized to improve FCNN performance.

Each neuron in an FCNN receives a weighted sum of output values from neurons in the previous layer, applies a linear or nonlinear transformation to the received sum of values, and then outputs the resulting value to other neurons of the next layer. The weights used in the input value calculation of each neuron are the learned weights (parameters) in the training process. The nonlinear transformations are applied through predetermined activation functions (*Figure 12.2*). FCNNs are known for coming up with complicated nonlinear relationships between input feature values and outputs, which makes them flexible in figuring out (maybe) different kinds of relationships between inputs and outputs. In FCNNs, activation functions that are applied to information that's been received in neurons are responsible for that complexity or flexibility:

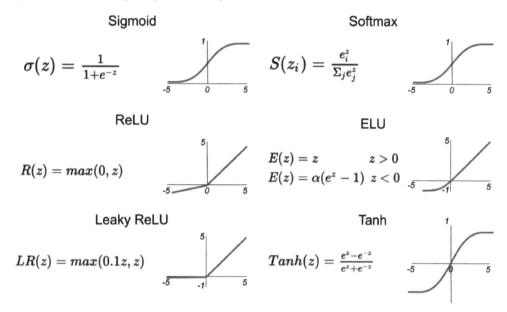

### Sigmoid

$$\sigma(z) = \frac{1}{1+e^{-z}}$$

### Softmax

$$S(z_i) = \frac{e_i^z}{\Sigma_j e_j^z}$$

### ReLU

$$R(z) = max(0, z)$$

### ELU

$$E(z) = z \qquad z > 0$$
$$E(z) = \alpha(e^z - 1) \quad z < 0$$

### Leaky ReLU

$$LR(z) = max(0.1z, z)$$

### Tanh

$$Tanh(z) = \frac{e^z - e^{-z}}{e^z + e^{-z}}$$

Figure 12.2 – Widely used activation functions in neural network modeling

Each of these activation functions, such as **rectified linear unit** (**ReLU**) and **exponential linear unit** (**ELU**), transform the values in a specific way, which makes them suitable for different layers and provides flexibility in neural network modeling. For example, the `sigmoid` and `softmax` functions are commonly used in output layers to transform the scores of the output neurons into values between zero and one for classification models; these are known as probabilities of predictions. There are also other activation functions such as **Gaussian error linear unit** (**GELU**) (Hendrycks and Gimpel, 2016) that have been used in more recent models such as **generative pre-trained transformer** (**GPT**), which will be explained in the next chapter. Here is the formula for GELU:

$$GELU\left(z\right) = 0.5z\left(1 + tanh\left(\sqrt{\tfrac{2}{\pi}}(z + 0.044715\,z^3)\right)\right)$$

Supervised learning has two main processes: predicting outputs and learning from the incorrectness or correctness of predictions. In FCNNs, predictions happen in forward propagation. The weights of the FCNNs between the input and first hidden layer are used to calculate the input values of the neurons of the first hidden layer and similarly for other layers in the FCNN (*Figure 12.3*). Going from input to output is called forward propagation or forward pass, which generates the output values (predictions) for each data point. Then, in the backward propagation (backpropagation) or backward pass, FCNN uses the predicted outputs and their differences with actual outputs to adjust its weights, resulting in better predictions:

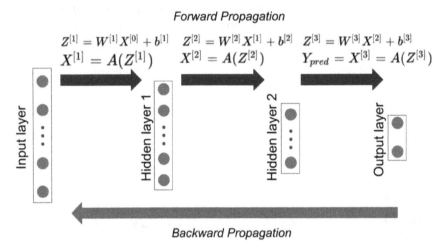

*Figure 12.3 – Schematic illustration of forward propagation and backpropagation for output prediction and parameter update, respectively*

The parameters of a neural network get determined in the training process using an optimization algorithm. Now, we will review some widely used optimization algorithms in neural network settings.

## Optimization algorithms

Optimization algorithms work behind the scenes, trying to minimize the loss function to identify the optimal parameters when you train a machine learning model. At each step in the training process, an optimization algorithm decides how to update each of the weights or parameters in a neural network, or other machine learning models. Most optimization algorithms rely on the gradient vector of the cost function to update the weights. The main difference is how the gradient vector is used and what data points are used to calculate it.

In gradient descent, all the data points are used to calculate the gradient of the cost function; then, the weights of the model get updated in the direction of maximum decrease of cost. Despite the effectiveness of this method for small datasets, it can become computationally expensive and unsuitable for large datasets as for every iteration of learning, the cost needs to be calculated for all the data points simultaneously. The alternative approach is **stochastic gradient descent** (**SGD**); instead of all data points, one data point gets selected in each iteration to calculate the cost and update the weights. But using one data point at a time causes a highly oscillating behavior in updating weights. Instead, we can use mini-batch gradient descent, which is commonly called SGD in tutorials and tools, in which instead of all data points or only one in each iteration, it will use a batch of data points to update the weights. The mathematics behind these three approaches is shown in *Figure 12.4*:

| **Gradient Descent** | **Stochastic Gradient Descent** | **Mini-batch Gradient Descent** |
| :---: | :---: | :---: |
| Considering all datapoints in each iteration | Considering all datapoints in each iteration | Considering a subset of datapoints at each iteration |
| $\theta = \theta - \eta.\nabla_\theta J(\theta)$ | $\theta = \theta - \eta.\nabla_\theta J(\theta; x^{(i)}; y^{(i)})$ | $\theta = \theta - \eta.\nabla_\theta J(\theta; x^{(i:i+n)}; y^{(i:i+n)})$ |

$J(\theta)$: Cost function      $\eta$: Learning rate      $\nabla_\theta J$: Gradient vector of cost function

Figure 12.4 – Gradient descent, stochastic gradient descent, and mini-batch gradient descent optimization algorithms

Other optimization algorithms have been suggested in recent years to improve the performance of neural network models across a variety of applications, such as the Adam optimizer (Kingma and Ba, 2014). One of the intuitions behind this approach is to avoid diminishing gradients in the optimization process. Getting further into the details of different optimization algorithms is beyond the scope of this book.

In neural network modeling, there are two important terms that you need to know the definition of: *epoch* and *batch size*. When training a neural network model using different frameworks, which we will review in the next section, you need to specify the *batch size* and the number of *epochs*. In each iteration of optimization, a subset of data points, or a mini-batch as in mini-batch gradient descent (*Figure 12.4*), gets used to calculate loss; then, the parameters of the model get updated using backpropagation. This process gets repeated to cover all the data points in the training data. Epoch is a term we use to specify how many times all the training data is used during the optimization process. For example, specifying an epoch of 5 means that the model gets trained until all the data points in the training process are used five times in the optimization process.

Now that you know the basics of neural network modeling, we are ready to introduce frameworks for neural network modeling.

## Frameworks for neural network modeling

Multiple frameworks have been used for neural network modeling:

- PyTorch (https://pytorch.org/)
- TensorFlow (https://www.tensorflow.org/learn)

- Keras (`https://keras.io/`)

- Caffe (`https://caffe.berkeleyvision.org/`)

- MXNet (`https://mxnet.apache.org/versions/1.9.1/`)

In this book, we will focus on PyTorch in practicing deep learning, but the concepts we'll introduce are independent of the framework you use in your projects.

## PyTorch for deep learning modeling

PyTorch is an open source deep learning framework, based on the `Torch` library, developed by Meta AI. You can easily integrate PyTorch with Python's scientific computing libraries in your deep learning projects. Here, we will practice using PyTorch by looking at a simple example of building an FCNN model using the MNIST digit dataset. It is a commonly used example and the objective is solely to understand how to train and test a deep learning model using PyTorch if you don't have experience with that.

First, we will import the required libraries and load the dataset for training and testing:

```
import torch
import torchvision
import torchvision.transforms as transforms
torch.manual_seed(10)
# Device configuration
device = torch.device(
    'cuda' if torch.cuda.is_available() else 'cpu')
# MNIST dataset
batch_size = 100
train_dataset = torchvision.datasets.MNIST(
    root='../../data',train=True,
    transform=transforms.ToTensor(),download=True)
test_dataset = torchvision.datasets.MNIST(
    root='../../data', train=False,
    transform=transforms.ToTensor())
# Data loader
train_loader = torch.utils.data.DataLoader(
    dataset=train_dataset,batch_size=batch_size,
    shuffle=True)

test_loader = torch.utils.data.DataLoader(
    dataset=test_dataset,  batch_size=batch_size,
    shuffle=False)
```

Next, we will determine the hyperparameters of the model and its input_size, which is the number of neurons in the input layer; this is the same as the number of features in our data. In this example, it is equal to the number of pixels in each image as we are considering each pixel as one feature to build an FCNN model:

```
input_size = 784
# size of hidden layer
hidden_size = 256
# number of classes
num_classes = 10
# number of epochs
num_epochs = 10
# learning rate for the optimization process
learning_rate = 0.001
```

Then, we will import torch.nn, from which we can add linear neural network layers for our FCNN model and write a class to determine the architecture of our network, which is a network with one hidden layer whose size is 256 (with 256 neurons):

```
import torch.nn as nn
class NeuralNet(nn.Module):
    def __init__(self, input_size, hidden_size,
        num_classes):
        super(NeuralNet, self).__init__()
        Self.fc_layer_1 = nn.Linear(input_size, hidden_size)
        self.fc_layer_2 = nn.Linear(hidden_size, num_classes)

    def forward(self, x):
        out = self.fc_layer_1(x)
        out = nn.ReLU()(out)
        out = self.fc_layer_2(out)
        return out

model = NeuralNet(input_size, hidden_size,
    num_classes).to(device)
```

The torch.nn.Linear() class adds a linear layer and has two input arguments: the number of neurons in the current and next layer, respectively. For the first, nn.Linear(), the first argument has to be equal to the number of features, while the second argument of the last nn.Linear() input argument in the network initialization class needs to be equal to the number of classes in the data.

Now, we must define our cross-entropy loss function and our optimizer object using the Adam optimizer from `torch.optim()`:

```
criterion = nn.CrossEntropyLoss()
optimizer = torch.optim.Adam(model.parameters(),
    lr=learning_rate)
```

We are now ready to train our model. As you can see in the following code block, we have a loop over epochs and another internal loop over each batch. Within the internal loop, we have three important steps that are common across most supervised models that use PyTorch:

1.  Get the output of the model for the data points within the batch.

2.  Calculate the loss using the true labels and the predicted output for the data points of that batch.

3.  Backpropagate and update the parameters of the model.

Next, we must train the model on the MNIST training set:

```
total_step = len(train_loader)
for epoch in range(num_epochs):
    for i, (images, labels) in enumerate(train_loader):
        images = images.reshape(-1, 28*28).to(device)
        labels = labels.to(device)
        # Forward pass to calculate output and loss
        outputs = model(images)
        loss = criterion(outputs, labels)
        # Backpropagation and optimization
        optimizer.zero_grad()
        loss.backward()
        optimizer.step()
```

At the end of epoch 10, we have a model with a loss of 0.0214 in the training set. Now, we can use the following code to calculate the accuracy of the model in the test set:

```
with torch.no_grad():
    correct = 0
    total = 0
    for images, labels in test_loader:
        images = images.reshape(-1, 28*28).to(device)
        labels = labels.to(device)
        outputs = model(images)
        _, predicted = torch.max(outputs.data, 1)
        total += labels.size(0)
        correct += (predicted == labels).sum().item()
```

```
print('Accuracy of the network on the test images:
    {} %'.format(100 * correct / total))
```

This results in 98.4% for the model in the MNIST test set.

There are more than 10 different optimization algorithms, including the Adam optimization algorithm, available in PyTorch (`https://pytorch.org/docs/stable/optim.html`), which helps you in training your deep learning models.

Next, we will discuss hyperparameter tuning, model interpretability, and fairness in deep learning settings. We will also introduce PyTorch Lightning, which will help you in your deep learning projects.

## Hyperparameter tuning for deep learning

In deep learning modeling, hyperparameters are key factors in determining its performance. Here are some of the hyperparameters of FCNNs you can work with to improve the performance of your deep learning models:

- **Architecture**: The architecture of an FCNN refers to the number of hidden layers and their sizes, or the number of neurons. More layers result in higher depth in a deep learning model and could result in more complex models. Although the depth of neural network models has been shown to improve performance on large datasets in many cases (Krizhevsky et al., 2012; Simonyan and Zisserman, 2014; Szegedy et al., 2015; He et al., 2016), the majority of the success stories behind the positive effect of higher depth on performance are outside of FCNNs. But architecture is still an important hyperparameter that needs to be optimized to find a high-performance model.

- **Activation functions**: Despite commonly used activation functions in each field and problem, you can still identify the best one for your problem. Remember that you don't have to use the same function across all layers, although we usually stick to one.

- **Batch size**: Changing batch size changes both the performance and speed of convergence of your models. But usually, it doesn't have a significant effect on performance, except in the steep part of the learning curve in the first few epochs.

- **Learning rate**: The learning rate determines the speed of convergence. A higher learning rate causes faster convergence but it might also cause oscillation around the local optimum point or even divergence. Algorithms such as the Adam optimizer control the diminishing convergence rate when we get closer to the local optima during the optimization process, but we can still play with the learning rate as a hyperparameter in deep learning modeling.

- **Number of epochs**: Deep learning models have a steep learning curve for the first few epochs, depending on the learning rate and batch size, and then start plateauing on performance. Using enough epochs is important to make sure you get the best possible model out of your training.

- **Regularization**: We talked about the importance of regulations in controlling overfitting and improving generalizability in *Chapter 5, Improving the Performance of Machine Learning Models*, by preventing the model from heavily relying on individual neurons and potentially improving generalizability. For example, if dropout is set to 0.2, each neuron has a 20% chance of getting zero out during training.

- **Weight decay**: This is a form of L2 regularization that adds a penalty to the weights of the neural network. We introduced L2 regularization in *Chapter 5, Improving the Performance of Machine Learning Models.*

You can use different hyperparameter optimization tools such as Ray Tune alongside PyTorch to train your deep learning models and optimize their hyperparameters. You can read more about it in this tutorial available on the PyTorch website: `https://pytorch.org/tutorials/beginner/hyperparameter_tuning_tutorial.html`.

In addition to hyperparameter tuning, PyTorch has different functionalities and associated libraries for tasks such as model interpretability and fairness.

### Model interpretability in PyTorch

We introduced multiple explainability techniques and libraries in *Chapter 6, Interpretability and Explainability in Machine Learning Modeling*, that can help you in explaining complex machine learning and deep learning models. Captum AI (`https://captum.ai/`) is another open source model interpretability library developed by Meta AI for deep learning projects using PyTorch. You can easily integrate Captum into your existing or future PyTorch-based machine learning pipelines. You can benefit from different explainability and interpretability techniques such as integrated gradients, GradientSHAP, DeepLIFT, and saliency maps through Captum.

### Fairness in deep learning models developed by PyTorch

We discussed the importance of fairness and introduced different notions, statistical measures, and techniques to help you in assessing and eliminating bias in your models as part of *Chapter 7, Decreasing Bias and Achieving Fairness*. FairTorch (`https://github.com/wbawakate/fairtorch`) and inFairness (`https://github.com/IBM/inFairness`) are two other libraries you can use for fairness and bias assessment for your deep learning modeling using PyTorch. You can benefit from inFairness in auditing, training, and post-processing your models for individual fairness. Fairtorch also provides you with tools to mitigate bias in classification and regression, though this is currently limited to binary classification.

### PyTorch Lightning

PyTorch Lightning is an open source, high-level framework that simplifies the process of developing and training deep learning models using PyTorch for you. Here are some of the features of PyTorch Lightning:

- **Structured code**: PyTorch Lightning organizes code into a Lightning Module that helps you in separating the model architecture, data handling, and training logic, making the code more modular and easier to maintain

- **Training loop abstraction**: You can avoid repetitive code for the training, validation, and testing loops using PyTorch Lightning

- **Distributed training**: PyTorch Lightning simplifies the process of scaling deep learning models across multiple GPUs or nodes

- **Experiment tracking and logging**: PyTorch Lightning integrates with experiment tracking and logging tools such as MLflow and Weights & Biases, which make monitoring your deep learning model training easier for you

- **Automatic optimization**: PyTorch Lightning automatically handles the optimization process, manages optimizers and learning rate schedulers, and makes it easier to switch between different optimization algorithms

Despite all these factors, there is more to deep learning modeling than FCNNs, as we'll see in the next chapter.

## Summary

In this chapter, you learned about deep learning modeling with FCNNs. We practiced using PyTorch with a simple deep learning model to help you start performing deep learning modeling using PyTorch if you haven't had that experience already. You also learned about the important hyperparameters of FCNNs, tools for model interpretability and fairness that you can use in deep learning settings, and PyTorch Lightning as an open source high-level framework to simplify deep learning modeling for you. You are now ready to learn more about PyTorch, PyTorch Lightning, and deep learning and start benefitting from them in your problems.

In the next chapter, you will learn about other more advanced types of deep learning models, including the convolutional neural network, transformer, and graph convolutional network models.

## Questions

1. Do the parameters of a neural network model get updated in backpropagation?

2. What is the difference between stochastic and mini-batch gradient descent?

3. Can you explain the difference between a batch and an epoch?

4. Can you provide an example of where you need to use the sigmoid and softmax functions in your neural network models?

## References

- LeCun, Yann, Yoshua Bengio, and Geoffrey Hinton. *Deep learning*. nature 521.7553 (2015): 436-444.

- Hinton, G. E., & Salakhutdinov, R. R. (2006). *Reducing the Dimensionality of Data with Neural Networks*. Science, 313(5786), 504-507.

- Abiodun, Oludare Isaac, et al. *State-of-the-art in artificial neural network applications: A survey.* Heliyon 4.11 (2018): e00938.

- Hendrycks, D., & Gimpel, K. (2016). *Gaussian Error Linear Units (GELUs).* arXiv preprint arXiv:1606.08415.

- Kingma, D. P., & Ba, J. (2014). *Adam: A Method for Stochastic Optimization.* arXiv preprint arXiv:1412.6980.

- Kadra, Arlind, et al. *Well-tuned simple nets excel on tabular datasets.* Advances in neural information processing systems 34 (2021): 23928-23941.

- Krizhevsky, A., Sutskever, I., & Hinton, G. E. (2012). *ImageNet classification with deep convolutional neural networks.* In Advances in neural information processing systems (pp. 1097-1105).

- Simonyan, K., & Zisserman, A. (2014). *Very deep convolutional networks for large-scale image recognition.* arXiv preprint arXiv:1409.1556.

- He, K., Zhang, X., Ren, S., & Sun, J. (2016). *Deep residual learning for image recognition.* In Proceedings of the IEEE conference on computer vision and pattern recognition (pp. 770-778).

- Szegedy, C., Liu, W., Jia, Y., Sermanet, P., Reed, S., Anguelov, D., ... & Rabinovich, A. (2015). *Going deeper with convolutions.* In Proceedings of the IEEE conference on computer vision and pattern recognition (pp. 1-9).

# 13

# Advanced Deep Learning Techniques

In the previous chapter, we reviewed the concept of neural network modeling and deep learning while focusing on fully connected neural networks. In this chapter, we will discuss more advanced techniques that let you use deep learning models across different data types and structures, such as images, texts, and graphs. These techniques are behind the majority of advancements across industries through artificial intelligence, such as in chatbots, medical diagnosis, drug discovery, stock trading, and fraud detection. Although we will present some of the most famous deep learning models across different data types, this chapter aims to help you understand the concepts and practice with PyTorch, and not provide you with state-of-the-art models for each data type or subject domain.

In this chapter, we will cover the following topics:

- Types of neural networks
- Convolutional neural networks for image shape data
- Transformers for language modeling
- Modeling graphs using deep neural networks

By the end of this chapter, you will have learned about **convolutional neural networks** (CNNs), transformers, and graph neural networks as the three important categories of deep learning modeling to develop high-performance models in your problems of interest. You will have also learned how to develop such models using PyTorch and Python.

# Technical requirements

The following requirements should be considered for this chapter as they will help you better understand the concepts, use them in your projects, and practice with the provided code:

- Python library requirements:

  - `torch` >= 2.0.0

  - `torchvision` >= 0.15.1

  - `transformers` >= 4.28.0

  - `datasets` >= 2.12.0

  - `torch_geometric` == 2.3.1

- You will require basic knowledge of the following:

  - Deep learning modeling and fully connected neural networks

  - How to use PyTorch for deep learning modeling

You can find the code files for this chapter on GitHub at `https://github.com/PacktPublishing/Debugging-Machine-Learning-Models-with-Python/tree/main/Chapter13`.

# Types of neural networks

The examples we have provided so far in this book have focused on tabular data either in machine learning or in deep learning modeling, as one category of machine learning modeling. However, machine learning, and especially deep learning, has been successful in tackling problems that deal with non-tabular, or unstructured, texts, images, and graphs. First, we'll introduce different problems that involve such data types in this section; then, we'll review deep learning techniques that can help you build reliable models for them.

## Categorization based on data type

Structured data, which is also referred to as tabular data, is data that can be organized into spreadsheets and structured databases. As we have used this data type in this book, we usually have different features and even output in the columns of a table, matrix, or DataFrame. The rows of a DataFrame represent different data points in the dataset. However, we have other types of data that are not structured, and reformatting them into a DataFrame or matrix results in a loss of information. *Figure 13.1* shows the three most important types of unstructured data – that is, sequence data such as text, image shape data such as family photos, and graphs such as social networks:

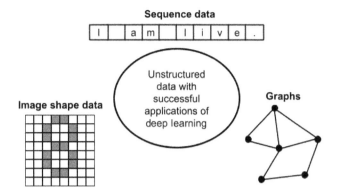

Figure 13.1 – Different data types that can be modeled using deep learning

*Table 13.1* provides some examples of problems and how their corresponding data fits within each category mentioned in *Figure 13.1*:

| Data Type | Examples |
|---|---|
| Sequence data | Text |
| | Time-series data such as stock prices |
| | Audio data as a sequence of sound waves |
| | Geolocation data as a sequence of object movement |
| | EEG data as a sequence of electrical activity of the brain |
| | ECG data as a sequence of electrical activity of the heart |
| Image shape data | Photographs |
| | Security and surveillance images |
| | Medical images such as X-rays or CT scans |
| | Visual arts and images of drawings and paintings |
| | Images captured by satellites, such as weather patterns |
| | Images captured using microscopes, such as images of cells |
| Graphs | Road networks |
| | Web graphs – connections between web pages |
| | Knowledge graphs – relationships between concepts |
| | Social networks – connections between individuals and groups |
| | Biological networks – connections between genes or other biological entities |

Table 13.1 – Examples of problems for each data type

Some of the challenges and issues with reformatting different data types into tabular data are as follows:

- Reformatting sequence data into a table shape data object results in a loss of information regarding the order of data, such as words

- Reformatting images into tabular format results in a loss of local patterns, such as the relationship between pixels of two-dimensional images

- Reformatting graphs into tabular data will eliminate dependency between data points or features

Now that we understand the importance of not reformatting all datasets and data types into tabular data, we can start working with different deep learning techniques to understand how we can build successful models for non-tabular data. We will start by looking at image shape data.

## Convolutional neural networks for image shape data

CNNs allow us to build deep learning models on image data without the need to reformat images into a tabular format. The name of this category of deep learning techniques comes from the concept of convolution, which in deep learning refers to applying a filter to image shape data to produce a secondary image shape feature map (shown in *Figure 13.2*):

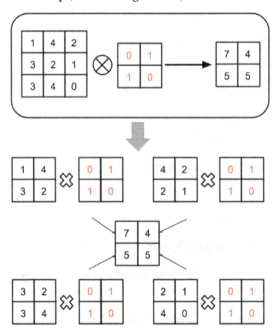

Figure 13.2 – A simple example of applying a predefined convolution filter to a 3x3 image shape data point

When training a deep learning model, for example using PyTorch, a convolution filter or other filters that we will introduce later in this chapter will not be predefined but rather learned through the learning process. Convolution and other filters and processes in CNN modeling let us use the methods under this category of deep learning techniques for different image shape data (as we saw in *Figure 13.1*).

The application of CNNs is beyond supervised learning for image classification, for which it might be most famous. CNNs have been used for different problems, including **image segmentation**, **resolution enhancements**, **object detection**, and more (*Figure 13.3*):

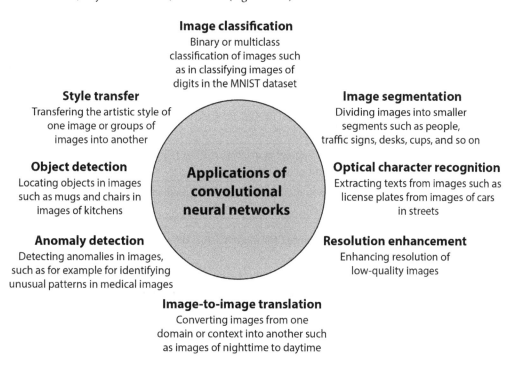

**Image classification**
Binary or multiclass classification of images such as in classifying images of digits in the MNIST dataset

**Style transfer**
Transfering the artistic style of one image or groups of images into another

**Image segmentation**
Dividing images into smaller segments such as people, traffic signs, desks, cups, and so on

**Object detection**
Locating objects in images such as mugs and chairs in images of kitchens

**Applications of convolutional neural networks**

**Optical character recognition**
Extracting texts from images such as license plates from images of cars in streets

**Anomaly detection**
Detecting anomalies in images, such as for example for identifying unusual patterns in medical images

**Resolution enhancement**
Enhancing resolution of low-quality images

**Image-to-image translation**
Converting images from one domain or context into another such as images of nighttime to daytime

Figure 13.3 – Some of the successful applications of convolutional neural networks

*Table 13.2* provides a list of high-performance models in different applications of CNNs that you can use in your projects or learn from to build even better models:

| Problem | Some of the Widely Used Models and Related Techniques |
|---------|-------------------------------------------------------|
| Image classification | ResNet (He et al., 2016); EfficientNets (Tan and Le, 2019); MobileNets (Howard et al., 2017; Sandler et al., 2018); Xception (Chollet, 2017) |
| Image segmentation | U-Net (Ronneberger et al., 2015); Mask R-CNN (He et al., 2017); DeepLab (Chen et al., 2017); PSPNet (Chao et al., 2017) |
| Object detection | Mask R-CNN (He et al., 2017); Faster R-CNN (Ren et al., 2015); YOLO (Redmon et al., 2016) |
| Image super-resolution | SRCNN (Dong et el., 2015); FSRCNN (Dong et al., 2016); EDSR (Lim et al., 2017) |
| Image-to-image translation | Pix2Pix (Isola et al., 2017); CycleGAN (Zhu et al., 2017) |
| Style transfer | Neural Algorithm of Artistic Style (Gatys et al., 2016); AdaIN-Style (Huang et al., 2017) |
| Anomaly detection | AnoGAN (Schlegl et al., 2017); RDA (Zhou et al., 2017); Deep SVDD (Ruff et al., 2018) |
| Optical character recognition | EAST (Zhou et al., 2017); CRAFT (Bake et al., 2019) |

Table 13.2 – High-performance CNN models across different problems

You can train CNN models on two-dimensional or three-dimensional image shape data. You can also build models that work on sequences of such data points, such as videos, as sequences of images. Some of the most famous models or approaches in terms of using CNNs on videos that you can play with are C3D (Tran et al., 2015), I3D (Carreira and Zisserman, 2017), and SlowFast (Feichtenhofer et al., 2019).

Next, we will learn about some of the ways we can assess the performance of CNN models.

## Performance assessment

You can use the performance measures presented in *Chapter 4, Detecting Performance and Efficiency Issues in Machine Learning Models*, such as ROC-AUC, PR-AUC, precision, and recall, for CNN classification models. However, there are other measures more specific to some of the problems presented in *Figure 13.3*, as follows:

- **Pixel accuracy**: This measure is defined as the ratio of correctly classified pixels to the total number of pixels. This measure works like accuracy and can be misleading when there is a class imbalance in the pixels.

- **Jaccard index**: The Jaccard index is defined as the intersection over the union and can be used to calculate the overlap between the predicted segmentation and the ground truth normalized by their union.

## CNN modeling using PyTorch

The process of CNN modeling in PyTorch is very similar to building fully connected neural networks, as we covered in the previous chapter. It starts with specifying the architecture of the network, then initializing the optimizer, and finally going through different epochs and batches to learn from training data points. Here, we want to practice CNN modeling in PyTorch using the **German Traffic Sign Recognition Benchmark (GTSRB)** dataset from the `torchvision` library. Examples of the images in this dataset are shown in *Figure 13.4*:

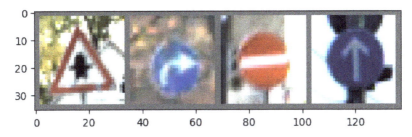

Figure 13.4 – Examples of images in the German Traffic Sign Recognition
Benchmark (GTSRB) dataset from torchvision

There are other filters and layers besides the convolution filter (`torch.nn.Conv2d`) available in `torch.nn` that you can use to train high-performance CNN models. One of those filters that is widely used besides `torch.nn.Conv2d` is `torch.nn.MaxPool2d`, which can be used as a pooling layer in CNN modeling (LeCun et al., 1989). You can read about the required arguments for these two filters on the PyTorch website (`https://pytorch.org/docs/stable/nn.html`).

Let's start practicing CNN modeling using the GTSRB dataset. First, we must load the data for model training and testing, and then specify the number of classes in the classification model:

```
transform = transforms.Compose([
    transforms.Resize((32, 32)),
    transforms.ToTensor(),
    transforms.Normalize((0.3337, 0.3064, 0.3171),
        ( 0.2672, 0.2564, 0.2629))
])
batch_size = 6
n_class = 43
# Loading train and test sets of
# German Traffic Sign Recognition Benchmark (GTSRB) Dataset.
trainset = torchvision.datasets.GTSRB(
```

```
        root='../../data',split = 'train',
        download=True,transform=transform)
trainloader = torch.utils.data.DataLoader(trainset,
        batch_size=batch_size,shuffle=True, num_workers=2)


testset = torchvision.datasets.GTSRB(
        root='../../data',split = 'test',
        download=True,transform=transform)
testloader = torch.utils.data.DataLoader(testset,
        batch_size=batch_size,shuffle=False,num_workers=2)
```

Then, we must define a neural network class, called Net, which determines the architecture of the network, including two layers of convolutional plus pooling filters, followed by ReLU activation functions, and then three layers of fully connected neural networks with ReLU activation functions:

```
import torch.nn as nn
import torch.nn.functional as F

class Net(nn.Module):
    def __init__(self):
        super().__init__()
        self.conv1 = nn.Conv2d(3, 6, 5)
        self.pool = nn.MaxPool2d(2, 2)
        self.conv2 = nn.Conv2d(6, 16, 5)
        self.fc1 = nn.Linear(16 * 5 * 5, 128)
        self.fc2 = nn.Linear(128, 64)
        self.fc3 = nn.Linear(64, n_class)

    def forward(self, x):
        x = self.pool(F.relu(self.conv1(x)))
        x = self.pool(F.relu(self.conv2(x)))
        x = torch.flatten(x, 1)
        x = F.relu(self.fc1(x))
        x = F.relu(self.fc2(x))
        x = self.fc3(x)
        return x
```

Then, we must initialize the network and optimizer, as follows:

```
import torch.optim as optim

net = Net()
```

```
criterion = nn.CrossEntropyLoss()
optimizer = optim.SGD(net.parameters(), lr=0.001,
    momentum=0.9)
```

Now, we are ready to train the network using the initialized architecture and the optimizer. Here, we will use three epochs to train the network. The batch sizes don't need to be specified here as they were determined when the data was loaded from `torchvision`, which was specified as 6 in this case (this can be found in this book's GitHub repository):

```
n_epoch = 3
for epoch in range(n_epoch):

    # running_loss = 0.0
    for i, data in enumerate(trainloader, 0):
        # get the input data
        inputs, labels = data
        # zero the parameter gradients
        optimizer.zero_grad()

        # output identification
        outputs = net(inputs)
        # loss calculation and backward propagation for parameter
  update
        loss = criterion(outputs, labels)
        loss.backward()
        optimizer.step()
```

The final calculated loss after 3 epochs is 0.00008.

This was a simple example of using PyTorch for CNN modeling. There are other functionalities in PyTorch that you can benefit from while building CNN models, such as data augmentation. We will discuss this next.

## Image data transformation and augmentation for CNNs

As part of the pre-training stages of a machine learning life cycle, you might need to transform your images, such as by cropping them, or implement data augmentation as a series of techniques for synthetic data generation to improve the performance of your models, as explained in *Chapter 5, Improving the Performance of Machine Learning Models*. *Figure 13.5* shows some simple examples of data augmentation, including rotation and scaling, that help you in generating synthetic but highly relevant data points to help your models:

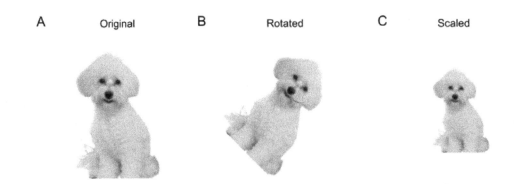

Figure 13.5 – Examples of rule-based data augmentation – (A) original
image, (B) rotated image, and (C) scaled image

Although there are simple examples of rules for data augmentation that you can implement in Python, there are many classes in PyTorch that you can use for both data transformation and augmentation, as explained at `https://pytorch.org/vision/stable/transforms.html`.

## Using pre-trained models

In a deep learning setting, often, we rely on pre-trained models either for inference or to further fine-tune for a specific problem we have at hand. CNNs are not an exception and you can find many pre-trained models in PyTorch for image classification or other applications of CNNs (`https://pytorch.org/vision/stable/models.html`). You can also find code examples at the same URL on how to use these models. You can find the necessary code to teach you how to fine-tune these models using new data at `https://pytorch.org/tutorials/beginner/finetuning_torchvision_models_tutorial.html`.

Although we've focused on applying CNNs to image data so far, they can be used to model any image shape data. For example, audio data can be transformed from the time domain into the frequency domain, resulting in image shape data that can be modeled using CNNs in combination with sequence modeling algorithms, as introduced later in this chapter (`https://pytorch.org/audio/main/models.html`).

In addition to images and image shape data, deep learning models and algorithms have been developed to properly model sequence data in a variety of applications, such as in **natural language processing** (**NLP**), which we will refer to as language modeling here for simplicity. In the next section, we will review transformers for language modeling to help you start benefiting from such models if you have a relevant idea or project at hand.

# Transformers for language modeling

Transformers were introduced in a famous paper called *Attention is All You Need* (Vaswani et al., 2017) as a new approach for sequence-to-sequence data modeling tasks such as translating statements from one language into another (that is, machine translation). These models are built on top of the idea of self-attention, which helps the model pay attention to other important parts of a sentence or sequence of information in the learning process during training. This attention mechanism helps the models better understand the relationships between the elements of input sequences – for example, between the words in the input sequences in language modeling. Models built using transformers usually work better than ones built using predecessor techniques such as **Long Short Term Memory** (**LSTM**) and **Recurrent Neural Networks** (**RNNs**) (Vaswani et al., 2017; Devlin et al., 2018).

*Figure 13.6* shows four traditional problems in language modeling that have been tackled successfully by transformer models:

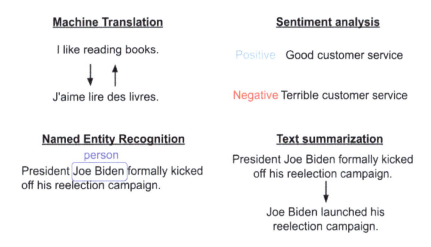

Figure 13.6 – Four traditional problems in language modeling for which
deep learning techniques have been used successfully

Some famous models have been used either directly or with some modifications across these or other language modeling tasks. Here are some examples:

- BERT (Devlin et al., 2018; `https://github.com/google-research/bert`)

- GPT (Radford et al., 2018) and its more recent versions (`https://openai.com/product/gpt-4`)

- DistilBERT (Sanh et al., 2019; `https://huggingface.co/docs/transformers/model_doc/distilbert`)

- RoBERTa (Liu et al., 2019; `https://github.com/facebookresearch/fairseq/tree/main/examples/roberta`)

- BART (Lewis et al., 2019; `https://github.com/huggingface/transformers/tree/main/src/transformers/models/bart`)

- XLNet (Yang et al., 2019; `https://github.com/zihangdai/xlnet/`)

- T5 (Raffel et al., 2020; `https://github.com/google-research/text-to-text-transfer-transformer`)

- LLaMA (Touvron et al., 2023; `https://github.com/facebookresearch/llama`)

Transformer models have also been used in other fields and sequence data, such as for electronic health records (Li et al., 2020), protein structure prediction (Jumpter et al., 2021), and time-series anomaly detection (Xu et al., 2021).

Generative modeling is another important concept in machine learning modeling for which transformers and CNNs have been successfully used. Examples of such models are different versions of GPT, such as GPT-4 (`https://openai.com/product/gpt-4`). You will learn about generative modeling in *Chapter 14, Introduction to Recent Advancements in Machine Learning*. There is an open **Large Language Model** (**LLM**) leaderboard that provides a list of up-to-date open source LLM models (`https://huggingface.co/spaces/HuggingFaceH4/open_llm_leaderboard`). You can also check the list of practical guide resources for LLMs at `https://github.com/Mooler0410/LLMsPracticalGuide`.

We don't want to get into the theoretical details behind transformers, but you will learn about the components of a transformer architecture while building one in PyTorch. However, other widely used performance measures are used in sequence data and language modeling, such as the following:

- **Perplexity** (`https://torchmetrics.readthedocs.io/en/stable/text/perplexity.html`)

- **Bilingual Evaluation Understudy** (**BLEU**) **score** (`https://torchmetrics.readthedocs.io/en/stable/text/bleu_score.html`)

- **Recall-Oriented Understudy for Gisting Evaluation** (**ROUGE**) **score** (`https://torchmetrics.readthedocs.io/en/stable/text/rouge_score.html`)

These measures help you in evaluating your sequence models.

## Tokenization

Before training and testing transformer models, we need to transform the data into the right format through a process called tokenization. Tokenization is about chunking data into smaller pieces such as words, as in **word tokenization**, or characters, as in **character tokenization**. For example, the sentence "I like reading books" can be transformed into its contained words – that is, ["I," "like," "reading," "books"]. When building a tokenizer, the maximum number of allowed tokens needs to be specified. For example, for a tokenizer with 1,000 tokens, the most frequent 1,000 words get used as tokens from a text provided to build the tokenizer. Then, each token will be one of those 1,000 most frequent tokens. After this, these tokens each get an ID; these numbers will be used later by neural network models for training and testing. The words and characters outside of the tokens of a tokenizer get a common value of, for example, 0 or 1. Another challenge in text tokenization is the different lengths of statements and sequences of words. To handle this challenge, a common ID, such as 0, is used before or after the IDs of tokens of words in each sequence of words or sentences in a process called padding.

The recent LLMs have different numbers of tokens in their tokenization process. For example, the **gpt-4-32k** model by OpenAI offers 32,000 tokens (`https://help.openai.com/en/articles/7127966-what-is-the-difference-between-the-gpt-4-models`), while Claude's LLM offers 100k tokens (`https://www.anthropic.com/index/100k-context-windows`). The difference in the number of tokens could impact the performance of the models in terms of the corresponding text-related tasks.

There are commonly used libraries for tokenization, such as Hugging Face's transformer (`https://huggingface.co/transformers/v3.5.1/main_classes/tokenizer.html`), SpaCy (`https://spacy.io/`), and NLTK (`https://www.nltk.org/api/nltk.tokenize.html`). Let's practice with Hugging Face's transformer library to better understand how tokenization works.

First, let's import `transformers.AutoTokenizer()` and then load the `bert-base-cased` and `gpt2` pre-trained tokenizers:

```
from transformers import AutoTokenizer
tokenizer_bertcased = AutoTokenizer.from_pretrained(
    'bert-base-cased')
tokenizer_gpt2 = AutoTokenizer.from_pretrained('gpt2')
```

To practice with these two tokenizers, we must make a list of two statements to use in the tokenization process:

```
batch_sentences = ["I know how to use machine learning in my
projects","I like reading books."]
```

Then, we must use each of the loaded tokenizers to tokenize and encode these two statements to the corresponding lists of IDs. First, let's use `gpt2`, as follows:

```
encoded_input_gpt2 = tokenizer_gpt2(batch_sentences)
```

The preceding code converts these two statements into the following two-dimensional lists, which include IDs for each of the tokens in each statement. For example, as both statements start with "I," the first ID for both of them is 40, which is the token for "I" in the `gpt2` tokenizer:

```
[[40, 760, 703, 284, 779, 4572, 4673, 287, 616, 4493],
 [40, 588, 3555, 3835, 13]]
```

Now, we will use `bert-base-cased`, but this time, we will ask the tokenizer to also use padding to generate lists of IDs of the same length and return the generated IDs in tensor format, which is suitable for use later in neural network modeling, such as using PyTorch:

```
encoded_input_bertcased = tokenizer_bertcased(
    batch_sentences, padding=True, return_tensors="pt")
```

The following tensor shows the same length for the generated IDs for both sentences:

```
tensor([[ 101,  146, 1221, 1293, 1106, 1329, 3395, 3776,
    1107, 1139, 3203,  102],
    [ 101,146, 1176, 3455, 2146, 119, 102, 0, 0, 0, 0, 0]])
```

We can also use decoding functionality from each of these tokenizers to convert the IDs back into the original statements. First, we must decode the generated IDs using gpt2:

```
[tokenizer_gpt2.decode(input_id_iter) for input_id_iter in encoded_
input_gpt2["input_ids"]]
```

This generates the following statements, which match the original input statements:

```
['I know how to use machine learning in my projects', 'I like reading
books.']
```

However, let's say we use the `bert-base-cased` tokenizer for decoding the IDs, as follows:

```
[tokenizer_bertcased.decode(input_id_iter) for input_id_iter in
encoded_input_bertcased["input_ids"]]
```

The resulting statements not only contain the original statements but also show how a padding token is decoded. This is shown as [PAD], [CLS], which is equivalent to the start of a sentence, and [SEP], which shows where another second sentence starts:

```
['[CLS] I know how to use machine learning in my projects [SEP]',
 '[CLS] I like reading books. [SEP] [PAD] [PAD] [PAD] [PAD] [PAD]']
```

## Language embedding

We can transform the identified IDs per word, or sentence if we tokenize sentences and statements, into more information-rich embeddings. The IDs themselves can be used as one-hot encodings, as discussed in *Chapter 4*, *Detecting Performance and Efficiency Issues in Machine Learning Models*, where each word gets a long vector with zeros for all elements and one for the token dedicated to the corresponding word. But these one-hot encodings don't provide us with any relationship between the words that work like data points in language modeling at the word level.

We can transform the words in a vocabulary into embeddings that can be used to capture semantic relationships between them and help our machine learning and deep learning models benefit from the new information-rich features across different language modeling tasks. Although models such as BERT and GPT-2 are not designed solely for embedding extraction for text, they can be used to generate embeddings for each word in a corpus of text. But there are other older methods such as Word2Vec (Mikolov et al., 2013), GloVe (Pennington et al., 2014), and fast-text (Bojanowski et al., 2017) that are designed for embedding generation. There are also more recent and more comprehensive models for word embedding such as Cohere (`https://txt.cohere.com/embedding-archives-wikipedia/`) that you can use to generate embeddings for text, in different languages, that you aim to embed and use for modeling.

## Language modeling using pre-trained models

There are pre-trained models that we can import into different deep learning frameworks, such as PyTorch, to use solely for inference or further fine-tuning with new data. Here, we want to practice this process with DistilBERT (Sanh et al., 2019), which is a faster and lighter version of BERT (Devlin et al., 2018). Specifically, we want to use `DistilBertForSequenceClassification()`, a model based on the DistilBERT architecture, that's been adapted for sequence classification tasks. In such processes, the model gets trained and can be used for inference for the task of assigning a label to a given sentence or statement. Examples of such label assignments are spam detection or semantic labeling, such as positive, negative, and neutral.

First, we will import the necessary libraries and classes from `torch` and `transformers`:

```
import torch
from torch.utils.data import DataLoader
from transformers import DistilBertTokenizerFast,
DistilBertForSequenceClassification, Trainer, TrainingArguments
```

Then, we will load the `imdb` dataset so that we can use it to train a model, as a fine-tuned version of `DistilBertForSequenceClassification()`:

```
from datasets import load_dataset
dataset = load_dataset("imdb")
```

Now, we can define a tokenizer function on top of the `DistilBertTokenizerFast()` tokenizer with `distilbert-base-uncased` as the pre-trained tokenizer:

```
tokenizer = DistilBertTokenizerFast.from_pretrained(
    "distilbert-base-uncased")

def tokenize(batch):
    return tokenizer(batch["text"], padding=True,
        truncation=True, max_length=512)
```

After, we can separate a small percentage (1%) of the imdb data for training and testing as we want to solely practice with this process, and using the whole dataset takes a long time in terms of training and testing:

```
train_dataset = dataset["train"].train_test_split(
    test_size=0.01)["test"].map(tokenize, batched=True)
test_dataset = dataset["test"].train_test_split(
    test_size=0.01)["test"].map(tokenize, batched=True)
```

Now, we can initialize the DistilBertForSequenceClassification() model while specifying the number of labels in the classification process. Here, this is 2:

```
model = DistilBertForSequenceClassification.from_pretrained(
    "distilbert-base-uncased", num_labels=2)
```

Now, we can train the model using separate training data from the imdb dataset for 3 epochs:

```
training_args = TrainingArguments(output_dir="./results",
    num_train_epochs=3,per_device_train_batch_size=8,
    per_device_eval_batch_size=8, logging_dir="./logs")

trainer = Trainer(model=model, args=training_args,
    train_dataset=train_dataset,eval_dataset=test_dataset)

trainer.train()
```

With that, the model has been trained and we can evaluate it on the separate test set from the imdb dataset:

```
eval_results = trainer.evaluate()
```

This results in a 0.35 evaluation loss.

There are many other available models you can use in your language modeling or inference tasks (for example, the PyTorch Transformers library: https://pytorch.org/hub/huggingface_pytorch-transformers/). There are also other sequence models, outside of language modeling, for areas such as the following:

- Audio modeling: https://pytorch.org/audio/main/models.html
- Time-series modeling: https://huggingface.co/docs/transformers/model_doc/time_series_transformer

- Forecasting: `https://pytorch-forecasting.readthedocs.io/en/stable/models.html`

- Video modeling: `https://pytorchvideo.org/)`

You can learn more about transformer modeling and how to make new architectures from scratch instead of using pre-trained models in PyTorch at `https://pytorch.org/tutorials/beginner/transformer_tutorial.html`.

In this section, you learned about modeling text as one type of sequence data. Next, we will cover modeling graphs, which are more complex data structures.

## Modeling graphs using deep neural networks

We can consider graphs as a more general structure of almost all non-tabular data we use for machine learning and deep learning modeling. Sequences can be considered **one-dimensional** (**1D**), while images or image shape data can be considered **two-dimensional** (**2D**) (see *Figure 13.7*). Earlier in this chapter, you learned how to start benefiting from CNNs and transformers in Python and PyTorch for sequence and image shape data. But more general graphs don't fit into these two graphs, which have predefined structures (see *Figure 13.7*), and we cannot simply model them using CNNs or sequence models:

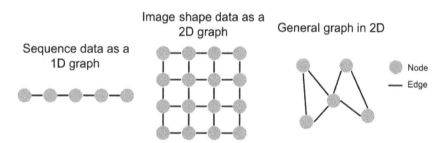

Figure 13.7 – Graph representation of different unstructured data types

Graphs have two important elements, called nodes and edges. The edges connect the nodes. The nodes and edges of graphs can have different characteristics that differentiate them from each other (see *Figure 13.8*):

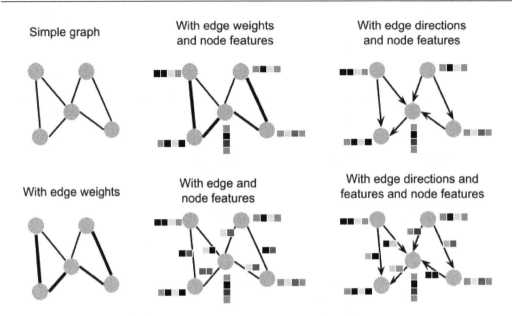

Figure 13.8 – Graph types according to their node and edge characteristics

We can have graphs where nodes have features, edges have weights or features, or edges have directions. Undirected graphs (graphs with undirected edges), for example, are useful for many applications, such as social media networks. Assuming each node in the graph of social media is a node, then the edges can determine which people are connected. The features of nodes in such graphs could be different characteristics of people in the social media network, such as their age, field of study or job title, city of residence, and so on. Directed graphs can be used in different applications, such as for causal modeling, which we'll discuss in *Chapter 15, Correlation versus Causality*.

As mentioned at the beginning of this section, techniques such as CNNs and transformers cannot be used directly on graphs. Due to this, we'll review other neural network techniques that can help you in modeling graphs in your projects.

## Graph neural networks

Graphs may have complicated structures as opposed to 2D images and 1D sequence data. However, we can model them using deep neural networks with the same idea as in CNNs and transformer models to rely on local patterns and relationships in the data. We can rely on local patterns in graphs and let the neural network learn from neighboring nodes instead of trying to learn information about the whole graph, which might contain thousands of nodes and millions of edges all at once. This is the idea behind **graph neural networks** (**GNNs**).

We can use GNNs for different tasks, such as the following:

- **Node classification**: We can aim to predict the class of each node in a graph using GNNs. For example, if you consider a graph of hotels in a city with edges being the shortest route between them, you can aim to predict which one gets filled in during the holidays. Or if you have a background in chemistry, you can use node classification to annotate amino acids in proteins using the 3D structure of proteins (Abdollahi et al., 2023).

- **Node selection**: Node selection for GNNs is a similar task to object detection for CNNs. We can design GNNs to identify and select nodes with specific characteristics, such as choosing people to suggest a product to in a graph of products and consumers.

- **Link prediction**: We can aim to predict unknown edges between already existing nodes or new nodes in a graph. For example, in a graph that's representative of a social media network, link prediction could be about predicting connections between people. Then, those individuals could be suggested to each other so that they can add each other to their networks of connections.

- **Graph classification**: Instead of aiming to predict or select nodes or edges, we can design GNNs to predict the characteristics of whole graphs (`https://chrsmrrs.github.io/datasets/`). In such cases, there could be graphs where each represents a data point, such as a drug molecule to be used in a GNN model for graph classification.

There are general taxonomies of different GNNs, such as the one suggested by Wu et al. (2020). But here, we want to focus on examples of widely used methods instead of getting too technical regarding the different categories of GNNs. Examples of methodologies that have been used successfully for modeling graphs are **Graph Convolutional Networks** (**GCNs**) (Kipf and Welling in 2016), **Graph Sample and Aggregation** (**GraphSAGE**) (Hamilton et al. in 2017), and **Graph Attention Networks** (**GATs**) (Veličković et al. in 2018). While most GNN techniques consider features for nodes, not all of them consider edge features. **Message Passing Neural Networks** (**MPNNs**) is an example of a technique that considers both node and edge features and was initially designed for producing graphs of drug molecules (Gilmer et al. in 2017).

You can build graphs from the data you have at hand or use publicly available datasets such as **Stanford Large Network Dataset Collection** (**SNAP**) to practice with different GNN techniques. SNAP has one of the largest collections of graph datasets you can download and start practicing with (`https://snap.stanford.edu/data/`).

Next, we will practice GNN modeling using PyTorch to help you better understand how to build such models in Python.

## GNNs with PyTorch Geometric

PyTorch Geometric is a Python library built upon PyTorch that helps you train and test GNNs. There is a series of tutorials you can benefit from to learn about GNN modeling using PyTorch Geometric (`https://pytorch-geometric.readthedocs.io/en/latest/notes/`

colabs.html). Here, we will practice the problem of node classification with code adapted from one of these tutorials (https://colab.research.google.com/drive/14OvFnAXgg xB8vM4e8vSURUp1TaKnovzX?usp=sharing#scrollTo=0YgHcLXMLk4o).

First, let's import the *CiteSeer* citation network dataset from Planetoid in PyTorch Geometric (Yang et al., 2016):

```python
from torch_geometric.datasets import Planetoid
from torch_geometric.transforms import NormalizeFeatures

dataset = Planetoid(root='data/Planetoid', name='CiteSeer',
    transform=NormalizeFeatures())
data = dataset[0]
```

Now, similar to initializing neural networks for FCNNs and CNNs, we must initialize a GCNet class for GNN modeling, but instead of using linear and convolutional layers, we will use GCNConv graph convolutional layers:

```python
import torch
from torch_geometric.nn import GCNConv
import torch.nn.functional as F
torch.manual_seed(123)


class GCNet(torch.nn.Module):
    def __init__(self, hidden_channels):
        super().__init__()
        self.gcn_layer1 = GCNConv(dataset.num_features,
            hidden_channels[0])
        self.gcn_layer2 = GCNConv(hidden_channels[0],
            hidden_channels[1])
        self.gcn_layer3 = GCNConv(hidden_channels[1],
            dataset.num_classes)

    def forward(self, x, edge_index):
        x = self.gcn_layer1(x, edge_index)
        x = x.relu()
        x = F.dropout(x, p=0.3, training=self.training)
        x = self.gcn_layer2(x, edge_index)
        x = x.relu()
        x = self.gcn_layer3(x, edge_index)

        return x
```

In the previous class, we used three GCNConv layers in combination with the ReLU activation function and dropout for regularization.

Now, we can use the defined GCNet class to initialize our model with hidden layers whose sizes are 128 and 16, both of which are arbitrary in this practice code. We must also initialize an optimizer while specifying the algorithm, which in this case is Adam, and a learning rate of 0.01 and a weight decay of 1e-4 for regularization:

```
model = GCNet(hidden_channels=[128, 16])
optimizer = torch.optim.Adam(model.parameters(), lr=0.01,
    weight_decay=1e-4)
criterion = torch.nn.CrossEntropyLoss()
```

Now, we can define our training function, which will be used for one-epoch training:

```
def train():
        model.train()
        optimizer.zero_grad()
        out = model(data.x, data.edge_index)
        loss = criterion(out[data.train_mask],
            data.y[data.train_mask])
        loss.backward()
        optimizer.step()
        return loss
```

With that, we are ready to go through a series of epochs and train the model. Please note that the following loop for training the model for 400 epochs might take a long time:

```
import numpy as np
epoch_list = []
loss_list = []
for epoch in np.arange(1, 401):
    loss = train()
    if epoch%20 == 0:
        print(f'Epoch: {epoch:03d}, Loss: {loss:.4f}')
        epoch_list.append(epoch)
        loss_list.append(loss.detach().numpy())
```

The following plot shows the learning curve (loss versus epoch) in the training process:

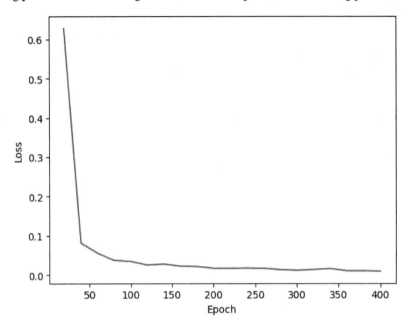

Figure 13.9 – The learning curve for the example GCN model on the CiteSeer dataset

We can also test the model on the test portion of the dataset, as follows:

```
model.eval()
pred = model(data.x, data.edge_index).argmax(dim=1)
test_correct = pred[data.test_mask] ==
    data.y[data.test_mask]
test_acc = int(test_correct.sum()) / int(
    data.test_mask.sum())
```

This results in an accuracy of 0.655. We can also generate a confusion matrix of the predictions on the test set:

```
from sklearn.metrics import confusion_matrix
cf = confusion_matrix(y_true = data.y, y_pred = model(
    data.x, data.edge_index).argmax(dim=1))
import seaborn as sns
sns.set()
sns.heatmap(cf, annot=True, fmt="d")
```

This results in the following matrix, shown as a heatmap. Although most of the predictions and true classes of data points match, many of them are misclassified and summarized outside of the diagonal elements of the confusion matrix:

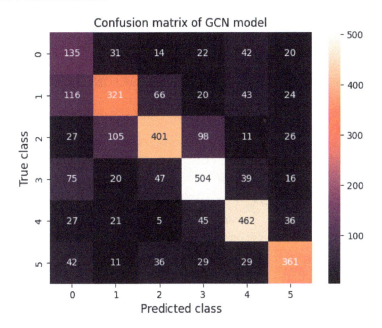

Figure 13.10 – Confusion matrix of the predictions over the test set
for the example GCN model on the CiteSeer dataset

In this section, we talked about techniques for modeling different data types and problems using deep learning. Now, you are ready to learn more about these advanced techniques and use them in your projects.

## Summary

In this chapter, you learned about advanced deep learning techniques, including CNNs, transformers, and GNNs. You were provided with some of the widely used or famous models that have been developed using each of these techniques. You also practiced building these advanced models either from scratch or fine-tuning them using Python and PyTorch. This knowledge helped you learn more about these techniques and start using them in your projects so that you can model images and image shape data, text and sequence data, and graphs.

In the next chapter, you will learn how recent advancements in generative modeling and prompt engineering, as well as self-supervised learning, can either help you in developing your projects or provide you with opportunities to develop interesting and useful tools and applications.

## Questions

1. What are some examples of problems you can use CNNs and GNNs for?

2. Does applying convolution preserve local patterns in images?

3. Could decreasing the number of tokens result in more mistakes in language models?

4. What is padding in the text tokenization process?

5. Are the network architecture classes we build for CNNs and GNNs in PyTorch similar?

6. When do you need edge features to build GNNs?

## References

- He, Kaiming, et al. *Deep residual learning for image recognition.* Proceedings of the IEEE conference on computer vision and pattern recognition. 2016.

- Tan, Mingxing, and Quoc Le. *Efficientnet: Rethinking model scaling for convolutional neural networks.* International conference on machine learning. PMLR, 2019.

- Howard, Andrew G., et al. *Mobilenets: Efficient convolutional neural networks for mobile vision applications.* arXiv preprint arXiv:1704.04861 (2017).

- Sandler, Mark, et al. *Mobilenetv2: Inverted residuals and linear bottlenecks.* Proceedings of the IEEE conference on computer vision and pattern recognition. 2018.

- Chollet, François. *Xception: Deep learning with depthwise separable convolutions.* Proceedings of the IEEE conference on computer vision and pattern recognition. 2017.

- Ronneberger, Olaf, Philipp Fischer, and Thomas Brox. *U-net: Convolutional networks for biomedical image segmentation.* Medical Image Computing and Computer-Assisted Intervention–MICCAI 2015: 18th International Conference, Munich, Germany, October 5-9, 2015, Proceedings, Part III 18. Springer International Publishing, 2015.

- He, Kaiming, et al. *Mask r-cnn.* Proceedings of the IEEE international conference on computer vision. 2017.

- Chen, Liang-Chieh, et al. *Deeplab: Semantic image segmentation with deep convolutional nets, atrous convolution, and fully connected crfs.* IEEE transactions on pattern analysis and machine intelligence 40.4 (2017): 834-848.

- Zhao, Hengshuang, et al. *Pyramid scene parsing network.* Proceedings of the IEEE conference on computer vision and pattern recognition. 2017.

- Ren, Shaoqing, et al. *Faster r-cnn: Towards real-time object detection with region proposal networks.* Advances in neural information processing systems 28 (2015).

- Redmon, Joseph, et al. *You only look once: Unified, real-time object detection.* Proceedings of the IEEE conference on computer vision and pattern recognition. 2016.

- Dong, Chao, et al. *Image super-resolution using deep convolutional networks*. IEEE transactions on pattern analysis and machine intelligence 38.2 (2015): 295-307.

- Dong, Chao, Chen Change Loy, and Xiaoou Tang. *Accelerating the super-resolution convolutional neural network*. Computer Vision–ECCV 2016: 14th European Conference, Amsterdam, The Netherlands, October 11-14, 2016, Proceedings, Part II 14. Springer International Publishing, 2016.

- Lim, Bee, et al. *Enhanced deep residual networks for single image super-resolution*. Proceedings of the IEEE conference on computer vision and pattern recognition workshops. 2017.

- Isola, Phillip, et al. *Image-to-image translation with conditional adversarial networks*. Proceedings of the IEEE conference on computer vision and pattern recognition. 2017.

- Zhu, Jun-Yan, et al. *Unpaired image-to-image translation using cycle-consistent adversarial networks*. Proceedings of the IEEE international conference on computer vision. 2017.

- Gatys, Leon A., Alexander S. Ecker, and Matthias Bethge. *Image style transfer using convolutional neural networks*. Proceedings of the IEEE conference on computer vision and pattern recognition. 2016.

- Huang, Xun, and Serge Belongie. *Arbitrary style transfer in real-time with adaptive instance normalization*. Proceedings of the IEEE international conference on computer vision. 2017.

- Schlegl, Thomas, et al. *Unsupervised anomaly detection with generative adversarial networks to guide marker discovery*. Information Processing in Medical Imaging: 25th International Conference, IPMI 2017, Boone, NC, USA, June 25-30, 2017, Proceedings. Cham: Springer International Publishing, 2017.

- Ruff, Lukas, et al. *Deep one-class classification*. International conference on machine learning. PMLR, 2018.

- Zhou, Chong, and Randy C. Paffenroth. *Anomaly detection with robust deep autoencoders*. Proceedings of the 23rd ACM SIGKDD international conference on knowledge discovery and data mining. 2017.

- Baek, Youngmin, et al. *Character region awareness for text detection*. Proceedings of the IEEE/CVF conference on computer vision and pattern recognition. 2019.

- Zhou, Xinyu, et al. *East: an efficient and accurate scene text detector*. Proceedings of the IEEE Conference on Computer Vision and Pattern Recognition. 2017.

- Tran, Du, et al. *Learning spatiotemporal features with 3d convolutional networks*. Proceedings of the IEEE international conference on computer vision. 2015.

- Carreira, Joao, and Andrew Zisserman. *Quo vadis, action recognition? a new model and the kinetics dataset*. Proceedings of the IEEE Conference on Computer Vision and Pattern Recognition. 2017.

- Feichtenhofer, Christoph, et al. *Slowfast networks for video recognition*. Proceedings of the IEEE/CVF international conference on computer vision. 2019.

- LeCun, Yann, et al. *Handwritten digit recognition with a back-propagation network*. Advances in neural information processing systems 2 (1989).

- Vaswani, Ashish, et al. *Attention is all you need*. Advances in neural information processing systems 30 (2017).

- Devlin, Jacob, et al. *Bert: Pre-training of deep bidirectional transformers for language understanding*. arXiv preprint arXiv:1810.04805 (2018).

- Touvron, Hugo, et al. *Llama: Open and efficient foundation language models*. arXiv preprint arXiv:2302.13971 (2023).

- Li, Yikuan, et al. *BEHRT: transformer for electronic health records*. Scientific reports 10.1 (2020): 1-12.

- Jumper, John, et al. *Highly accurate protein structure prediction with AlphaFold*. Nature 596.7873 (2021): 583-589.

- Xu, Jiehui, et al. *Anomaly transformer: Time series anomaly detection with association discrepancy*. arXiv preprint arXiv:2110.02642 (2021).

- Yuan, Li, et al. *Tokens-to-token vit: Training vision transformers from scratch on imagenet*. Proceedings of the IEEE/CVF international conference on computer vision. 2021.

- Liu, Yinhan, et al. *Roberta: A robustly optimized bert pretraining approach*. arXiv preprint arXiv:1907.11692 (2019).

- Lewis, Mike, et al. *Bart: Denoising sequence-to-sequence pre-training for natural language generation, translation, and comprehension*. arXiv preprint arXiv:1910.13461 (2019).

- Radford, Alec, et al. *Improving language understanding by generative pre-training*. (2018).

- Raffel, Colin, et al. *Exploring the limits of transfer learning with a unified text-to-text transformer*. The Journal of Machine Learning Research 21.1 (2020): 5485-5551.

- Sanh, Victor, et al. *DistilBERT, a distilled version of BERT: smaller, faster, cheaper and lighter*. arXiv preprint arXiv:1910.01108 (2019).

- Yang, Zhilin, et al. *Xlnet: Generalized autoregressive pretraining for language understanding*. Advances in neural information processing systems 32 (2019).

- Mikolov, Tomas, et al. *Efficient estimation of word representations in vector space*. arXiv preprint arXiv:1301.3781 (2013).

- Pennington, Jeffrey, Richard Socher, and Christopher D. Manning. *Glove: Global vectors for word representation*. Proceedings of the 2014 conference on empirical methods in natural language processing (EMNLP). 2014.

- Bojanowski, Piotr, et al. *Enriching word vectors with subword information*. Transactions of the association for computational linguistics 5 (2017): 135-146.

- Wu, Zonghan, et al. *A comprehensive survey on graph neural networks*. IEEE transactions on neural networks and learning systems 32.1 (2020): 4-24.

- Abdollahi, Nasim, et al. *NodeCoder: a graph-based machine learning platform to predict active sites of modeled protein structures*. arXiv preprint arXiv:2302.03590 (2023).

- Kipf, Thomas N., and Max Welling. *Semi-supervised classification with graph convolutional networks*. arXiv preprint arXiv:1609.02907 (2016).

- Hamilton, Will, Zhitao Ying, and Jure Leskovec. *Inductive representation learning on large graphs*. Advances in neural information processing systems 30 (2017).

- Velickovic, Petar, et al. *Graph attention networks*. stat 1050.20 (2017): 10-48550.

- Gilmer, Justin, et al. *Neural message passing for quantum chemistry*. International conference on machine learning. PMLR, 2017.

- Yang, Zhilin, William Cohen, and Ruslan Salakhudinov. *Revisiting semi-supervised learning with graph embeddings*. International conference on machine learning. PMLR, 2016.

# 14

# Introduction to Recent Advancements in Machine Learning

Supervised learning was the focus of the majority of successful applications of machine learning across different industries and application domains until 2020. However, other techniques, such as generative modeling, later caught the attention of developers and users of machine learning. So, an understanding of such techniques will help you to broaden your understanding of machine learning capabilities beyond supervised learning.

In this chapter, we will cover the following topics:

- Generative modeling
- Reinforcement learning
- Self-supervised learning

By the end of this chapter, you will have learned about the meaning, widely used techniques, and benefits of generative modeling, **reinforcement learning** (**RL**), and **self-supervised learning** (**SSL**). You will also practice some of these techniques using Python and PyTorch.

# Technical requirements

The following requirements are applicable to this chapter as they will help you better understand the concepts, be able to use them in your projects, and practice with the provided code:

- Python library requirements:

  - `torch` >= 2.0.0

  - `torchvision` >= 0.15.1

  - `matplotlib` >= 3.7.1

You can find the code files for this chapter on GitHub at `https://github.com/PacktPublishing/Debugging-Machine-Learning-Models-with-Python/tree/main/Chapter14`.

# Generative modeling

Generative modeling, or more generally Generative AI, provides you with the opportunity to generate data that is close to an expected or reference set of data points or distributions, commonly referred to as realistic data. One of the most successful applications of generative modeling has been in language modeling. The success story of **Generative Pre-trained Transformer** (**GPT**)-4 and ChatGPT (`https://openai.com/blog/chatgpt`), a chatbot built on top of GPT-4 and GPT-3.5, and similar tools such as Perplexity (`https://www.perplexity.ai/`), resulted in the rise in interest among engineers, scientists, people in different businesses such as finance and healthcare, and many other job roles in generative modeling. When using Chat-GPT or GPT-4, you can ask a question or provide the description of an ask, called a prompt, and then these tools generate a series of statements or data to provide you with the answer, information, or text you asked for.

In addition to the successful application of generative modeling in text generation, many other applications of generative modeling can help you in your work or studies. For example, GPT-4 and its previous versions or other similar models, such as LLaMA (Touvron et al., 2023), can be used for code generation and completion (`https://github.com/features/copilot/` and `https://github.com/sahil280114/codealpaca`). You can write the code you are interested in generating and it generates the corresponding code for you. Although the generated code might not work as expected all the time, it is usually close to what is expected, at least after a couple of trials.

There have also been many other successful applications of generative modeling, such as in image generation (`https://openai.com/product/dall-e-2`), drug discovery (Cheng et al., 2021), fashion design (Davis et al., 2023), manufacturing (Zhao et al., 2023), and so on.

Beginning in 2023, many traditional commercial tools and services started integrating Generative AI capabilities. For example, you can now edit photos using Generative AI in Adobe Photoshop simply by explaining what you need in plain English (`https://www.adobe.com/ca/products/photoshop/generative-fill.html`). WolframAlpha also combined its power of symbolic computation with Generative AI, which you can use to ask for specific symbolic processes in plain English (`https://www.wolframalpha.com/input?i=Generative+Adversarial+Networks`). Khan Academy (`https://www.khanacademy.org/`) designed a strategy to help teachers and students benefit from Generative AI, specifically ChatGPT, instead of it being harmful to the education of students.

These success stories have been achieved by relying on different deep learning techniques designed for generative modeling, which we will briefly review next.

## Generative deep learning techniques

There are multiple generative modeling approaches with available the APIs available in PyTorch or other deep learning frameworks, such as TensorFlow. Here, we will review some of them to help you start learning more about how they work and how you can use them in Python.

### Transformer-based text generation

You already learned that transformers, introduced in 2017 (Vaswani et al., 2017), are used to generate the most successful recent language models in *Chapter 13*, *Advanced Deep Learning Techniques*. However, these models are not useful only for tasks such as translation, which is traditional in natural language processing, but can be used in generative modeling to help us generate meaningful text, for example, in response to a question we ask. This is the approach behind GPT models, Chat-GPT, and many other generative language models. The process of providing a short text, as an ask or a question, is also called prompting, in which we need to provide a good prompt to get a good answer. We will talk about optimal prompting in the *Prompt engineering for text-based generative models* section.

### Variational autoencoders (VAEs)

Autoencoders are techniques with which you can reduce the number of features to an information-rich set of embeddings, which you can consider a more complicated version of **principal component analysis (PCA)** to better understand it. It does that by first attempting to encode the original space to the new embedding (called encoding), then decode the embeddings, and regenerate the original features for each data point (called decoding). In a VAE (Kingma and Welling, 2013), instead of one set of features (embeddings), it generates a distribution for each new feature. For example, instead of reducing the original 1,000 features to 100 features, each having one float value, you get 100 new variables, each being a normal (or Gaussian) distribution. The beauty of this process is that then you can select different values from these distributions for each variable and generate a new set of 100 embeddings. In the process of decoding them, these embeddings get decoded and a new set of features with the original size (1,000) gets generated. This process can be used for different types of data such as images (Vahdat et al., 2020) and graphs (Simonovsky et al., 2018; Wengong et al., 2018). You can find a collection of VAEs implemented in PyTorch at `https://github.com/AntixK/PyTorch-VAE`.

### *Generative Adversarial Networks (GANs)*

In this technique introduced in 2014 (Goodfellow et al., 2020), a discriminator that works like a supervised classification model and a generator work alongside each other. The generator, which could be a neural network architecture for generating the desired data types, such as images, generates images aiming to fool the discriminator into recognizing the generated data as real data. The discriminator learns to remain good at distinguishing generated data from real data. The generated data in some cases is called fake data, as in technologies and models such as deepfakes (`https://www.businessinsider.com/guides/tech/what-is-deepfake`). However, the generated data can be used as opportunities for new data points to be used in different applications, such as drug discovery (Prykhodko et al., 2019). You can use `torchgan` to implement GANs (`https://torchgan.readthedocs.io/en/latest/`).

As there has been an emerging generation of prompt-based technologies built on top of generative models, we will provide a better understanding of how to optimally design prompts next.

## Prompt engineering for text-based generative models

Prompt engineering is not only a recent topic in machine learning but has also become a highly paid job title. In prompt engineering, we aim to provide optimal prompts to generate the best possible result (for example, text, code, and images) and identify issues with the generative models as opportunities for improving them. A basic understanding of large language and generative models, your language proficiency, and domain knowledge for domain-specific data generation can help you in better prompting. There are free resources that you can use to learn about prompt engineering, such as a course by Andrew Ng and OpenAI (`https://www.deeplearning.ai/short-courses/chatgpt-prompt-engineering-for-developers/`) and some introductory content about prompt engineering released by Microsoft (`https://learn.microsoft.com/en-us/azure/cognitive-services/openai/concepts/prompt-engineering`). However, we will not leave you to learn this topic from scratch by yourself. We will provide you with some guidance for optimal prompting here that will help you improve your prompting skills.

### *Targeted prompting*

In our daily conversations, either at work, university, or home, there are ways we try to make sure the person across from us better understands what we mean, and as a result, we get a better response. For example, if you tell your friend, "Give me that" instead of "Give me that bottle of water on the desk," there is a chance that your friend won't give you the bottle of water or get confused about what exactly you are referring to. In prompting, you can get better responses and data generated, such as images, if you clearly explain what you want for a very specific task. Here are a few techniques to use for better prompting:

- **Be specific about the ask**: You can provide specific information such as the format of the data you would like to be generated, such as bullet points or code, and the task you are referring to, such as writing an email versus a business plan.

- **Specify who the data is getting generated for**: You can even specify an expertise or job title for whom the data is getting generated, such as generating a piece of text for a machine learning engineer, business manager, or software developer.

- **Specify time**: You can specify whether you want information about the date when technology got released, the first time something was announced, the chronological order of events, the change in something such as the net worth of a famous rich person such as Elon Musk over time, and so on.

- **Simplify the concepts**: You can provide a simplified version of what you ask to make sure the model doesn't get confused by the complexity of your prompt.

Although these techniques will help you in better prompting, there is still a chance of getting false answers with high confidence if you ask for a text response or unrelated data generation. This is what is usually referred to as a hallucination. One of the ways to decrease the chance of irrelevant or wrong responses or data generation is to provide tests for the model to use. When we write functions and classes in Python, we can design unit tests to make sure their output meets the expectation, as discussed in *Chapter 8, Controlling Risks Using Test-Driven Development.*

## Generative modeling using PyTorch

You can develop generative models based on different techniques discussed earlier in this chapter using PyTorch. We want to practice with VAEs here. With VAEs, the aim is to identify a probability distribution for a lower-dimensional representation of data. For example, the model learns about the mean and variance (or log variance) for the representations of the input parameters, assuming normal or Gaussian distribution for the latent space (that is, the space of the latent variables or representations).

We first import the required libraries and modules and load the `Flowers102` dataset from PyTorch:

```
transform = transforms.Compose([
    transforms.Resize((32, 32)),
    transforms.ToTensor()
])

train_dataset = datasets.Flowers102(root='./data',
    download=True, transform=transform)
train_loader = DataLoader(train_dataset, batch_size=32,
    shuffle=True)
```

Then, we define a class for the VAE as follows in which two linear layers are defined to encode the input pixels of images. Then, the mean and variance of the probability distribution of latent space are also defined by two linear layers for decoding the latent variables back to the original number of inputs to generate images similar to the input data. The learned mean and variance of the distribution in latent space will be then used to generate new latent variables and potentially generate new data:

```python
class VAE(nn.Module):
    def __init__(self):
        super(VAE, self).__init__()
        self.encoder = nn.Sequential(
            nn.Linear(32 * 32 * 3, 512),
            nn.ReLU(),
            nn.Linear(512, 128),
            nn.ReLU(),
        )self.fc_mean = nn.Linear(128, 32)
        self.fc_var = nn.Linear(128, 32)
        self.decoder = nn.Sequential(
            nn.Linear(32, 128),
            nn.ReLU(),
            nn.Linear(128, 512),
            nn.ReLU(),
            nn.Linear(512, 32 * 32 * 3),
            nn.Sigmoid(),
        )
    def forward(self, x):
        h = self.encoder(x.view(-1, 32 * 32 * 3))
        mean, logvar = self.fc_mean(h), self.fc_var(h)
        std = torch.exp(0.5*logvar)
        q = torch.distributions.Normal(mean, std)
        z = q.rsample()
        return self.decoder(z), mean, logvar
```

We now initialize the defined VAE class and determine the Adam optimizer as the optimization algorithm with 0.002 as the learning rate:

```python
model = VAE()
optimizer = optim.Adam(model.parameters(), lr=2e-3)
device = torch.device("cuda" if torch.cuda.is_available() else "cpu")
model.to(device)
```

We then define a loss function using `binary_cross_entropy` as follows to compare the regenerated pixels with the input pixels:

```python
def loss_function(recon_x, x, mu, logvar):
    BCE = nn.functional.binary_cross_entropy(recon_x,
        x.view(-1, 32 * 32 * 3), reduction='sum')
    KLD = -0.5 * torch.sum(
        1 + logvar - mu.pow(2) - logvar.exp())
    return BCE + KLD
```

Now we are ready to train the model using the `Flowers102` dataset we loaded before:

```python
n_epoch = 400

for epoch in range(n_epoch):
    model.train()
    train_loss = 0
    for batch_idx, (data, _) in enumerate(train_loader):
        data = data.to(device)
        optimizer.zero_grad()
        recon_batch, mean, logvar = model(data)
        loss = loss_function(recon_batch, data, mean,
            logvar)
        loss.backward()
        train_loss += loss.item()
        optimizer.step()

    print(f'Epoch: {epoch} Average loss: {
        train_loss / len(train_loader.dataset):.4f}')
```

We can then use this trained model to generate images that almost look like flowers (see *Figure 14.1*). Upon hyperparameter optimization, such as changing the model's architecture, you can achieve better results. You can review hyperparameter optimization in deep learning in *Chapter 12, Going Beyond ML Debugging with Deep Learning*.

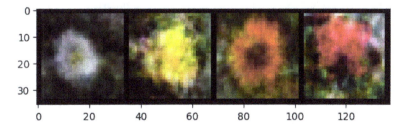

Figure 14.1 – Example images generated by the simple VAE we developed earlier

This was a simple example of generative modeling using PyTorch. In spite of the success of generative modeling, part of the recent success of tools developed using generative models, such as Chat-GPT, is due to the smart use of reinforcement learning, which we will discuss next.

# Reinforcement learning

**Reinforcement learning (RL)** is not a new idea or technique. The initial idea dates back to the 1950s, when it was introduced by Richard Bellman with the concept of the Bellman equation (Sutton and Barto, 2018). However, its recent combination with human feedback, which we will explain in the next section, provided a new opportunity for its utility in developing machine learning technologies. The general idea of RL is to learn by experience, or interaction with a specified environment, instead of using a collected set of data points for training, as in supervised learning. An agent is considered in RL, which learns how to improve actions to get a greater reward (Kaelbling et al., 1996). The agent learns to improve its approach to taking action, or policy in more technical terminology, iteratively after receiving the reward of the action taken in the previous step.

In the history of RL, two important developments and utilities resulted in an increase in its popularity including the development of Q-learning (Watkins, 1989) and combining RL and deep learning (Mnih et al., 2013) using Q-learning. In spite of the success stories behind RL and the intuition that it mimics learning by experience as humans do, it has been shown that deep reinforcement learning is not data efficient and requires large amounts of data or iterative experience, which makes it fundamentally different from human learning (Botvinick et al., 2019).

More recently, **reinforcement learning with human feedback** (**RLHF**) was used as a successful application of reinforcement learning to improve the results of generative models, which we will discuss next.

## Reinforcement learning with human feedback (RLHF)

With reinforcement learning with human feedback, the reward is calculated based on the feedback of humans, either experts or non-experts, depending on the problem. However, the reward is not like a predefined mathematical formula considering the complexity of the problems such as language modeling. The feedback provided by humans results in improving the model step by step. For example, the training process of a RLHF language model can be summarized as follows (`https://huggingface.co/blog/rlhf`):

1. Training a language model, which is referred to as pretraining.
2. Data collection and training the reward model.
3. Fine-tuning the language model with reinforcement learning using the reward model.

However, learning how to use PyTorch to design RLHF-based models could be helpful to better understand this concept.

## RLHF with PyTorch

One of the major challenges in benefitting from RLHF is designing an infrastructure for human feedback collection and curation, then providing them to calculate the reward, and then improving the main pre-trained model. Here, we don't want to get into that aspect of RLHF but rather go through a simple code example to understand how such feedback can be incorporated into a machine learning model. There are good resources, such as `https://github.com/lucidrains/PaLM-rlhf-pytorch`, that help you to improve your understanding of RLHF and how to implement it using Python and PyTorch.

Here, we will use GPT-2 (`https://huggingface.co/transformers/v1.2.0/_modules/pytorch_transformers/modeling_gpt2.html`) as the pre-trained model. First, we import the necessary libraries and modules and initialize the model, tokenizer, and optimizer, which is chosen to be Adam:

```
import torch
from transformers import GPT2LMHeadModel, GPT2Tokenizer
from torch import optim
from torch.utils.data import DataLoader

# Pretrain a GPT-2 language model
tokenizer = GPT2Tokenizer.from_pretrained('gpt2')
model = GPT2LMHeadModel.from_pretrained('gpt2')
optimizer = optim.Adam(model.parameters(), lr=1e-3)
```

Now, assuming we collected the human feedback and formatted it properly, we can use it to create a DataLoader from PyTorch:

```
dataloader = DataLoader(dataset, batch_size=1, shuffle=True)
```

The next step is to design a reward model, for which we use a two-layer fully connected neural network:

```
class Reward_Model(torch.nn.Module):
    def __init__(self, input_size, hidden_size, output_size):
        super(RewardModel, self).__init__()
        self.fc_layer1 = torch.nn.Linear(input_size,
            hidden_size)
        self.fc_layer2 = torch.nn.Linear(hidden_size,
            output_size)

    def forward(self, x):
        x = torch.relu(self.fc_layer1(x))
        x = self.fc_layer2(x)
        return x
```

We then initialize the reward model using the previously defined class:

```
reward_model = Reward_Model(input_size, hidden_size, output_size)
```

We are now ready to improve our pre-trained model using the collected human feedback and the reward model. If you pay attention to the following code, the main difference between this simple loop over epochs and batches for model training compared to neural networks without a reward model is the reward calculation and then using it for loss calculation:

```
for epoch in range(n_epochs):
    for batch in dataloader:
        input_ids = tokenizer.encode(batch['input'],
            return_tensors='pt')
        output_ids = tokenizer.encode(batch['output'],
            return_tensors='pt')
        reward = reward_model(batch['input'])
        loss = model(input_ids, labels=output_ids).loss * reward
        loss.backward()
        optimizer.step()
        optimizer.zero_grad()
```

This was a very simple example of designing RLHF-based model improvement, used to help you better understand the concept. Resources such as `https://github.com/lucidrains/PaLM-rlhf-pytorch` will help you to implement more complex ways of incorporating such human feedback for improving your models.

Next, let's go through another interesting topic in machine learning, called self-supervised learning.

## Self-supervised learning (SSL)

**Self-supervised learning (SSL)** is not a new concept. It's similar to RL, but it gained attention after its combination with deep learning due to its effectiveness in learning data representations. Examples of such models are Word2vec for language modeling (Mikolov et al., 2013) and Meta's RoBERTa models trained using SSL, which achieved state-of-the-art performance on several language modeling tasks. The idea of SSL is to define an objective for the machine learning model that doesn't rely on pre-labeling or the quantification of data points – for example, predicting the positions of objects or people in videos for each time step using previous time steps, masking parts of images or sequence data, and aiming to refill those masked sections. One of the widely used applications of such models is in RL to learn representations of images and text, and then use those representations in other contexts, for example, in supervised modeling of smaller datasets with data labels (Kolesnikov et al., 2019, Wang et al., 2020).

There are multiple techniques under the umbrella of SSL, three of which are as follows:

- **Contrastive learning**: The idea of contrastive learning is to learn representations that result in similar data points being closer to each other compared to dissimilar data points (Jaiswal et al., 2020).

- **Autoregressive models**: In autoregressive modeling, the model aims to predict the next data points, either based on time or a specific sequence order, given the previous ones. This is a very popular technique in language modeling, where models such as GPT predict the next word in a sentence (Radford et al., 2019).

- **Self-supervision via inpainting**: In this approach, we mask parts of the data and train the models to fill in the missing parts. For example, a portion of an image might be masked, and the model is trained to predict the masked portion. Masked autoencoder is an example of such a technique in which the masked portions of images are refilled in the decoding process of the autoencoder (Zhang et al., 2022).

Next, we will practice with a simple example of self-supervised modeling using Python and PyTorch.

## Self-supervised learning with PyTorch

From a programming perspective, the main difference between deep learning for SSL compared to supervised learning is in defining the objectives and data for training and testing. Here, we want to practice with **self-supervision via inpainting** using a masked image autoencoder based on convolutional layers. We also use the same `Flowers102` dataset we used to practice with RLHF.

We first define the neural network class using two encoding and decoding `torch.nn.Conv2d()` layers as follows:

```
class Conv_AE(nn.Module):
    def __init__(self):
        super(Conv_AE, self).__init__()
        # Encoding data
        self.encoding_conv1 = nn.Conv2d(3, 8, 3, padding=1)
        self.encoding_conv2 = nn.Conv2d(8, 32, 3,padding=1)
        self.pool = nn.MaxPool2d(2, 2)
        # Decoding data
        self.decoding_conv1 = nn.ConvTranspose2d(32, 8, 2,
            stride=2)
        self.decoding_conv2 = nn.ConvTranspose2d(8, 3, 2,
            stride=2)

    def forward(self, x):
        # Encoding data
        x = torch.relu(self.encoding_conv1(x))
```

```
x = self.pool(x)
x = torch.relu(self.encoding_conv2(x))
x = self.pool(x)
# Decoding data
x = torch.relu(self.decoding_conv1(x))
x = self.decoding_conv2(x)
x = torch.sigmoid(x)

return x
```

We then initialize the model, specify `torch.nn.MSELoss()` as the criterion for comparison of predicted and true images, and `torch.optim.Adam()` as the optimizer with a learning rate of `0.001`:

```
model = Conv_AE().to(device)
criterion = nn.MSELoss()
optimizer = torch.optim.Adam(model.parameters(), lr=0.001)
```

The following function helps us to implement masking on random 8x8 portions of each image, which then the autoencoder learns to fill:

```
def create_mask(size=(32, 32), mask_size=8):
    mask = np.ones((3, size[0], size[1]), dtype=np.float32)
    height, width = size
    m_height, m_width = mask_size, mask_size
    top = np.random.randint(0, height - m_height)
    left = np.random.randint(0, width - m_width)
    mask[:, top:top+m_height, left:left+m_width] = 0
    return torch.from_numpy(mask)
```

Then, we train the model for 200 epochs as follows. As you can see in *Figure 14.2*, the images first get masked, and then in the decoding step, the autoencoder attempts to rebuild the full image, including the masked portions:

```
n_epoch = 200
for epoch in range(n_epoch):
    for data in train_loader:
        img, _ = data
        # Creating mask for small part in training images
        mask = create_mask().to(device)
        img_masked = img * mask
        img = img.to(device)
        img_masked = img_masked.to(device)

        optimizer.zero_grad()
```

```
outputs = model(img_masked)
loss = criterion(outputs, img)
loss.backward()
optimizer.step()
```

As you can see in the examples of the resulting refilled images shown in *Figure 14.2*, the model could find the patterns correctly. However, with proper hyperparameter optimization and designing models with better neural network architectures, you can achieve higher performance and better models.

Figure 14.2 – Example images (first row), their masked versions (second row), and regenerated versions (third row) using the convolutional autoencoder model

You can read more about SSL and the other techniques provided in this chapter using the provided resources and references to better understand these concepts.

## Summary

In this chapter, you gained a high-level understanding of recent advancements in machine learning modeling beyond supervised learning, including generative modeling, reinforcement learning, and self-supervised learning. You also learned about optimal prompting and prompt engineering to benefit from tools and applications built on top of generative models that accept text prompts as input from users. You were provided with the relevant code repositories and functionalities available in Python and PyTorch that will help you to start learning more about these advanced techniques. This knowledge helps you not only better understand how they work if you come across them but also start building models of your own using these advanced techniques.

In the next chapter, you will learn about the benefits of identifying causal relationships in machine learning modeling and practice with Python libraries that help you in implementing causal modeling.

## Questions

1.  What are examples of generative deep learning techniques?

2.  What are examples of generative text models that use transformers?

3.  What are generators and discriminators in GANs?

4.  What are some of the techniques you can use for better prompting?

5.  Could you explain how RL could be helpful in importing the results of generative models?

6.  Briefly explain contrastive learning.

## References

- Cheng, Yu, et al. "*Molecular design in drug discovery: a comprehensive review of deep generative models.*" Briefings in bioinformatics 22.6 (2021): bbab344.

- Davis, Richard Lee, et al. "*Fashioning the Future: Unlocking the Creative Potential of Deep Generative Models for Design Space Exploration.*" Extended Abstracts of the 2023 CHI Conference on Human Factors in Computing Systems (2023).

- Zhao, Yaoyao Fiona, et al., eds. "*Design for Advanced Manufacturing.*" Journal of Mechanical Design 145.1 (2023): 010301.

- Touvron, Hugo, et al. "*Llama: Open and efficient foundation language models.*" arXiv preprint arXiv:2302.13971 (2023).

- Vaswani, Ashish, et al. "*Attention is all you need.*" Advances in neural information processing systems 30 (2017).

- Kingma, Diederik P., and Max Welling. "*Auto-encoding variational bayes.*" arXiv preprint arXiv:1312.6114 (2013).

- Vahdat, Arash, and Jan Kautz. "*NVAE: A deep hierarchical variational autoencoder.*" Advances in neural information processing systems 33 (2020): 19667-19679.

- Simonovsky, Martin, and Nikos Komodakis. *"Graphvae: Towards generation of small graphs using variational autoencoders." Artificial Neural Networks and Machine Learning–ICANN 2018: 27th International Conference on Artificial Neural Networks*, Rhodes, Greece, October 4-7, 2018, Proceedings, Part I 27. Springer International Publishing (2018).

- Jin, Wengong, Regina Barzilay, and Tommi Jaakkola. *"Junction tree variational autoencoder for molecular graph generation." International conference on machine learning*. PMLR (2018).

- Goodfellow, Ian, et al. *"Generative adversarial networks." Communications of the ACM* 63.11 (2020): 139-144.

- Karras, Tero, Samuli Laine, and Timo Aila. *"A style-based generator architecture for generative adversarial networks." Proceedings of the IEEE/CVF conference on computer vision and pattern recognition* (2019).

- Prykhodko, Oleksii, et al. *"A de novo molecular generation method using latent vector based generative adversarial network." Journal of Cheminformatics* 11.1 (2019): 1-13.

- Sutton, Richard S., and Andrew G. Barto. *Reinforcement learning: An introduction*. MIT Press (2018).

- Kaelbling, Leslie Pack, Michael L. Littman, and Andrew W. Moore. *"Reinforcement learning: A survey." Journal of artificial intelligence research* 4 (1996): 237-285.

- Watkins, Christopher John Cornish Hellaby. *Learning from delayed rewards*. (1989).

- Mnih, Volodymyr, et al. *"Playing atari with deep reinforcement learning."* arXiv preprint arXiv:1312.5602 (2013).

- Botvinick, Matthew, et al. *"Reinforcement learning, fast and slow." Trends in cognitive sciences* 23.5 (2019): 408-422.

- Kolesnikov, Alexander, Xiaohua Zhai, and Lucas Beyer. *"Revisiting self-supervised visual representation learning." Proceedings of the IEEE/CVF conference on computer vision and pattern recognition* (2019).

- Wang, Jiangliu, Jianbo Jiao, and Yun-Hui Liu. *"Self-supervised video representation learning by pace prediction." Computer Vision–ECCV 2020: 16th European Conference*, Glasgow, UK, August 23–28, 2020, Proceedings, Part XVII 16. Springer International Publishing (2020).

- Jaiswal, Ashish, et al. *"A survey on contrastive self-supervised learning." Technologies* 9.1 (2020): 2.

- Radford, Alec, et al. *"Language models are unsupervised multitask learners."* OpenAI blog 1.8 (2019): 9.

- Zhang, Chaoning, et al. *"A survey on masked autoencoder for self-supervised learning in vision and beyond."* arXiv preprint arXiv:2208.00173 (2022).

# Part 5:
# Advanced Topics
# in Model Debugging

In the concluding part of this book, we will address some of the most pivotal topics in machine learning. We will begin by explaining differences between correlation and causality, shedding light on their distinct implications in model development. Transitioning to the topic of security and privacy, we will discuss the pressing concerns, challenges, and techniques that ensure our models are both robust and respectful of user data. We will wrap up the book with an explanation of human-in-the -loop machine learning, emphasizing the synergy between human expertise and automated systems, and how this collaboration paves the way for more effective solutions.

This part has the following chapters:

- *Chapter 15, Correlation versus Causality*
- *Chapter 16, Security and Privacy in Machine Learning*
- *Chapter 17, Human-in-the-Loop Machine Learning*

# 15

# Correlation versus Causality

In previous chapters of this book, you learned how to train, evaluate, and build high-performance and low-bias machine learning models. However, the algorithms and example methods we used to practice the concepts that were introduced in this book do not necessarily provide you with a causal relationship between features and output variables in a supervised learning setting. In this chapter, we will discuss how causal inference and modeling could help you increase the reliability of your models in production.

In this chapter, we will cover the following topics:

- Correlation as part of machine learning models

- Causal modeling to reduce risks and improve performance

- Assessing causation in machine learning models

- Causal modeling using Python

By the end of this chapter, you will have learned about the benefits of causal modeling and inference compared to correlative modeling and practice with available Python functionalities to identify the causal relationship between features and output variables.

## Technical requirements

You need the following for this chapter as they will help you better understand the concepts, use them in your projects, and practice with the provided code:

- Python library requirements:

  - dowhy == 0.5.1

  - bnlearn == 0.7.16

- `sklearn >= 1.2.2`
- `d3blocks == 1.3.0`

- You will also require basic knowledge of machine learning model training, validation, and testing

The code files for this chapter are available on GitHub at `https://github.com/PacktPublishing/Debugging-Machine-Learning-Models-with-Python/tree/main/Chapter15`.

## Correlation as part of machine learning models

The majority of machine learning modeling and data analysis projects result in correlative relationships between features and output variables in supervised learning settings and statistical modeling. Although these relationships are not causal, identifying causal relationships is of high value, even if it's not a necessity in most problems we try to solve. For example, we can define medical diagnosis as *"The identification of the diseases that are most likely to be causing the patient's symptoms, given their medical history."* (Richens et al., 2020).

Identifying causal relationships resolves issues in identifying misleading relationships between variables. Relying solely on correlations rather than causality could result in spurious and bizarre associations such as the following (`https://www.tylervigen.com/spurious-correlations; https://www.buzzfeednews.com/article/kjh2110/the-10-most-bizarre-correlations`):

- US spending on science, space, and technology correlates with suicides by hanging, strangulation, and suffocation
- Total revenue generated by arcades correlates with computer science doctorates awarded in the US
- US crude oil imports from Norway correlates with drivers killed in collisions with railway trains
- Eating organic food correlates with autism
- Obesity correlates with the debt bubble

You can find more of these spurious correlations in the sources for these examples.

Relying on correlations versus causation could decrease the reliability of different aspects of technology development and improvement processes such as AB testing. For example, understanding "if we get more visitors to search, we'll see an increase in purchases and revenue" (`https://conversionsciences.com/correlation-causation-impact-ab-testing/`) helps in proper decision-making and investment in technology development.

Now that you understand the problems with relying solely on correlative relationships, let's discuss what causal modeling means in a machine learning setting.

# Causal modeling to reduce risks and improve performance

Causal modeling helps in eliminating unreliable correlative relationships between variables. Eliminating such unreliable relationships reduces the risks of wrong decision-making across different domains of applications for machine learning, such as healthcare. Decisions in healthcare, such as diagnosing diseases and assigning effective treatment regimens to patients, have a direct effect on quality of life and survival. Hence, decisions need to be based on reliable models and relationships in which causal modeling and inference could help us (Richens et al., 2020; Prosperi et al., 2020; Sanchez et al., 2022).

Causal modeling techniques help in eliminating bias, such as confounding and collider bias, in our models (Prosperi et al., 2020) (*Figure 15.1*). An example of such bias is smoking as a confounder of the relationship between yellow fingers and lung cancer (Prosperi et al., 2020). As shown in *Figure 15.1*, the existence of collider variables results in correlative, but biased and unreal, associations between some of the input variables and outcome. Also, not having some of the variables that could be confounding in our modeling could result in us concluding other variables are associated with the outcome:

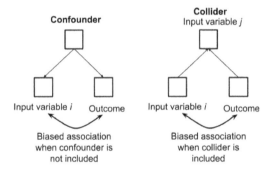

Figure 15.1 – Schematic representation of confounding and collider bias

Next, we will mention some concepts and techniques in causal modeling such as causal inference and how to test causation in a machine learning model.

# Assessing causation in machine learning models

Calculating the correlation between features and outcomes in machine learning modeling has been a common approach in many fields and industries. For example, we can simply calculate the Pearson correlation coefficient to identify correlative features with the target variable. There are also features in many of our machine learning models that contribute to the prediction of outcomes not as causal but rather as correlative predictors. There are several ways to differentiate between such correlative and causal features with the available functionalities in Python. Here are a few examples:

- **Experimental design**: One way to establish causality is to conduct experiments where we measure the effect of changes in the causal feature on the target variable. However, such experimental studies may not always be feasible or ethical.

- **Feature importance**: We can use explainability techniques, as presented in *Chapter 6, Interpretability and Explainability in Machine Learning Modeling*, to identify feature importance and use such information to discriminate between correlation and causality.

- **Causal inference**: Causal inference methods aim to identify the causal relationship between variables. You can use causal inference to determine whether a change in one variable causes a change in another variable.

We discussed different explainability techniques such as SHAP, LIME, and counterfactual explanations in *Chapter 6, Interpretability and Explainability in Machine Learning Modeling*. You can use these techniques to identify features that are not causal in your models. For example, features with low SHAP values most probably are not causal in the model under investigation. If there is a feature with low importance in the local approximation, according to LIME, then it is likely to not be causal regarding the output of your model. Or if changing a feature has little or no effect on the output of your model, through counterfactual analysis, then it is likely not a causal feature.

We can also use another technique, called **permutation feature importance**, which is also considered under the umbrella of explainability techniques to identify features with a low chance of being causal. In this approach, we change the values of a feature and measure the effect of change on the model's performance. Then we can identify features with low effects that are likely to not be causal.

We already practiced explainability techniques in *Chapter 6, Interpretability and Explainability in Machine Learning Modeling*. We will focus on causal inference for the remainder of this chapter.

## Causal inference

In causal inference, we aim to identify and understand the causal relationship between variables in a dataset or model. In this process, we might rely on different statistical and machine learning techniques to analyze data and infer causal relationships between variables. *Figure 15.2* shows five such methods: **experimental design**, **observational studies**, **propensity score matching**, **instrumental variables**, and **machine learning-based methods**:

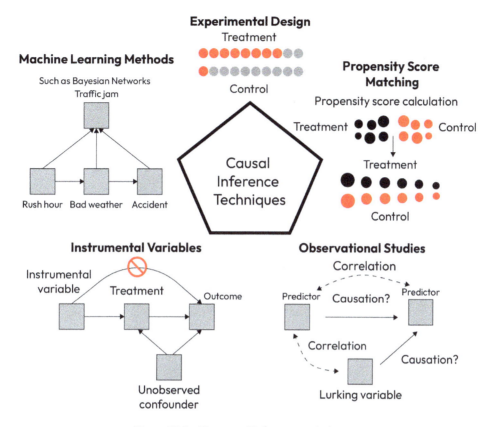

Figure 15.2 – Five causal inference techniques

In **experimental design,** you design experiments to compare outcome variables for samples with differences in a treatment variable, or different conditions based on a specific feature or characteristics. Examples of treatment and outcome variables are provided in *Table 15.1* to help you understand the difference between these two terms:

| Treatment Variable | Outcome Variable |
|---|---|
| Education level | Income level |
| Smoking | Lung cancer |
| Physical activity | Cardiovascular health |
| Family income | Academic performance |

Table 15.1 – Examples of treatment and outcome variables in causal modeling

In **observational studies**, we use observational data, instead of controlled experiments, and try to identify causal relationships by controlling confounding variables. **Propensity score matching** matches treatment and control groups based on the probability of receiving the treatment given the observed variables. **Instrumental variables** is used to overcome a common problem in observational studies where the treatment and outcome variables are jointly determined by other variables, or confounders, that are not included in the model. This approach starts with identifying an instrument that is correlated with the treatment variable and uncorrelated with the outcome variable, except through its effect on the treatment variable. **Machine learning-based methods** are other categories of techniques where machine learning methods such as Bayesian networks and decision trees are used to identify causal relationships between variables and outcomes.

## Bayesian networks

You can benefit from Bayesian networks in causal modeling and identifying causal relationships between variables. Bayesian networks are graphical models that show the relationship between variables through **directed acyclic graphs** (**DAGs**), where each variable, including the input features and outputs, is a node and directions show the relationship between variables (*Figure 15.3*):

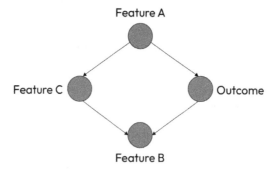

Figure 15.3 – Illustrating an example Bayesian network

What this network tells us is that higher values of **Feature A** and **Feature B** make it more likely for the outcome to occur. Note that the features could be numerical or categorical. Although the directions, such as from Feature A to the outcome (*Figure 15.3*), don't necessarily mean causality, Bayesian networks can be used for estimating the causal effects of variables on the outcome while controlling the confounding variables.

From a probabilistic perspective, the network can be used to simplify the joint probability of all the variables, including the features and outcome, as follows:

$$p(F_A, F_B, F_C, Outcome) = p(Outcome|F_A, F_B)p(F_B|F_C)p(F_C|F_A)p(F_A)$$

Here, $p(Outcome|F_A, F_B)$ is the **conditional probability distribution** (**CPD**) of the outcome given the values of Features A and B, $p(F_B|F_C)$ is the CPD of Feature B given Feature C, $p(F_C|F_A)$ is the CPD of Feature C given Feature A, and $p(F_A)$ is the probability of Feature A that is not conditional to other features as no edge is directed toward it in the graph. These CPDs can help us estimate the effect of change one feature value has on another. It tells us about the likelihood of the occurrence of one variable given the occurrence of one or more variables. You will learn how to make a Bayesian network in a data-driven way for a given dataset and how to identify the CPDs of the network using Python by the end of this chapter.

There are several methods available in Python for causal inference. We'll cover these next.

# Causal modeling using Python

Several Python libraries provide you with easy-to-use functionalities for using causal methods and conducting causal inference. Some of these are as follows:

- dowhy (https://pypi.org/project/dowhy/)

- pycausalimpact (https://pypi.org/project/pycausalimpact/)

- causalnex (https://pypi.org/project/causalnex/)

- econml (https://pypi.org/project/econml/)

- bnlearn (https://pypi.org/project/bnlearn/)

In the next few subsections, we will review dowhy and bnlearn.

## Using dowhy for causal effect estimation

First, we want to practice with a propensity score matching approach that is useful when you have a treatment variable in mind – for example, when you want to identify the effect of a drug on patients and have other variables in the model, such as their diet, age, sex, and so on. Here, we will use the breast cancer dataset of scikit-learn, where the target variable is a binary outcome telling us about the cells, from masses of breast cancer patients, as being from malignant or benign masses. Here, we will use the mean *radius* feature – the mean distance from the center to points on the perimeter – as the treatment variable.

First, we must import the required libraries and modules in Python:

```
import pandas as pd
import numpy as np
from sklearn.datasets import load_breast_cancer
import dowhy
from dowhy import CausalModel
```

Then, we must load the breast cancer dataset and convert it into a DataFrame:

```
breast_cancer = load_breast_cancer()
data = pd.DataFrame(breast_cancer.data,
```

```
        columns=breast_cancer.feature_names)
data['target'] = breast_cancer.target
```

Now, we need to convert the numerical values of the treatment variable, the mean radius, into a binary as propensity scoring matching only accepts binary treatment variables:

```
data['mean radius'] = data['mean radius'].gt(data[
    'mean radius'].values.mean()).astype(int)
data=data.astype({'mean radius':'bool'}, copy=False)
```

We also need to make a list of common causes, which in this case we consider as being all the other attributes in the dataset:

```
common_causes_list = data.columns.values.tolist()
common_causes_list.remove('mean radius')
common_causes_list.remove('target')
```

Now, we can build a model using `CausalModel()` from dowhy by specifying the data, treatment, outcome variable, and common causes. The `CausalModel()` object helps us estimate the causal effect of the `treatment` variable (mean radius) on the outcome variable (`target`):

```
model = CausalModel(
    data=data,
    treatment='mean radius',
    outcome='target',
    common_causes=common_causes_list
)
```

Now, we can estimate the causal effect of the specified treatment variable, the mean radius, on the target variable. Note that propensity score matching, which we're using here, is applicable only for discrete treatment variables:

```
identified_est = model.identify_effect()
estimate = model.estimate_effect(identified_est,
    method_name='backdoor.propensity_score_matching')
```

The `estimate` value is -0.279, which means that the probability of the outcome is decreased by ~28% with the high mean radius as the treatment variable. This propensity score is the conditional probability of receiving the treatment (high mean radius) given a set of observed covariates. The backdoor adjustment controls the confounding variables, which are associated with both the treatment and outcome variables.

We can also use `refute_estimate()` to assess the validity of our hypothesis regarding the causal variables and their data-driven estimated effects on the outcome. For example, we can use the `'placebo_treatment_refuter'` method, which replaces the specified treatment variable with an independent random variable. If our assumption of causality between the treatment and outcome is correct, then the new estimate goes close to zero. Here is the code to check the validity of our assumption using `'placebo_treatment_refuter'`:

```
refute_results = model.refute_estimate(identified_estimand,
    estimate, method_name='placebo_treatment_refuter',
    placebo_type='permute', num_simulations=40)
```

This results in the new effect of 0.0014, which is an assurance about the validity of our assumption. However, the *p*-value estimate, which is another output of this command, is 0.48, which shows the level of statistical confidence.

A low *p*-value from `refute_estimate()` does not mean that the treatment variable is not causal. A low *p*-value shows the sensitivity of the estimated causal effect to the specific assumption being tested. The significance of the refutation result does not imply the absence of a causal relationship between the treatment variable and the outcome variable.

## Using bnlearn for causal inference through Bayesian networks

One of the libraries that exists in both the Python and R programming languages for Bayesian network learning and inference is `bnlearn`. We can learn a Bayesian network for a given dataset using this library and then use the learned graph to infer causal relationships.

To practice with `bnlearn`, we must install and then import this library and load the Sprinkler dataset that exists as part of it:

```
import bnlearn as bn
df = bn.import_example('sprinkler')
```

Next, we must fit a `structure_learning()` model to generate a Bayesian network or a DAG:

```
DAG = bn.structure_learning.fit(df)
```

Then, we must define the properties of the nodes and visualize the DAG, as follows:

```
# Set some colors to the edges and nodes
node_properties = bn.get_node_properties(DAG)
node_properties['Sprinkler']['node_color']='#00FFFF'
node_properties['Wet_Grass']['node_color']='#FF0000'
node_properties['Rain']['node_color']='#A9A9A9'
node_properties['Cloudy']['node_color']='#A9A9A9'

# Plotting the Bayesian Network
bn.plot(DAG,
    node_properties=node_properties,
```

```
          interactive=True,
          params_interactive={'notebook':True,
                'cdn_resources': 'remote'})
```

This results in the network shown in *Figure 15.4*. As shown in this DAG, `'Sprinkler'` could be a causal variable for both cloudy weather and wet grass. And wet grass could be potentially caused by rain and sprinklers. But there are functionalities to quantify these dependencies:

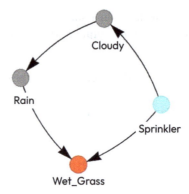

Figure 15.4 – Learned DAG using bnlearn for the Sprinkler dataset

You can use `independence_test()` as follows to test the dependency of the variables:

```
bn.independence_test(DAG, df, test = 'chi_square',
    prune = True)
```

*Table 15.2* includes a summary of the output of the previous command, clearly showing the significance of the dependency of the paired variables in the DAG:

| Source | Target | p-value (from chi_sqare test) | chi-square |
|---|---|---|---|
| Cloudy | Rain | 1.080606e-87 | 394.061629 |
| Sprinkler | Wet_Grass | 1.196919e-23 | 100.478455 |
| Sprinkler | Cloudy | 8.383708e-53 | 233.906474 |
| Rain | Wet_Grass | 3.886511e-64 | 285.901702 |

Table 15.2 – Summary of using bnlearn.independence_test() on the Sprinkler dataset

You can also use `bnlearn.parameter_learning.fit()` to learn about the CPDs, as follows:

```
model_mle = bn.parameter_learning.fit(DAG, df,
    methodtype='maximumlikelihood')
# Printing the learned Conditional Probability Distribution (CPDs)
bn.print_CPD(model_mle)
```

*Figure 15.5* shows the CPDs of the `Cloudy`, `Rain`, and `Sprinkler` variables. These CPDs, in combination with the identified DAG (*Figure 15.4*), provide the required information to not only identify potentially causal relationships between the variables but also do a quantitative assessment of them:

```
[bnlearn] >CPD of Cloudy:
+-----------+--------------------+--------------------+
| Sprinkler | Sprinkler(0)       | Sprinkler(1)       |
+-----------+--------------------+--------------------+
| Cloudy(0) | 0.3256150506512301 | 0.8511326860841424 |
+-----------+--------------------+--------------------+
| Cloudy(1) | 0.6743849493487699 | 0.1488673139158576 |
+-----------+--------------------+--------------------+
[bnlearn] >CPD of Rain:
+---------+--------------------+-------------+
| Cloudy  | Cloudy(0)          | Cloudy(1)   |
+---------+--------------------+-------------+
| Rain(0) | 0.8073770491803278 | 0.177734375 |
+---------+--------------------+-------------+
| Rain(1) | 0.19262295081967212| 0.822265625 |
+---------+--------------------+-------------+
[bnlearn] >CPD of Sprinkler:
+--------------+-------+
| Sprinkler(0) | 0.691 |
+--------------+-------+
| Sprinkler(1) | 0.309 |
+--------------+-------+
```

Figure 15.5 – Examples of CPDs identified by bnlearn for the Sprinkler dataset

In this chapter, you practiced using causal modeling, but there is much more to this topic. This is one of the most important topics in machine learning and you will benefit from learning more about this subject.

## Summary

In this chapter, you learned about the difference between correlative and causal relationships, the importance of causal modeling, and techniques such as Bayesian networks for causal inference. Later, we went through Python practices to help you start working with causal modeling and inference in your projects so that you can identify more reliable relationships between variables in your datasets and design reliable models.

In the next chapter, you will learn techniques for preserving privacy and ensuring security while maximizing the benefits of using private and proprietary data in building reliable machine learning models.

## Questions

1. Could you have a feature that is highly correlated with the output but not causal in a supervised learning model?

2. What is the difference between experimental design and observation studies for causal inference?

3. What are the requirements for using instrumental variables for causal inference?

4. Could relationships in a Bayesian network necessarily be considered causal?

# References

- Schölkopf, Bernhard. *Causality for machine learning*. Probabilistic and Causal Inference: The Works of Judea Pearl. 2022. 765-804.

- Kaddour, Jean, et al. *Causal machine learning: A survey and open problems*. arXiv preprint arXiv:2206.15475 (2022).

- Pearl, Judea. *Bayesian networks*. (2011).

- Richens, Jonathan G., Ciarán M. Lee, and Saurabh Johri. *Improving the accuracy of medical diagnosis with causal machine learning*. Nature communications 11.1 (2020): 3923.

- Prosperi, Mattia, et al. *Causal inference and counterfactual prediction in machine learning for actionable healthcare*. Nature Machine Intelligence 2.7 (2020): 369-375.

- Sanchez, Pedro, et al. *Causal machine learning for healthcare and precision medicine*. Royal Society Open Science 9.8 (2022): 220638.

# 16

# Security and Privacy in Machine Learning

In the digital world that we live in, preserving the privacy of users' data and their personal information, as well as ensuring the security of their digital information and assets, are of great importance in technology development. This is not an exception for technologies built on top of machine learning models. We briefly talked about this topic in *Chapter 3*, *Debugging toward Responsible AI*. In this chapter, we will provide you with more details to help you start your journey in learning more about privacy preservation and ensuring security in developing machine learning models and technologies.

In this chapter, we will cover the following topics:

- Encryption techniques and their use in machine learning
- Homomorphic encryption
- Differential privacy
- Federated learning

By the end of this chapter, you will understand the challenges in preserving privacy and ensuring security in machine learning settings, and learn a few techniques to tackle those challenges.

## Technical requirements

The following requirements are applicable to this chapter as they will help you better understand the concepts, be able to use them in your projects, and practice with the provided code:

- Python library requirements:
  - `numpy` >= 1.22.4
  - `matplotlib` >= 3.7.1

- `tenseal >= 0.3.14`
- `pycryptodome = 3.18.0`
- `pycryptodomex = 3.18.0`

If you are a Mac user and run into issues with `tenseal` installation, you can install it directly by cloning its repository, as explained at `https://github.com/OpenMined/TenSEAL/issues`.

The code files for this chapter are available on GitHub at `https://github.com/PacktPublishing/Debugging-Machine-Learning-Models-with-Python/tree/main/Chapter16`.

# Encryption techniques and their use in machine learning

We can use different encryption techniques to encrypt raw data, processed data for model training and inference, model parameters, or other sensitive information that needs to be secured. There is a term called *key*, usually a string of numbers or letters, which is important in the majority of encryption techniques. The key gets processed by encryption algorithms for encoding and decoding data. There are several encryption techniques, some of which include the following (Bhanot et al., 2015; Dibas et al., 2021):

- **Advanced Encryption Standard** (**AES**): AES is one of the strongest encryption algorithms that protects data. AES accepts different key sizes: 128, 192, or 256 bits.

- **Rivest-Shamir-Adleman (RSA) security**: RSA, which is one of the most secure encryption algorithms, is a public-key encryption algorithm that is widely used for secure data transmission.

- **Triple Data Encryption Standard (DES)**: Triple DES is an encryption method that uses a 56-bit key to encrypt data blocks.

- **Blowfish**: Blowfish is a symmetric-key encryption technique used as an alternative to the DES encryption algorithm. Blowfish is fast and highly effective for data encryption. It splits data, for example, strings and messages, into blocks of 64 bits and encrypts them individually.

- **Twofish**: Twofish, which is Blowfish's successor, is a symmetric encryption algorithm that deciphers 128-bit data blocks.

Next, we are going to use Python to practice the use of AES for data encryption, which is one of the most common encryption techniques.

## Implementing AES encryption in Python

Here we want to practice with AES for data encryption in Python. The sole purpose of this practice is to help you better understand how you can benefit from Python for data encryption, how easy it is to encrypt and decrypt data in Python, and how you can benefit from it to preserve data privacy and ensure security in machine learning settings.

We first import `Cryptodome.Cipher.AES()` for ciphering (encrypting) and deciphering (decrypting) and `Cryptodome.Random.get_random_bytes()` for key generation:

```
from Cryptodome.Cipher import AES
from Cryptodome.Random import get_random_bytes
```

We can use AES for encryption of text such as `My name is Ali` or other types of information. Here, we want to use it for encrypting what is called SMILES, which is a sequence representing a chemical compound. For example, `CC(=O)NC1=CC=C(C=C1)O` represents a famous drug called Acetaminophen (source: `https://pubchem.ncbi.nlm.nih.gov/compound/Acetaminophen`):

```
data = b'CC(=O)NC1=CC=C(C=C1)O'
key_random = get_random_bytes(16)
cipher_molecule = AES.new(key_random, AES.MODE_EAX)
ciphertext, tag = cipher_molecule.encrypt_and_digest(data)

out_encrypt = open("molecule_enc.bin", "wb")
[out_encrypt.write(x) for x in (cipher_molecule.nonce, tag,
    ciphertext) ]
out_encrypt.close()
```

We can then decrypt and securely load the data back if we have the key:

```
in_encrypt = open("molecule_enc.bin", "rb")
nonce, tag, ciphertext = [in_encrypt.read(x) for x in (16,
    16, -1) ]
in_encrypt.close()
# let's assume that the key is somehow available again
decipher_molecule = AES.new(key_random, AES.MODE_EAX,nonce)
data = decipher_molecule.decrypt_and_verify(ciphertext,tag)
print('Decrypted data: {}'.format(data))
```

This regenerates the sequence we encrypted, `CC(=O)NC1=CC=C(C=C1)O`.

In this example, AES helped us to encrypt information about drugs, which could be important for pharmaceutical and biotechnology companies in the process of developing a new drug. However, you can use AES via Python to encrypt other types of data.

Next, we want to talk about another technique called homomorphic encryption.

# Homomorphic encryption

Another technique that lets us implement computations on encrypted data is called **homomorphic encryption**. This capability is helpful in machine learning settings, for example, in using a model for inference on encrypted data without the need for decryption. However, implementing fully homomorphic encryption can be complex, computationally expensive, and memory-inefficient (Armknecht et al., 2015; Gentry et al., 2009; Yousuf et al., 2020).

There are a few Python libraries that can help us practice with homomorphic encryption schemes, such as the following:

- TenSEAL (https://github.com/OpenMined/TenSEAL), which can be integrated with PyTorch and NumPy
- PySEAL (https://github.com/Huelse/PySEAL)
- HElib (https://github.com/homenc/HElib)

Let's see a simple example of using homomorphic encryption using TenSEAL.

We first import the TenSEAL library and generate a context object using tenseal.context(). The context object generates and stores the necessary keys required by an encrypted computation:

```
import tenseal as ts
context = ts.context(ts.SCHEME_TYPE.BFV,
    poly_modulus_degree=4096, plain_modulus=1032193)
```

The poly_modulus_degree parameter is used to determine the degree of the polynomial modulus, which is a polynomial with integer coefficients. The plain_modulus parameter is used to specify the modulus for encoding plaintext messages into polynomials that can be encrypted and processed homomorphically. If the plain_modulus parameter is too small, the messages may overflow and cause incorrect results, while if it is too large, the ciphertexts may become too large and slow down the homomorphic operations.

In the previous code, we used the **Brakerski-Fan-Vercauteren** (**BFV**) scheme. BFV is a homomorphic encryption scheme that supports integer arithmetic. It consists of different polynomial-time algorithms for generating the public and secret keys, encrypting a plaintext message, decrypting a ciphertext message, adding and subtracting two ciphertexts, and multiplying two ciphertexts. The ciphertext is encrypted information that is unreadable by us or a computer without the proper cipher, or algorithm for performing encryption or decryption, to decrypt it.

Now we define a list of three numbers:

```
plain_list = [50, 60, 70]
```

We then implement decryption using the `context` object defined before:

```
encrypted_list = ts.bfv_vector(context, plain_list)
```

We then first implement an operation process as follows:

```
add_result = encrypted_vector + [1, 2, 3]
```

The resulting `add_result` list would be `[51, 62, 73]`, which is an element-wise summation of the original list of values `[50, 60, 70]` and `[1, 2, 3]`.

Although homomorphic encryption, or other encryption techniques, seems to be very secure, it still requires access to secret keys, for example, on the cloud server, which could lead to security concerns. There are solutions to reduce such risks, for example, by using key management services such as AWS KMS (`https://aws.amazon.com/kms/`) or **Multi-Factor Authentication** (**MFA**).

Next, we will briefly review **differential privacy** (**DP**) as a technique for preserving the privacy of individual data points.

## Differential privacy

The objective of **differential privacy** is to ensure that the removal or addition of individual data points does not affect the outcome of the modeling. For example, by adding random noise to a normal distribution, it tries to make the features of individual data points obscure. The effect of noise in learning could be eliminated based on the *law of large numbers* (Dekking et al., 2005) if a large number of data points is accessible. To better understand this concept, we want to generate a random list of numbers and add noise to them from a normal distribution to help you better understand why this technique works. In this process, we will also define some widely used technical terminology.

We first define a function called `gaussian_add_noise()` to add *Gaussian* noise to a query list of values:

```
def gaussian_add_noise(query_result: float,
    sensitivity: float, epsilon: float):

        std_dev = sensitivity / epsilon
        noise = np.random.normal(loc=0.0, scale=std_dev)
        noisy_result = query_result + noise

    return noisy_result
```

In the previous function, we used `sensitivity` and `epsilon` as input arguments of the function, whose meaning we can simplify as follows:

- `sensitivity`: The level of noise that is needed in the DP mechanism get determined by sensitivity parametrizes. Sensitivity tells us about the impact of a change on the result of the query. Larger `sensitivity` values result in better privacy but a less accurate response.

- `epsilon (Privacy budget)`: The privacy budget is a parameter that limits the extent of the deviation between the noisy and query data. A smaller `epsilon` value will result in better privacy but a less accurate response.

We then use a simple `for` loop to generate random values following a normal distribution as query values and then add noise to them using the defined `gaussian_mechanism()` function:

```
query_list = []
noisy_list = []
for iter in range(1000):
    # Generating a random value between 0 and 100
    query_val = np.random.rand()*100
    noisy_val = gaussian_add_noise(query_val, sensitivity,
        epsilon_budget)

    query_list.append(query_val)
    noisy_list.append(noisy_val)

print('Mean of the original distribution:

    {}'.format(np.mean(query_list)))
print('Mean of the nosiy distribution:
    {}'.format(np.mean(noisy_list)))

print('Standard deviation of the original distribution:
    {}'.format(np.std(query_list)))
print('Standard deviation of the nosiy distribution:
    {}'.format(np.std(noisy_list)))
```

The resulting noisy and query distributions are very similar, with an average of 0.78 and 0.82 and a standard deviation of 99.32 and 99.67, respectively. *Figure 16.1* shows the scatter plot of the two lists of values. You can change the distance between the query and noisy values by playing with the `sensitivity` and `epsilon` parameters.

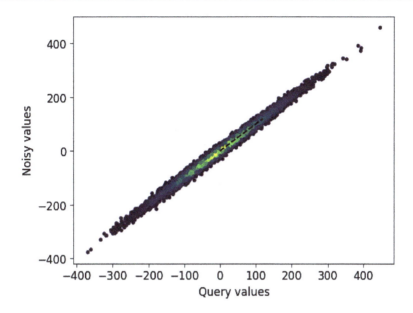

Figure 16.1 – Comparison of the values of variables before and after noise addition

There are also Python libraries that you can use to implement DP, such as the following:

- **IBM Differential Privacy Library** (`Diffprivlib`) (`https://github.com/IBM/differential-privacy-library`)

- `PyDP` (`https://github.com/OpenMined/PyDP`)

- `Opacus` (`https://github.com/pytorch/opacus`)

The last topic we want to introduce in this chapter is called **federated learning**, which helps us to go beyond privacy preservation for a central storage system.

## Federated learning

**Federated learning** (FL) relies on the idea of decentralizing learning, data analysis, and inference, therefore allowing the user data to be kept within individual devices or local databases (Kaissis et al., 2020; Yang et al., 2019). Through FL, we can benefit from the data of local devices and users, which cannot be stored in a centralized data storage system, to train and improve our machine learning models. As shown in *Figure 16.2*, a local device or user can provide local data to update the global model and the model we are training and improve the central server. The global model then gets updated and improved and provides updated inferences to the local users and devices.

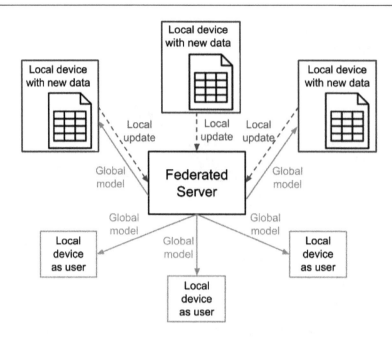

Figure 16.2 – Schematic representation of updating a model using local data
and feeding the global model back to the local devices and users

There are several Python libraries you can benefit from in implementing FL, such as the following:

- PySyft (https://github.com/OpenMined/PySyft)

- TensorFlow Federated (https://www.tensorflow.org/federated)

- FedML (https://github.com/FedML-AI/FedML)

- Flower (https://github.com/adap/flower)

- FATE (https://github.com/FederatedAI/FATE)

However, the challenge of using FL in practice is beyond programming or infrastructure design. In spite of this great alternative to storing user data locally, there are still ethical, legal, and business challenges in benefitting from FL in different applications. Healthcare is a great example of a domain where FL can benefit the most but legal and ethical challenges still exist, slowing down its implementation in practice. Many institutes, hospitals, pharmaceutical companies, and government agencies still require the data used for modeling, even through FL, to go through the usual ethics, legal, and business approval processes that exist for full access to the data, without the need for FL. However, there is hope that as FL algorithms and the associated infrastructure get better, agencies, hospitals, and institutions will also come up with solutions to benefit from this technique.

In addition to what we covered in this chapter on data privacy and security, you can review the important topics of attacks in machine learning settings in *Chapter 3, Debugging toward Responsible AI*. You can also check other resources such as the great article by Papernot et al., 2018 titled *Sok: Security and privacy in machine learning* to learn more about these important topics

## Summary

In this chapter, you learned about some of the most important concepts and techniques that help you in preserving privacy and ensuring security including data encryption techniques, homomorphic encryption, differential privacy, and federated learning. You learned how homomorphic encryption provides the possibility of different types of operation and machine learning inference compared to traditional data encryption techniques. You also learned how we can ensure data privacy by adding noise to the data, in differential privacy, or work with decentralized data and omit the need to transfer raw data, as in federated learning. You also practiced some of them in Python. This knowledge could be a starting point for you to learn about these concepts further and benefit from them in your machine learning projects.

In the next chapter, you will learn about the importance of integrating human feedback into machine learning modeling and the techniques that will help you on this topic.

## Questions

1. Explain three encryption techniques that could help you in your machine learning projects.
2. What is the benefit of homomorphic encryption in a machine learning setting?
3. What is differential privacy?
4. What are the non-technical challenges in the use of federated learning or differential privacy?

## References

- Shafahi, Ali, et al. "*Adversarial training for free!*" *Advances in Neural Information Processing Systems* 32 (2019).

- Gaur, Shailendra Singh, Hemanpreet Singh Kalsi, and Shivani Gautam. "*A Comparative Study and Analysis of Cryptographic Algorithms: RSA, DES, AES, BLOWFISH, 3-DES, and TWOFISH.*"

- Bhanot, Rajdeep, and Rahul Hans. "*A review and comparative analysis of various encryption algorithms.*" *International Journal of Security and Its Applications* 9.4 (2015): 289-306.

- Dibas, Hasan, and Khair Eddin Sabri. "*A comprehensive performance empirical study of the symmetric algorithms: AES, 3DES, Blowfish and Twofish.*" *International Conference on Information Technology (ICIT)*. IEEE (2021).

- Armknecht, Frederik, et al. *"A guide to fully homomorphic encryption."* Cryptology ePrint Archive (2015).

- Gentry, Craig. *A fully homomorphic encryption scheme.* Stanford University, 2009.

- Yousuf, Hana, et al. *"Systematic review on fully homomorphic encryption scheme and its application."* Recent Advances in Intelligent Systems and Smart Applications (2020): 537-551.

- Yang, Qiang, et al. *"Federated machine learning: Concept and applications."* ACM Transactions on Intelligent Systems and Technology (TIST) 10.2 (2019): 1-19.

- Abadi, Martin, et al. *"Deep learning with differential privacy."* Proceedings of the 2016 ACM SIGSAC conference on computer and communications security (2016).

- Dekking, Frederik Michel, et al. *A Modern Introduction to Probability and Statistics: Understanding why and how.* Vol. 488. London: Springer (2005).

- Kaissis, Georgios A., et al. *"Secure, privacy-preserving and federated machine learning in medical imaging."* Nature Machine Intelligence 2.6 (2020): 305-311.

- Yang, Qiang, et al. *"Federated machine learning: Concept and applications."* ACM Transactions on Intelligent Systems and Technology (TIST) 10.2 (2019): 1-19.

- Papernot, Nicolas, et al. *"Sok: Security and privacy in machine learning."* IEEE European Symposium on Security and Privacy (EuroS&P). IEEE (2018).

# 17
# Human-in-the-Loop Machine Learning

Machine learning modeling is more than just machine learning developers and engineers sitting behind their computers to build and revise components of a machine learning life cycle. Incorporating feedback from domain experts, or even the non-expert crowd, is key in bringing more reliable and application-oriented models to production. This concept, which is called human-in-the-loop machine learning, is about benefiting from human intelligence and expert knowledge in different stages of a life cycle to further improve the performance and reliability of our models.

In this chapter, we will cover the following topics:

- Humans in the machine learning life cycle
- Human-in-the-loop modeling

By the end of this chapter, you will know about the benefits and challenges of incorporating human intelligence in your machine learning modeling projects.

## Humans in the machine learning life cycle

Developing and improving different components of a machine learning life cycle to bring a reliable and high-performance model to production is a collaborative effort that can benefit from expert and non-expert human feedback (*Figure 17.1*):

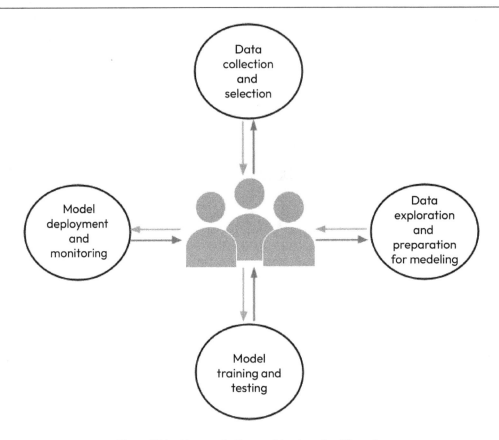

Figure 17.1 – Humans in the machine learning life cycle

For example, a radiologist can help in annotating radiological images while most people with good vision capabilities can easily label cat and dog images. But incorporating human feedback is not limited to data annotation at the beginning of a life cycle.

We can benefit from human intelligence and expertise to improve data preparation, feature engineering, and representation learning aspects of a life cycle, as well as model training and testing, and eventually model deployment and monitoring. In each of these stages, human feedback can be incorporated either passively or actively, which allows us to bring a better model into production.

Passive human-in-the-loop is about collecting feedback and information from experts and non-experts and benefitting from that the next time we revise components of the corresponding machine learning modeling system. In this process, the feedback and extra information help in identifying opportunities for improving the components of the life cycle and identifying data and concept drift to bring a better model into production. In active human-in-the-loop machine learning, the infrastructure and one or all of the life cycle components need to be designed in a way that the extra human-in-the-loop information and data can be actively and continuously incorporated to improve data analysis and modeling.

First, we will review expert feedback collection and how to effectively benefit from it in improving our models.

## Expert feedback collection

The ultimate goal of building a piece of technology on top of one or multiple machine learning modes is to provide a tool for users, experts, or non-experts for a specific objective, such as healthcare image classification, stock price prediction, credit risk estimation, and product recommendation in platforms such as Amazon. For example, we can collect feedback for data annotation or later in the production stage for drift detection. We can then use this feedback to improve our models. However, this feedback could extend beyond the purposes of just data annotation or identifying data and concept drift.

We can incorporate expert feedback for four major purposes: data generation and annotation, data filtering, model selection, and model monitoring. Expert feedback collection for annotation and monitoring is generally similar to non-expert data collection except for the fact that in some applications, expertise is of necessity, such as in classifying radiological images.

For model selection, we can use expert feedback to not need to rely exclusively on the performance measures we use for model performance assessment and, consequently, select the best model, but to detect red flags according to wrong predictions or rely on explainability information for our models, such as if features that contribute the most in terms of predictions are of lowest relevance.

We can also benefit from experts' feedback in monitoring our models. Drift detection, as discussed in *Chapter 11, Avoiding and Detecting Data and Concept Drifts*, is crucial to ensure the reliability of our models in production. In many applications, users of our models could be experts in specific domains, such as healthcare and drug discovery. In such cases, we need to make sure we continuously collect their feedback and use this to detect and eliminate drifts in our models.

Collecting feedback from experts as users of our machine learning models should not be limited to getting their binary response of "good" versus "bad." We need to provide enough information about our models and their predictions and ask experts to provide their feedback, as follows:

- **Provide sufficient information**: When asking for feedback from expert users of our models, we need to provide sufficient information to get better and more relevant feedback. For example, in addition to the performance of our model in testing and production, or wrong and correct predictions for a specific set of data points, we can also provide explainability information on how the model came up with its decision for those data points. This type of information could help the users provide better feedback that will help us in improving our models.

- **Don't ask for translations**: Many of the users of our models might have limited statistical and machine learning modeling knowledge. So, asking them to convert their opinions and ideas into technical terms would limit efficient feedback collection. You need to provide sufficient information and ask for their feedback and have a back-and-forth conversation to convert their insights into actionable items for model improvement.

- **Design for automated feedback collection**: Although it is better to not ask for translations, as pointed out earlier, you can move toward more automated feedback collection using clear and detailed questions and proper infrastructure design to collect the feedback and incorporate it into your models. For example, you can use machine learning explainability and ask whether the most informative features used by the model for predicting the output of a specific set of data points are relevant to the task or not.

Human-in-the-loop has its own challenges, such as in preserving privacy when third-party companies are needed to monitor models and pipelines, or when there would be specific legal barriers in sharing data coming from collaborators and business partners with others in our teams and organizations. We need to keep these challenges in mind when we're designing so that we can benefit from human feedback in our machine learning life cycles.

Although we can collect feedback in different stages of the machine learning life cycle to improve our models, there are techniques such as active learning (which we will cover next) that can help us bring a better model with lower cost into production.

## Human-in-the-loop modeling

Despite more high-quality annotated data points being more valuable, the cost of annotating data, specifically when domain expertise is of necessity, could be very high. Active learning is a strategy that helps us in generating and labeling data to improve the performance of our models at a lower cost. In an active learning setting, we aim to benefit from a model with a limited amount of data and iteratively select new data points to be labeled, or their continuous value identified, with the aim of achieving higher performance (Wu et al., 2022; Ren et al., 2021; Burbidge et al., 2007). The model queries new instances to be annotated by experts or non-experts, or their labels or continuous values are identified via any computational or experimental technique. However, instead of the instances being selected randomly, there are techniques for new instance selection to help us in achieving better models with a lower number of instances and iterations (*Table 17.1*). Each of these techniques has its advantages and disadvantages. For example, *uncertainty sampling* is simple but its effect on performance might be limited if uncertainty in the predicted output of instances is not highly correlated with model error:

| Data-Centric | Model-Centric |
|---|---|
| Uncertainty sampling | Expected model change |
| Selecting instances with the most uncertainty (in inference), which could be instances closest to the decision boundary in classification problems | Selecting instances that know their labels results in the biggest impact on the current model |
| Density-weighted uncertainty sampling | Estimation of error reduction |
| Selecting instances that not only have the highest uncertainty but also are representative of many other data points that rely on the density of data in feature space | Selecting instances that know their labels would result in the biggest future error reduction |
| Query-by-committee | Variance reduction |
| Multiple models (the committee) get trained and instances with the highest disagreement in their prediction get selected | Selecting instances that know their labels would result in the most reduction in the model's uncertainty about its parameters |

Table 17.1 – Active learning techniques for instance election to be annotated in each step

In this chapter, we focused on introducing concepts and techniques behind human-in-the-loop. However, there are Python libraries such as modAL (https://modal-python.readthedocs.io/en/latest/) that can help you in implementing some of these techniques in your projects to bring human feedback into your machine learning life cycle.

## Summary

In this chapter, you learned about some of the important concepts in human-in-the-loop machine learning, which can help you in better establishing collaboration between you and your team with experts or non-experts so that you can incorporate their feedback into your machine learning modeling projects.

This was the last chapter of this book. I hope you learned enough about different approaches to improve your machine learning models and build better ones so that you can start your journey toward becoming an expert in this domain.

## Questions

1.  Is human-in-the-loop machine learning limited to data annotation and labeling?

2.  What is the difference between uncertainty sampling and density-weighted uncertainty sampling in selecting instances in each step of an active learning process?

## References

- Amershi, Saleema, et al. *Power to the people: The role of humans in interactive machine learning.* Ai Magazine 35.4 (2014): 105-120.

- Wu, Xingjiao, et al. *A survey of human-in-the-loop for machine learning.* Future Generation Computer Systems 135 (2022): 364-381.

- Ren, Pengzhen, et al. *A survey of deep active learning.* ACM computing surveys (CSUR) 54.9 (2021): 1-40.

- Burbidge, Robert, Jem J. Rowland, and Ross D. King. *Active learning for regression based on query by committee.* Intelligent Data Engineering and Automated Learning-IDEAL 2007: 8th International Conference, Birmingham, UK, December 16-19, 2007. Proceedings 8. Springer Berlin Heidelberg, 2007.

- Cai, Wenbin, Ya Zhang, and Jun Zhou. *Maximizing expected model change for active learning in regression.* 2013 IEEE 13th international conference on data mining. IEEE, 2013.

- Roy, Nicholas, and Andrew McCallum. *Toward optimal active learning through monte carlo estimation of error reduction.* ICML, Williamstown 2 (2001): 441-448.

- Donmez, Pinar, Jaime G. Carbonell, and Paul N. Bennett. *Dual strategy active learning.* Machine Learning: ECML 2007: 18th European Conference on Machine Learning, Warsaw, Poland, September 17-21, 2007. Proceedings 18. Springer Berlin Heidelberg, 2007.

# Assessments

## Chapter 1 – Beyond Code Debugging

1. Yes – here is an example that was provided in this chapter:

```python
def odd_counter(num_list: list):
    """
    :param num_list: list of integers to be checked for
identifying odd numbers
    :return: return an integer as the number of odd numbers in
the input list
    """
    odd_count = 0
    for num in num_list:
        if (num % 2) == 0:
            print("{} is even".format(num))
        else:
            print("{} is even".format(num))
            odd_count += 1

    return odd_count

num_list = [1, 2, 5, 8, 9]
print(odd_counter(num_list))
```

2. Here are their definitions:

   - `AttributeError`: This type of error is raised when an attribute is used for an object that it is not defined for. For example, `isnull` is not defined for a list. So, `my_list.isnull()` results in `AttributeError`.

   - `NameError`: This error is raised when you try to call a function, class, or other names and modules that are not defined in your code. For example, if you haven't defined a `neural_network` class in your code but call it in your code as `neural_network()`, you will get a `NameError` message.

3. Higher dimensionality makes a sparser feature space and could reduce the confidence of the model in identifying generalizable decision boundaries in a classification setting.

4. When you get an error message in Python, it usually provides you with the necessary information to find the issue. This information creates a report-like message about the lines of your code that the error occurred in, the types of errors, and the function or class calls that resulted in such errors. This report-like message is called a **traceback** in Python.

5. **Incremental programming**: Writing code for every small component, then testing it and writing test codes using PyTest, for example, could help you avoid issues with each function or class you wrote. It also helps you ensure the outputs of one module that feed another module as its input are compatible.

   **Logging**: When you develop functions and classes in Python, you can benefit from logging to log information, errors, and other kinds of messages to help you in identifying potential sources of issues when you get an error message.

6. For example, if you use experts, such as radiologists, to annotate medical images for a cancer diagnosis, then the confidence on the label of images could be different. And these confidences could be considered in the modeling phase either in the data collection process, such as by asking more experts to annotate the same images, or in the modeling process, such as by assigning a weight to each image based on the confidence in labeling. The features of your data could also have different qualities. For example, you might have highly sparse features that have mostly zero values across the data points or features that might have different levels of confidence. For example, a measurement feature will have lower confidence if you use a measurement tape to capture millimeter differences between the sizes of objects, such as dice, compared to using the same tape to capture differences between bigger objects, such as furniture.

7. You can control underfitting and overfitting by controlling model complexity.

8. Yes, it is possible. The data that's used for training and testing machine learning models could become out of date. For example, the changes in the trends of the clothing market could make predictions of a model for clothing recommendation unreliable.

9. By playing with model hyperparameters alone, you can't develop the best possible model. In the same way, by increasing the quality and quantity of your data and keeping your model hyperparameters the same, you also can't achieve the best performance possible. So, data and hyperparameters work hand in hand.

# Chapter 2 – Machine Learning Life Cycle

1. Examples of cleaning processes are filling in missing values in your data and removing outliers.

2. One-hot encoding generates a new feature for each category of categorical features. Label encoding keeps the same features and just replaces each category with a number assigned to that category.

3. The simplest way of detecting outliers is by using quantiles of the distribution of variable values. Data points that are beyond the upper and lower bounds are considered outliers. The lower and upper bounds can be calculated as $Q1-a.IQR$ and $Q3+a.IQR$, where $a$ can be a real value

between 1.5 and 3. The common value of $a$ that is also used by default in drawing a boxplot is 1.5, but having higher values makes the process of outlier identification less stringent and lets fewer data points be detected as outliers.

4.  If you want to deploy a model in doctors' personal computers in hospitals to be used directly by clinicians, you need to consider all difficulties and planning needed to set up the proper production environment and all the software dependencies. You also need to make sure their local system has the necessary hardware requirements. These are not among the considerations if you want to deploy a model behind chatbots in a banking system.

# Chapter 3 – Debugging toward Responsible AI

1.  **Data collection bias**: Data that is collected could have biases such as gender bias, as in Amazon's applicant sorting examples, race bias, as in COMPAS, socioeconomic biases, as in hospitalization examples, or other kinds of biases.

    **Sampling bias**: Another source of data bias could be in the process of sampling data points or sampling the population in the data collection stage of the life cycle. For example, in sampling students to fill in a survey, our sampling process could be biased toward girls or boys, rich or poor student families, or high- versus low-grade students.

2.  **Perfect-knowledge white-box attacks**: The attacker knows everything about the system.

    **Zero-knowledge black-box attacks**: The attacker doesn't have any knowledge of the system itself but collects information through predictions of the model in production.

3.  The encryption process transforms the information, data, or algorithm into a new (that is, encrypted) form. The encrypted data can be decrypted (that is, become human-readable or machine understandable) if the individual has access to the encryption key (that is, a password-style key necessary for the decryption process). In this way, getting access to the data and algorithm without the encryption key will be almost impossible or very difficult.

4.  **Differential privacy** tries to ensure that the removal or addition of individual data points does not affect the outcome of modeling. It attempts to learn from patterns within groups of data points. For example, by adding random noise from a normal distribution, it tries to make the features of individual data points obscure. The effect of noise in learning could be eliminated based on the law of large numbers if a large number of data points will be accessible.

    **Federated learning** relies on the idea of decentralizing learning, data analysis, and inference, thus allowing the user's data to be kept within individual devices or local databases.

5.  Transparency helps in building trust in users and could potentially increase the number of users that trust and use your models.

# Chapter 4 – Detecting Performance and Efficiency Issues in Machine Learning Models

1.  In a primary diagnostic test, with more accurate follow-up tests, we want to make sure we do not lose any patients with the disease we are testing for. So, we need to aim to decrease false negatives, while trying to decrease false positives at the same time. So, we can aim to maximize **recall** while controlling for **precision** and **specificity**.

2.  In such cases, you want to make sure you have the **precision** to control risks and suggest good investment opportunities. This might result in a lower **recall**, which is okay as a bad investment could result in a significant loss of capital for individual investors. Here, we don't want to consider the details of investment risk management and want to have a high-level understanding of how to select a good performance measure. If you are an expert in this field, consider your knowledge and select a good performance measure that satisfies the requirements you are aware of.

3.  ROC-AUC is a summary measure. Two models with the same ROC-AUCs could have different predictions for individual data points.

4.  **MCC** focuses on predicted labels, while **log-loss** cares about predicted probabilities for the tested data points. So, a lower **log-loss** does not necessarily result in a lower **MCC**.

5.  Not necessarily. $R^2$ doesn't take into account data dimensionality (that is, the number of features, inputs, or independent variables). A model with more features could result in a higher $R^2$, while it might not necessarily be a better model.

6.  It depends on the performance measure and test data used for assessing the generalizability of the model. We need to use the right performance measure for our objective in production, and use a set of data points for model testing that will be more reflective of unseen data in production.

# Chapter 5 – Improving the Performance of Machine Learning Models

1.  Adding more training data points could help to reduce variance while adding more features could help to reduce bias. However, there is no guarantee of a reduction of variance through the addition of new data points or whether new features will be helpful in reducing variance.

    **Assigning weights during optimization**: You can assign a weight to each data point, according to the confidence of class labels, when training machine learning models.

    **Ensemble learning**: If you consider a distribution of the quality or confidence score of each data point, then you can build different models using data points from each part of this distribution and then combine the predictions of the models for example using their weighted average.

    **Transfer learning**: You can train a model on a large dataset with different levels of label confidence (see *Figure 5.3*), excluding very low-confidence data and then fine-tune it on the very high-confidence part of your dataset.

2. By increasing confidence in identifying the decision boundary, in a classification setting, where the minority class is sparse.

3. If we use Borderline-SMOTE, the new synthetically generated data points would be close to the majority-class data points, which helps in identifying a generalizable decision boundary.

   In DSMOTE, **DBSCAN** is used to divide data points of the minority class into three groups of core samples, borderline samples, and noise (that is, outlying) samples, and then the core and borderline samples only get used for oversampling.

4. Searching over the whole possible combinations of hyperparameters is not necessary, as explained in this chapter.

5. Yes, L1 regularization can eliminate the contribution of features to the regularization process.

6. Yes, it is possible.

# Chapter 6 – Interpretability and Explainability in Machine Learning Modeling

1. Explainability can help improve performance, such as by reducing the sensitivity of models to small feature value changes, increasing data efficiency in model training, trying to help in proper reasoning in models, and avoiding spurious correlations.

2. **Local explainability** helps us understand the behavior of a model close to a data point in feature space. Although these models meet local fidelity criteria, features that have been identified to be locally important might not be globally important, and vice versa.

   **Global explainability** techniques try to go beyond local explainability and provide global explanations to the models.

3. Linear models, although interpretable, usually have low performance. Instead, we could benefit from more complex models, with higher performance, and use explainability techniques to understand how the model comes up with its predictions.

4. Yes, it does. Explainability techniques could help us understand what models are major contributors to predictions for one set of data points.

5. SHAP can determine how each feature contributes to a model's prediction. As features work cooperatively in determining the decision boundaries of classification models and eventually affecting model predictions, SHAP tries to first identify the marginal contribution of each feature and then provide Shapely values as an estimate of each feature in cooperation with the whole feature set to predict a model.

   LIME is an alternative to SHAP for **local explainability** that explains the predictions of any classifier or regressor, in a model-agnostic way, by approximating a model locally with an interpretable model.

6. Counterfactual examples, or explanations, help us identify what needs to be changed in an instance to change the outcome of a classification model. These counterfactuals could help in identifying actionable paths in many applications, such as finance, retail, marketing, recruiting, and healthcare. For example, we can use them to suggest to a bank customer how they can change the rejection to their loan application.

7. As presented in the *Counterfactual generation using Diverse Counterfactual Explanations (DiCE)* section, not all counterfactuals are feasible according to the definition and meaning of each feature. For example, if we want to suggest to a 30-year-old individual to change their outcome, suggesting that they need to wait until they get to their 50s is not an effective and actionable suggestion. Also, suggesting a change of `hours_per_week` of work from 38 to >80 is not feasible.

# Chapter 7 – Decreasing Bias and Achieving Fairness

1. No. There might be proxies in our models for sensitive attributes, but not in our models.

2. Salary and income (in some countries), occupation, a history of a felony charge.

3. Not necessarily. Satisfying fairness according to **demographic parity** wouldn't necessarily result in a model being fair according to **equalized odds**.

4. **Demographic parity** is a group fairness definition to ensure that a model's predictions are not dependent on a given sensitive attribute, such as ethnicity or sex.

   **Equalized odds** is satisfied when a given prediction is independent of the group of a given sensitive attribute and the real output.

5. Not necessarily. For example, there could be feature proxies for `'sex'` among top contributors to model predictions.

6. We can use explainability techniques to identify potential biases in our models and then plan to improve them toward fairness. For example, we can identify fairness issues between male and female groups.

# Chapter 8 – Controlling Risks Using Test-Driven Development

1. `pytest` is a simple-to-use Python library you can use to design unit tests. The designed tests can then be simply used to test changes in your code and control risks of potential mistakes throughout the development process and future changes in your code.

2. In programming for data analysis and machine learning modeling, we need to use data that is in different variables or data objects, comes from a file in your local machine or the cloud, is queried from a database, or comes from a URL to our tests. Fixtures help us in these processes by removing the need to repeat the same code across our tests. Attaching a fixture function

to a test will run it and return data to the test before each test runs. We can use the examples provided on the `pytest` documentation page for fixtures (`https://docs.pytest.org/en/7.1.x/ how-to/fixtures.html`).

3.  Differential testing attempts to check two versions of a piece of software, as base and test versions, on the same input and compare the outputs. This process helps identify whether the outputs are the same and identify unexpected differences. In differential testing, the base version is already verified and considered as the approved version while the test version needs to be checked against the base version in producing the correct output.

4.  `mlflow` is a widely used machine learning experiment tracking library that we can use in Python. Keeping track of our machine learning experiments will help us to reduce the risks of invalid conclusions and selecting unreliable models. Experiment tracking in machine learning is about saving information about the experiments, such as the data that has been used, the testing performance and the metric used for performance assessment, and the algorithms and the hyperparameters used for modeling.

# Chapter 9 – Testing and Debugging for Production

1.  **Data drift**: Data drift happens if the characteristics and meaning of features or independent variables in production differ from the modeling stage. Imagine you used a third-party tool to generate a score for the health or financial situation of people. The algorithm behind that tool could change over time, and its range and meaning will not be the same when your model gets used in production. If you have not updated your model accordingly, then your model will not work as expected as the meaning of the value of the features will not be the same between the data used for training and the user data after deployment.

    **Concept drift**: Concept drift is about any change in the definition of output variables. For example, real decision boundaries between training data and production could be different because of concept drift, meaning the effort in training might result in a decision boundary far from reality in production.

2.  **Model assertions** can help you detect issues early on, such as input data drift or other unexpected behaviors that might affect the model's performance. We can consider model assertions as a set of rules that get checked during the model's training, validation, or even during deployment to ensure that the model's predictions meet the predefined conditions. Model assertions can help us in many ways, such as detecting and diagnosing issues with the model or input data, allowing us to address them before they impact the model's performance.

3.  Here are some examples of the components of integration testing:

    •   **Testing data pipelines**: We need to evaluate that the data preprocessing components before model training, such as data wrangling, are consistent between the training and deployment stages.

- **Testing APIs**: If our machine learning model is exposed through an API, we can test the API endpoints to ensure they handle requests and responses correctly.

- **Testing model deployment**: We can use integration testing to assess the model's deployment process, whether it's deployed as a standalone service, within a container, or embedded in an application. This process helps us ensure that the deployment environment provides the necessary resources, such as CPU, memory, and storage, and that the model can be updated if needed.

- **Testing interactions with other components**: We need to verify that our machine learning model works seamlessly with databases, user interfaces, or third-party services. This may include testing how the model's predictions are stored, displayed, or used within the application.

- **Testing end-to-end functionality**: We can use end-to-end tests that simulate real-world scenarios and user interactions to validate that the model's predictions are accurate, reliable, and useful in the context of the overall application.

4. IaC and configuration management tools such as Chef, Puppet, and Ansible can be used to automate the deployment, configuration, and management of software and hardware infrastructures. These tools could help us ensure consistency and reliability across different environments. First, we need to define two important terminologies, client and server, before describing what these IaC tools are for us:

- **Chef** (`https://www.chef.io/products/chef-infrastructure-management`): Chef is an open source configuration management tool that relies on a client-server model, where the Chef server stores the desired configuration, and the Chef client applies it to the nodes.

- **Puppet** (`https://www.puppet.com/`): Puppet is another open source configuration management tool that works in a client-server model or as a standalone application. Puppet enforces desired configurations across nodes by periodically pulling them from the Puppet master server.

- **Ansible** (`https://www.ansible.com/`): Ansible is an open source and easy-to-use configuration management, orchestration, and automation tool that employs an agentless architecture to communicate and apply configurations to nodes.

# Chapter 10 – Versioning and Reproducible Machine Learning Modeling

1. **MLflow**: We introduced MLflow for experiment tracking and model monitoring in previous chapters, but you can also use it for data versioning (`https://mlflow.org/`).

   **DVC**: An open source version control system for managing data, code, and ML models. It is designed to handle large datasets and integrates with Git (`https://dvc.org/`).

**Pachyderm**: A data versioning platform that provides reproducibility, provenance, and scalability in machine learning workflows (`https://www.pachyderm.com/`).

2. No. Different versions of the same data file could be stored with the same name and restored and retrieved when needed.

3. A simple change of the random state when splitting data into training and test sets or during model initialization could result in different parameter values and performances for training and evaluation sets.

# Chapter 11 – Avoiding and Detecting Data and Concept Drifts

1. **Magnitude**: We might face different magnitudes of difference in the data distribution resulting in drift in our machine learning models. Small changes in the data distribution may be difficult to detect, while large changes may be more noticeable.

   **Frequency**: Drifts might occur in different frequencies.

2. The Kolmogorov–Smirnov test can be used for data drift detection.

# Chapter 12 – Going Beyond ML Debugging with Deep Learning

1. Yes, in the forward pass, parameters that are already calculated get used for output generation; then, the difference between the real and predicted output gets used in the backpropagation process to update the weights.

2. In stochastic gradient descent, one data point is used per iteration to optimize and update the model weights, while in mini-batch gradient descent, a mini-batch (small subset) of data points gets used.

3. Each batch or mini-batch is a small subset of data points in the training set that gets used to calculate the loss and update the model's weights. In each epoch, multiple batches get iterated to cover all training data.

4. The sigmoid and softmax functions are commonly used in output layers to transform the scores of the output neurons to values of between zero and one for classification models. This is called the probability of predictions.

# Chapter 13 – Advanced Deep Learning Techniques

1. CNNs can be used for image classification or segmentation – for example, for radiological images to identify malignancies (tumor regions). On the other hand, GNNs can be used in social and biological networks.

2. Yes, it does.

3. It might result in more mistakes.

4. To handle this challenge, a common ID, such as 0, gets used before or after IDs of tokens of words in each sequence of words or sentences in a process called padding.

5. The classes we build for CNNs and GNNs have similar code structures.

6. Edge features help you include some vital information, depending on the application. For example, in chemistry, you can determine the type of chemical bond as an edge feature, while the nodes could be the atoms in the graphs.

# Chapter 14 – Introduction to Recent Advancements in Machine Learning

1. Transformer-based text generation, VAEs, and GANs.

2. Different versions of LLaMA and GPT.

3. The generator, which could be a neural network architecture for generating desired data types, such as images, generates images aiming to fool the discriminator into recognizing the generated data as real data. The discriminator learns to remain good at recognizing generated data compared to real data.

4. You can improve your prompting by being specific about the question and specifying for whom the data is being generated.

5. In RLHF, the reward is calculated based on the feedback of humans, either experts or non-experts, depending on the problem. But the reward is not like a predefined mathematical formula considering the complexity of problems such as language modeling. The feedback provided by humans results in improving the model step by step.

6. The idea of contrastive learning is to learn representations that result in similar data points being closer to each other compared to dissimilar data points.

# Chapter 15 – Correlation versus Causality

1. Yes. You can have features that are highly correlated with the output in supervised learning that aren't causal.

2. One way to establish causality is to conduct experiments, as in **experimental design**, where we measure the effect of changes in the causal feature on the target variable. However, such experimental studies may not always be feasible or ethical. In **observational studies**, we use observational data, instead of controlled experiments, and try to identify causal relationships by controlling confounding variables.

3. **Instrumental variables** is used in causal aim to overcome a common problem in observational studies where the treatment and outcome variables are jointly determined by other variables, or confounders, that are not included in the model. This approach starts with identifying an instrument that is correlated with the treatment variable and uncorrelated with the outcome variable, except through its effect on the treatment variable.

4. The directions, from a feature to the outcome, don't necessarily mean causality. But *Bayesian* networks can be used for estimating the causal effects of variables on the outcome while controlling the confounding variables.

# Chapter 16 – Security and Privacy in Machine Learning

1. **Advanced Encryption Standard** (**AES**): AES is one of the strongest encryption algorithms that protects data. AES accepts different key sizes: 128, 192, or 256 bits.

   **Triple Data Encryption Standard** (**DES**): Triple DES is an encryption method that uses a 56-bit key to encrypt data blocks.

   **Blowfish**: Blowfish is a symmetric-key encryption technique used as an alternative to the DES encryption algorithm. Blowfish is fast and highly effective for data encryption. It splits data, for example, strings and messages, into blocks of 64 bits and encrypts them individually.

2.  We can use a model for inference on encrypted data without the need for decryption.

3. The objective of **differential privacy** (**DP**) is to ensure that the removal or addition of individual data points does not affect the outcome of the modeling. For example, by adding random noise to a normal distribution, it tries to make the features of individual data points obscure.

4. The challenge of using FL or DP in practice goes beyond programming or infrastructure design. In spite of this great alternative to storing user data locally, there are still ethical, legal, and business challenges when benefitting from FL in different applications.

# Chapter 17 – Human-in-the-Loop Machine Learning

1. No. For example, you can bring human experts into the loop through *active learning*.

2. In **uncertainty sampling**, data points get selected solely based on uncertainty in inference. But in **density-weighted uncertainty sampling**, instances get selected not only based on their highest uncertainty but also to be representative of the many other data points that rely on the density of data in the feature space.

# Index

www.packtpub.com

Subscribe to our online digital library for full access to over 7,000 books and videos, as well as industry leading tools to help you plan your personal development and advance your career. For more information, please visit our website.

## Why subscribe?

- Spend less time learning and more time coding with practical eBooks and Videos from over 4,000 industry professionals

- Improve your learning with Skill Plans built especially for you

- Get a free eBook or video every month

- Fully searchable for easy access to vital information

- Copy and paste, print, and bookmark content

Did you know that Packt offers eBook versions of every book published, with PDF and ePub files available? You can upgrade to the eBook version at www.packtpub.com and as a print book customer, you are entitled to a discount on the eBook copy. Get in touch with us at customercare@packtpub.com for more details.

At www.packtpub.com, you can also read a collection of free technical articles, sign up for a range of free newsletters, and receive exclusive discounts and offers on Packt books and eBooks.

# Other Books You May Enjoy

If you enjoyed this book, you may be interested in these other books by Packt:

**Python Machine Learning - Second Edition**

Sebastian Raschka, Vahid Mirjalili

ISBN: 978-1-78712-593-3

- Understand the key frameworks in data science, machine learning, and deep learning
- Harness the power of the latest Python open source libraries in machine learning
- Master machine learning techniques using challenging real-world data
- Master deep neural network implementation using the TensorFlow library
- Ask new questions of your data through machine learning models and neural networks
- Learn the mechanics of classification algorithms to implement the best tool for the job
- Predict continuous target outcomes using regression analysis
- Uncover hidden patterns and structures in data with clustering
- Delve deeper into textual and social media data using sentiment analysis

**Python Machine Learning By Example**

Yuxi (Hayden) Liu

ISBN: 978-1-78355-311-2

- Exploit the power of Python to handle data extraction, manipulation, and exploration techniques
- Use Python to visualize data spread across multiple dimensions and extract useful features
- Dive deep into the world of analytics to predict situations correctly
- Implement machine learning classification and regression algorithms from scratch in Python
- Be amazed to see the algorithms in action
- Evaluate the performance of a machine learning model and optimize it
- Solve interesting real-world problems using machine learning and Python as the journey unfolds

**Python Machine Learning Cookbook - Second Edition**

Giuseppe Ciaburro, Prateek Joshi

ISBN: 978-1-78980-845-2

- Use predictive modeling and apply it to real-world problems
- Explore data visualization techniques to interact with your data
- Learn how to build a recommendation engine
- Understand how to interact with text data and build models to analyze it
- Work with speech data and recognize spoken words using Hidden Markov Models
- Get well versed with reinforcement learning, automated ML, and transfer learning
- Work with image data and build systems for image recognition and biometric face recognition
- Use deep neural networks to build an optical character recognition system

## Packt is searching for authors like you

If you're interested in becoming an author for Packt, please visit authors.packtpub.com and apply today. We have worked with thousands of developers and tech professionals, just like you, to help them share their insight with the global tech community. You can make a general application, apply for a specific hot topic that we are recruiting an author for, or submit your own idea.

## Share your thoughts

Once you've read *Debugging Machine Learning Models with Python*, we'd love to hear your thoughts! Scan the QR code below to go straight to the Amazon review page for this book and share your feedback.

https://packt.link/r/1-800-20858-8

Your review is important to us and the tech community and will help us make sure we're delivering excellent quality content.

# Download a free PDF copy of this book

Thanks for purchasing this book!

Do you like to read on the go but are unable to carry your print books everywhere?

Is your eBook purchase not compatible with the device of your choice?

Don't worry, now with every Packt book you get a DRM-free PDF version of that book at no cost.

Read anywhere, any place, on any device. Search, copy, and paste code from your favorite technical books directly into your application.

The perks don't stop there, you can get exclusive access to discounts, newsletters, and great free content in your inbox daily

Follow these simple steps to get the benefits:

1.  Scan the QR code or visit the link below

https://packt.link/free-ebook/978-1-80020-858-2

2.  Submit your proof of purchase
3.  That's it! We'll send your free PDF and other benefits to your email directly

www.ingramcontent.com/pod-product-compliance
Lightning Source LLC
Chambersburg PA
CBHW060111090326
40690CB00064B/4755